AFRICAN HISTORICAL DICTIONARIES

Edited by Jon Woronoff

1. *Cameroon*, by Victor T. Le Vine and Roger P. Nye. 1974

2. *The Congo* (*Brazzaville*), by Virginia Thompson and Richard Adloff. 1974

3. *Swaziland*, by John J. Grotpeter. 1975

4. *The Gambia*, by Harry A. Gailey. 1975

5. *Botswana*, by Richard P. Stevens. 1975

6. *Somalia*, by Margaret F. Castagno. 1975

7. *Dahomey*, by Samuel Decalo. 1975

Historical Dictionary
of
The Republic of
BOTSWANA

by

Richard P. Stevens

African Historical Dictionaries, No. 5

The Scarecrow Press, Inc.

Metuchen, N. J.   1975

Library of Congress Cataloging in Publication Data

Stevens, Richard P   1931-
    Historical dictionary of the Republic of
Botswana.

    (African historical dictionaries ; no. 5)
    Bibliography: p.
    1. Botswana--History--Dictionaries. I. Title.
II. Series.
DT791.S8   968'.1'003   75-16489
ISBN 0-8108-0857-9

to

CHRIS, JANE and SONS

in a free Zimbabwe

ACKNOWLEDGMENT

I am indebted to various persons whose help was indispensable in collecting, researching and checking the information presented here. In the first place, any work dealing with the history of Botswana must rely upon the solid foundations laid by Professor Anthony Sillery of Oxford University, former Resident Commissioner of Bechuanaland. I have borrowed freely from his various works. Ambassador A. M. Dambe and Mr. B. C. Thema, Minister of Education, graciously read through the entire manuscript and made helpful corrections and suggestions. My research assistant at Lincoln University, Miss Debra Walker, was of great help in gathering together basic resources. The library of Lincoln University extended me every facility and Miss Gabrielle Miner, Special Collections librarian, was especially helpful. Dr. Samir Zoghby of the Africa Section of the Library of Congress gave invaluable help in locating data and checking materials for accuracy. Needless to say any errors of omission or commission are my own responsibility.

As usual, I am indebted to my secretary, Mrs. Barbara Coyle, for her devoted and tireless efforts in the preparation of the manuscript.

R. P. S.

University of Khartoum, Sudan
September 1974

CONTENTS

EDITOR'S FOREWORD

Over the past two decades, Africa has ceased being the Dark Continent and has become an increasingly researched and documented part of the world. But such is the expanse of its area and the variety of its nations, that it will take many decades to shed sufficient light. For that reason, the African Historical Dictionaries have been covering, one by one, the emerging states of Africa, some of which have never been described in a single comprehensive book. Once just another of the High Commission Territories, only recently a sovereign state, much remains to be known about Botswana, sandwiched into the prosperous and explosive southern portion of the continent. Yet a big step has been taken with the publication of this volume.

The most valuable aspect of this dictionary is that, without neglecting the political and economic weight of its unfortunate neighbors, the history of Botswana is considered primarily from within and dealt with in a way that highlights the specific characteristics of a country following its own destiny. Despite a small population, a surprisingly large number of ethnic groups are cooperating in this attempt at nation-building. Here, the history of each one of these groups is described, as are the persons and events that led to the creation and development of the state. And this is done with the wealth of detail and intimate insight that could only come from an old friend.

Professor Richard P. Stevens first went to the region in 1962-63, when he served as Chairman of the Department of Political Science at Pius XII University College in Lesotho. Several other visits were made over the years. As a recognized authority, Professor Stevens wrote numerous articles and sections in various encyclopedias and books. In 1967, he authored the first major work on the independent states: Lesotho, Botswana, and Swaziland: The Former High Commission Territories in Southern Africa. But a lot has happened since 1967, and this volume devoted exclusively to Botswana is able to build on his accumulated knowledge and bring the story up to date.

Jon Woronoff, Series Editor

NOTE ON SPELLING

The orthography of the Setswana (the indigenous) language has developed in a totally haphazard way, and only since 1972 has there been any official attempt to standardize spellings. "Bechuana" is the way Botswana was spelled by early white travelers and missionaries but it has also been written as Beetjuana, Booshuana, Bootchuana, Bichwana and Buchuana.

In Setswana, Ba is the plural of the noun-class of people. A Motswana is a single citizen; the Batswana are the people. Bo is the place prefix. The terminal eng is the ordinary locative. Se is the language prefix. Thus, Setswana is the Tswana language; Sekgatla is the Kgatla dialect. Spellings of the various tribes sometimes include the Ba prefix but in keeping with recent usage it has been omitted in this text.

The intrusion of an Afrikaans element has complicated the spelling of many words. Thus, "g" often represents the South African "g" which is equivalent to the German "ch." Consequently, the name Khama is sometimes spelled Kgama. Many words in Setswana begin with the "gh" sound such as kgotla (tribal council) or kgosi (chief).

ABBREVIATIONS

ANC	African National Congress
BCU	Botswana Cooperative Union
BDC	Botswana Development Corporation
BDP	Botswana Democratic Party [formerly, Bechuanaland Democratic Party]
BIP	Botswana Independent Party
BMC	Botswana Meat Commission
BNF	Botswana National Front
BPFP	Bechuanaland Protectorate Federal Party
BPP	Botswana People's Party [formerly, Bechuanaland People's Party]
BRST	Botswana Roan Selection Trust
BSAC	British South Africa Company
BSAP	British South Africa Police
CDA	Community Development Assistant
CDD	Community Development Department
CDWF	Commonwealth Development and Welfare Fund
DDC	District Development Committee
EAC	European Advisory Council
LMS	London Missionary Society
NA	Native Authority
OAU	Organization of African Unity
PAC	Pan African Congress
UBLS	University of Botswana, Lesotho and Swaziland
UN	United Nations
UNHCR	United Nations High Commissioner for Refugees
WCC	World Council of Churches

BOTSWANA

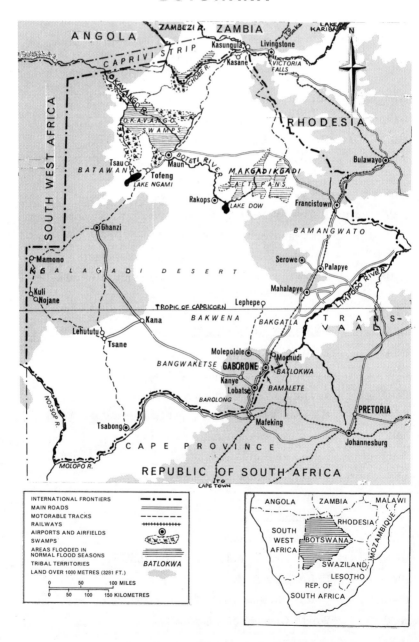

INTRODUCTION

The Land and the People

Botswana, the area of which is estimated at some 220,000 square miles (569,800 square kilometres), is about the size of France. It is entirely land-locked, being bounded on the south and east by the Republic of South Africa; on the west and north by South West Africa (Caprivi Strip), and on the northeast by Rhodesia. Botswana touches Zambia at the confluence of the Zambezi and Chobe Rivers in the extreme north. This part of the border, several hundred yards long, is a source of controversy with South Africa (through its political relationship with South West Africa).

The country is a vast tableland at a mean altitude of some 3300 feet (approximately 1000 metres), but with elevations of up to 5000 feet. A plateau broken with small hills which runs from the South African border near Lobatse to a point west of Kanye and thence northwards to the Rhodesian border near Bulawayo, forms a watershed between the main natural divisions of Botswana.

The most fertile area of the country, inhabited by some 80 per cent of the population, comprises the central watershed and the lands between it and the Limpopo River, which forms part of the eastern boundary with South Africa. There is just sufficient rainfall for growing food crops, and the presence of an easily tapped underground water table and ample grass of good feeding quality combine to make this a good cattle-rearing area.

To the west of the watershed conditions are far less favorable. The extreme southwestern triangle lying between the confluence of the Molopo and Nossop Rivers consists mainly of dry savannah and scrub-land merging gradually to the northwest into the Kgalagadi Desert. The desert itself, a fairly level, sometimes sandy tract, covered with thorn bush and grass, riverless and with only the minimum of surface water, covers all the central and western areas of Botswana stretching far over the border into South West Africa.

11

In places such as the Ghanzi plateau, underground potable
water near the surface has been tapped and cattle are kept.

In the extreme northwest lies the area known as
Ngamiland, of which the main feature is the Okavango River.
Rising in Angola, this considerable river, after crossing the
Caprivi Strip of South West Africa, enters Botswana and very
soon dissipates most of its flow in the 6500 square miles of
the Okavango swamps, or into the sand-bed of the Boteti
River.   Under exceptional conditions the Okavango floods the
Makgadikgadi salt pans.   Some of the Okavango waters also
flow into the Chobe River, which forms part of Botswana's
northern boundary.   Round the perimeter of the swamps, and
along the northeastern border from Kasane to Francistown,
there is forest and dense bush and conditions are reasonably
favorable for cattle raising and some tillage.

Climate

The northern part of Botswana lies just within the
tropics, and the climate is generally sub-tropical but varies
according to altitude and latitude.   In the hottest month, January, mean maximum temperatures vary from $86°F$ ($30°C$)
to $94°F$ ($34.4°C$).   In winter (August) a dry seasonal wind
sweeps in from the Atlantic across the Kgalagadi, bringing
dust and sandstorms.   July is the coldest month, mean minimum temperatures varying from just over $33°F$ ($0.5°C$) in
the Kgalagadi to $47°F$ ($8.3°C$) in the far north.

Population

A census held in 1971 showed that the total population
of the country was then 630,000 persons, comprising about
600,000 Africans, 4000 Europeans, 3500 persons of mixed
race, and about 500 Asians.   In addition, there were an estimated 11,000 nomads.   At any given moment approximately
35,000 males are temporarily absent, mainly laboring in South
Africa and Rhodesia.   Overall population density is 2.5 persons per square mile with rural densities ranging from 0 to
6 per square mile.   The annual rate of population increase
is believed to be at least 3 per cent.

The African population, apart from some 29,000 Bushmen (also known as the Sarwa), are Batswana (Tswana) of
Southern Sotho stock.   The Sarwa belong to the Naron, Auen,

Kung and Herkum groups; about 10,000 are nomads in the
Kgalagadi. The Batswana people are divided into eight principal tribal groups, each occupying its own separate territory
with its own traditional chiefs and retaining an inalienable
communal ownership over its tribal lands. Associated with
each of the dominant tribes are smaller related or formerly
subjected tribes. Only the Sarwa and the few thousand Europeans are not included in this traditional system. The largest tribe is the Ngwato (Bamangwato), which, numbering
about 200,000, comprises about one-third of the total population and owns one-fifth of all the land; its territory lies to
the east. The next two largest tribes are the Kwena (Bakwena) and the Ngwaketse (Bangwaketse), who live in the southeast near Gaborone; each tribe numbers about 70,000. The
other smaller tribes are the Kgatla (Bakgatla), numbering
32,000; the Malete (Bamalete), numbering 14,000; and the
Tlokwa (Batlokwa), numbering 4000--all of whom live in the
southeast; the Rolong (Barolong), numbering 11,000, who
overspill into South Africa; and the Tawana (Batawana), numbering 42,000, who live on the South West African border.
Unlike most African tribes, the Tswana, or Batswana, have
a tradition of living in large towns often located at great distances from their grazing lands. The inhabitants are largely
cattle farmers. The cattle are often located in remote areas
where cattle posts are maintained. There is a seasonal concentration of people in large central villages, such as Serowe,
Kanye, and Molepolole.

In the 19th century, several large blocks of land were
transferred from African to European ownership around Lobatse, Gaborone, and Tuli in the southeast; Ganzi in the west;
and on the banks of the Molopo River in the south. In 1869
The Tati Concession in the Francistown District (now North
East District) gave a private company the right to exploit a
potentially rich mining area of more than 2000 square miles;
these rights have since been taken by the Botswana government. A company formed in 1914 until recently exercised
the right to grant farming and mining concessions, and held
land rights in the district, all of which have also been taken
over by the government; the company now retains prospecting
rights over barely 300 square miles.

Although thousands of young people leave their villages
every year to seek work in South Africa, or in pursuit of
further education in the towns, there is still little urbanization. The only local magnets for employment outside the traditional sector are the six small towns stretched along the rail-

way line that runs across the country and links it to South
Africa and Rhodesia.

The capital, Gaborone (18, 000), although it has grown
rapidly into an administrative center since becoming the capital, is still much smaller in population than Serowe (36, 000),
the Ngwato capital, which lies 35 miles from the nearest rail-
head.   Francistown (19, 000) is the commercial center of the
Tati Concession area, which is dominated by Europeans,
mainly from South Africa.   Lobatse (12, 000), the nearest of
the six towns to Mafeking across the South African border,
is another center of commerce.   Other population centers,
traditional or modern, are Selebi-Pikwe (est. 27, 000); Kanye
(40, 000 seasonal); Maun (10, 000); Molepolole (10, 000); Ramotswa (12, 000); Mochudi (7000).

History

Like that of other Sotho peoples, the early history of
the Batswana is shrouded in legend.   Historians believe the
Batswana to be part of the Bantu-speaking tribes which moved
south from Central Africa about the time of the birth of
Christ.   But it was not until the 19th century that Botswana's
history became documented when such missionary figures as
Livingstone and Moffat moved northward towards the Zambezi
through Botswana.   As is the case today, the majority of the
people lived on the eastern border of the country staying in
large tribal villages.   It was not until the beginning of the
19th century, when a common threat appeared from outside
the country's borders, that the various tribes came together.

This threat came through the expansion of the Zulu nation under their great leader Chaka.   Some of the tribes
which did not join the Zulus were forced westward, and under
such leaders as Sebetoane and Manthatisi, began to enter and
raid the country.   This grew to a climax with Mzilikazi,
Chaka's lieutenant, who fled from his commander and settled
first of all north of Zeerust close to the southeastern border
of present day Botswana.   He made continual raids across
the border into the Batswana lands plundering cattle.   Although then driven farther north by the Boer settlers in South
Africa, he continued to raid the Batswana from what is now
Rhodesia.

The Boer settlers moving into the Transvaal became
the potential plunderers of the Batswana in the south and the

tribes lived in continual fear of raiding parties from the Boer
Republic of the Transvaal.

The Batswana could offer no resistance to these potential invaders and, helped by such missionary figures as
MacKenzie and Price, and later Lloyd and Willoughby, three
of the main chiefs, led by Khama III, the great-grandfather
of the present President of Botswana, appealed to the British
for help. In answer to their request a military mission by
the British under Sir Charles Warren entered the country in
1884 to stop the Boer raiders and in the following year Britain
declared Bechuanaland as far north as Serowe a British Protectorate. This was later extended to the present northern
boundary of the country. However, in the south the Boers
had already taken land and started farms. This land, which
belonged to the Rolong tribe, was lost to the Batswana and
eventually became part of South Africa. For the next ten
years the Batswana lived a comparatively peaceful life, protected by the occasional presence of British troops which
patrolled the southern borders of the country.

Then in 1894, a new threat faced the country. Cecil
Rhodes and the British settlers in South Africa started to ex-
pand northwards and Rhodes, seeing the importance of Bechuanaland as "the Suez Canal to the North, " tried to have
the country incorporated in his British South Africa Company.
Once again the Batswana united against this threat and Khama
III, with two other chiefs, went to Britain to object to Rhodes'
plans and seek the personal protection of Queen Victoria.

After a long struggle lasting several months during
which the British Government tried to ignore the Chiefs,
Bechuanaland was formally declared a Protectorate in 1895
and this began 70 years of British administration. The British also finally decided to take an active interest in Bechuanaland because they feared that the Boers in the Transvaal
would link up with the German settlers in South West Africa
and thereby cut off British expansion north into Rhodesia.

Even under British rule the Chiefs remained leaders
of the individual tribes. It was not until 1920, with the establishment of the African Advisory Council, that any political
advancement was made. Despite opposition from the chiefs,
the Act of Union which created South Africa in 1909 provided
for the possibility of including Bechuanaland and the other
two protectorates, Swaziland and Batsutoland (now Lesotho).
This threat to the independence of the country was not removed until 1960, when South Africa left the Commonwealth.

It was mainly due to this expectation--that Bechuanaland would become part of South Africa--that the successive
British administrators in Bechuanaland did very little to develop the country. Few Batswana were trained in administration or any other skills and even the capital of the country
remained until 1965 at Mafeking outside Botswana's borders.

Very little progress was made towards political advancement until 1950 when a Joint Advisory Council, made up
from the African and European Councils, formed in 1920 and
1921, was formed. In 1961 a new Constitution gave the country limited legislative powers under the Legislative Council.
At the same time political parties were being formed which
pressed for total independence. Four years later, in March
1965, Britain granted Bechuanaland internal self-government
following a general election based on universal adult suffrage.

In the elections, the Bechuanaland Democratic Party
(BDP), led by Dr. Seretse Khama, won 28 of the 31 seats
in the Legislative Assembly. The Bechuanaland People's
Party (BPP), led by Mr. P. G. Matante, won 3 seats; the
Botswana Independence Party (BIP), which also contested the
elections, failed to win any.

The 1965 constitution introduced a system of responsible government under which, subject to certain responsibilities and reserve powers vested in Her Majesty's Commissioner, the executive government of Bechuanaland would be
controlled by ministers drawn from and responsible to an
elected legislative chamber. The Executive Council was replaced by a Cabinet (presided over until 21 September 1965
by her Majesty's Commissioner and subsequently by the Prime
Minister) consisting of a Prime Minister together with his
deputy and six other ministers chosen by him from the members of the Legislative Assembly. Dr. Seretse Khama, as
leader of the political party which held a majority of the seats
in the assembly, was appointed by Her Majesty's Commissioner
to be Bechuanaland's first Prime Minister. The Legislative
Assembly, from which the Cabinet was drawn, replaced the
former Legislative Council. It consisted of 31 elected members, 4 members specially elected by the assembly itself,
and the Attorney-General who had no vote in the assembly.

There was also a House of Chiefs (consisting of the
eight principal tribal chiefs ex officio and four other chiefs
elected by and from the sub-chiefs) which advised the Government and had special consultative powers where matters of

tribal concern were affected by bills introduced into the Legislative Assembly.

Although in most matters the executive government of
Bechuanaland was controlled by the Cabinet, Her Majesty's
Commissioner under the 1965 constitution retained a general
reserve executive power.   He also retained responsibility,
acting in his own discretion, for external affairs, defense
and internal security, and public service.

The Bechuanaland Democratic Party, which formed
the Government under Dr. Seretse Khama after winning the
general election of March 1965, stated in its election manifesto that it would work for the independence of Bechuanaland
within the shortest possible time.   Proposals for an independence constitution, prepared by the Government, were de-
bated and endorsed by both the House of Chiefs and the Legislative Assembly.   The proposals were subsequently presented for discussion at the Bechuanaland Independence Conference held in London during February 1966, when it was
agreed that the Bechuanaland Protectorate should become an
independent sovereign state, the Republic of Botswana, on
September 30, 1966.

THE DICTIONARY

ANC   see   AFRICAN NATIONAL CONGRESS

AFRICAN ADVISORY COUNCIL. Founded in 1920 as the Native Advisory Council, its function was to discuss with the Resident Commissioner all matters affecting African interests which the members desired to bring forward. While in principle the selection of the representatives to the council rested with the tribal kgotlas, in practice the choice was usually exercised by the chiefs. In the Bechuanaland Protectorate each chief or Native Authority could express his separate opinion, so that the Bechuana spoke officially with divided voices. The council did afford a useful link between the administration and the recognized voice of the people, thus laying the groundwork for constitutional advance. One of the most important functions performed by the Council was in providing a platform for the expression of vehement opposition to the incorporation of the Protectorate in the Union of South Africa. The administration used the African Advisory Council as a proving ground for proposed legislation. Obtaining the prior, often perfunctory, approval of the chiefs, added a necessary measure of legitimacy to new regulations when they were presented to the populace. The Council was also employed as a tool to limit the necessity for direct administrative intervention in local affairs.

AFRICAN NATIONAL CONGRESS (ANC). A South African political party, founded in 1912, that became prominent after World War II when it demanded the abolition of all racial discrimination. From its inception the Congress enjoyed support from the traditional chieftainship in Bechuanaland and the other High Commission Territories. After its banning in 1960 by the South African government the Congress went underground and a new, radical strategy was adopted. In Bechuanaland the ANC presence was for a while represented by Motsamai Mpho, the first secretary-general of the Bechuanaland People's Party. (See also MATTHEWS, Z. K.: MATTHEWS, J.; MPHO;

19

PAN AFRICAN CONGRESS.)

AFRIKAANERS   see   BOERS

AGRICULTURE   see   ECONOMY, INTERNAL--(2) Agriculture

AGUDA, AKINOLA, the Honorable Justice (1923-).   Chief
Justice of Botswana.   Born at Akure in the Western
State of Nigeria, and called to the English Bar in July
1952.   From 1957 he was appointed Senior Crown Coun-
sel and on May 2, 1968, a Judge of the High Court of
the Western State of Nigeria.   He held many other ap-
pointments in the same state before being appointed Chief
Justice of Botswana on February 4, 1972, under the
terms of a technical agreement signed between Nigeria
and Botswana in 1971.   He has published widely both
articles and books, the best known of his books being
Principles of Criminal Liability in Nigerian Law: Practice and Procedure in the High Courts of Nigeria and
Law of Evidence in Nigeria.

AHA HILLS.   A hilly region in western Ngamiland near the
South West Africa border.   Elevations reach 1070 meters.

AMERICAN METAL CLIMAX, Inc.   see   ECONOMY, INTER-
NAL--(4) Mining

ANGLICAN CHURCH.   The Anglican Church in Botswana broke
its historical association with Rhodesia in June 1972 and
became a separate diocese with its own bishop, the Rt.
Rev. Charles Shannon Mallory.   Bishop Mallory, formerly archdeacon of Ovamboland in South West Africa (Nami-
bia) and chaplain of the diocese in Grahamstown was
senior lecturer in theology at the University of Makerere
in East Africa before his arrival in Botswana.   Bishop
Mallory was consecrated and enthroned in Gaborone on
December 31, 1972, as Botswana's first Anglican Bishop.

ANGLO-AMERICAN CORPORATION.   South African corporation formed in 1917 by Sir Ernest Oppenheimer (1880-
1957) with American backing and controlled since his
death by his son, Harry Oppenheimer.   One of the world's
largest mining and financial empires, the corporation,
through its De Beers Group, has taken over the mining
concessions originally obtained in the Tati area by Cecil
Rhodes.   See also ECONOMY, INTERNAL--(4) Mining.

ANIMAL LIFE. A wide spectrum of wildlife is found in
Botswana and provides one of the country's most valuable resources. Nearly 30,000 square miles, one sev-
enth of the country, has been declared as national park
or game reserve. Animals include elephant, hippopotamus, giraffe, lion, buffalo, zebra, leopard, cheetah,
over two dozen varieties of antelope, wild dogs, warthog,
genets, serval, a vast range of lesser mammals and
over 530 varieties of birds. Crocodiles, poisonous
snakes, including cobra and puff adder, abound.

ARDEN-CLARKE, SIR CHARLES (1898-1962). British colonial administrator. From Nigeria he went to Bechuanaland
and in 1934 and from 1936 to 1942 was its resident commissioner. From 1942 to 1946 he held a similar post
in Basutoland, becoming Governor of Sarawak in 1946
and of the Gold Coast (now Ghana) in 1949.

-B-

BCU see BOTSWANA COOPERATIVE UNION

BDC see BOTSWANA DEVELOPMENT CORPORATION

BDP see BOTSWANA DEMOCRATIC PARTY

BIP see BOTSWANA INDEPENDENCE PARTY

BMC see BOTSWANA MEAT COMMISSION

BNF see BOTSWANA NATIONAL FRONT

BPFP see BECHUANALAND PROTECTORATE FEDERAL
    PARTY

BPP see BOTSWANA PEOPLE'S PARTY

BSAC see BRITISH SOUTH AFRICA COMPANY

BSAP see BRITISH SOUTH AFRICA POLICE

BA. Prefix indicating plural of a people. See under name
    of people--e.g., Kgatla for Bakgatla.

BALANCE OF PAYMENTS see ECONOMY, EXTERNAL--
    (2) Balance of Payments

BAMANGWATO CONCESSIONS. An area of land granted to
the British South Africa Company in 1893 by Chief Khama
of the Ngwato. In 1931 Tshekedi Khama, Acting Chief
and Regent, urged the cancellation of the concession and
declared his tribe's opposition to all mining in their country. In 1932 a new agreement was signed between the
tribe and the Company which provided for the cession by
the Company to the High Commissioner in trust for the
tribe of two strips in the Tuli Block. At the same time,
the British Government ceded to the tribe a large area
to the north of the Ngwato reserve, while in return for
the new agreement and an acceptable mining law, the
Company made over to the Crown an area near Gaborone.
In 1934 the Company abandoned the concession and the
two strips in the Tuli Block were transferred back from
the tribe to the Company. The Ngwato retained the
Crown Lands made over to them.

BAMANGWATO CONCESSIONS LTD. see ECONOMY, IN-
TERNAL--(4) Mining

BANKING see ECONOMY, INTERNAL--(9) Banking

BANTU. The term Bantu was formerly the name given only
to a group of languages spoken by the many tribes which
today are found scattered over a very large part of the
African continent, south of a line drawn from the East
African great lakes to the Indian Ocean, and extending to
the southernmost point of the Cape Province, South Africa. These languages are spoken by all the peoples south
of the Zambezi including the Batswana, with the exception
of the disappearing Hottentots and Sarwa. But while the
term was originally applied only to the group of languages, today it is the peoples themselves that are usually
meant, and the word embraces many tribes of Negroid
origin, each of which has its own tribal name.

BAROLONG FARMS see ROLONG

BATHOEN, CHIEF (d. 1910). Chief of the Ngwaketse (Bangwaketse), a sub-tribe of the Batswana, from 1889, on
the death of his father, Gaseitsiwe. He came into prominence in 1895 through visiting England with Khama, Chief
of the Ngwato, and Chief Sebele of the Kwena. He and
his companions were received by Queen Victoria, whose
sovereignty he agreed to accept. Later, he objected to
having control of his territory made over to the Chartered

Company and submitted a protest. During the South African War he furnished wagons to the British military authorities. A convert to Christianity, he abolished many practices deemed incompatible with Christianity or opposed to the welfare of the tribe. His tribal capital was Kanye. See also NGWAKETSE.

BATHOEN II, CHIEF GASEITSIWE SEEPAPITSO, C. B. E. (1908-). Son of Seepapitso, grandson of Bathoen I, educated at Tiger Kloof and Lovedale (South Africa). Paramount Chief of Ngwaketse 1928-69; Chairman of the African Advisory Council 1937-47 and 49-58; member of the Legislative Council and Executive Council 1961; Director of the Botswana Meat Commission 1965-69; Member of the Council of the University of Botswana, Lesotho and Swaziland, 1967-69; Director of the Botswana Exploration and Mining Company 1968- ; Chairman of the Botswana National Museum and Art Gallery 1968- ; Member of Parliament, House of Assembly 1969- ; President of the Botswana National Front 1970- .

BATSWANA see TRIBAL STRUCTURE (also see "Population" portion of the Introduction)

BECHUANALAND BORDER POLICE see BRITISH SOUTH AFRICA POLICE (BSAP)

BECHUANALAND DEMOCRATIC PARTY see BOTSWANA DEMOCRATIC PARTY

BECHUANALAND PEOPLE'S PARTY see BOTSWANA PEOPLE'S PARTY (BPP)

BECHUANALAND PROTECTORATE FEDERAL PARTY (BPFP). Founded by Leetile Disang Raditladi in 1959 at the time when a Legislative Council for Bechuanaland was first established. A member of the Ngwato chiefly House, who had quarrelled with Tshekedi Khama and was banished between 1937 and 1957 from the tribal area, Raditladi felt that the country was in need of political parties to replace "rule by one man." Among the founding members of the party were representatives of the eight major tribes in Bechuanaland. The BPFP announced that it aimed to work for the unity of these tribes while enhancing the institution of chieftainship. The party called for the removal of the chiefs from party politics and the establishment of a chamber of chiefs with considerable

power. In a conservative vein, it condemned calls for
a black majority in the Legislative Council and denounced
as dangerous calls for early independence. The party
made little headway and by 1962 had ceased to exist.

BIRWA   see   TULI BLOCK DISTRICT; KHAMA III

BOER WAR   see   SOUTH AFRICAN WAR

BOERS (AFRIKAANERS). The name applies to South Africans
of Dutch or Huguenot descent, especially to early settlers of the Transvaal and the Orange Free State. As
early as 1852 the Transvaalers attacked the Kwena and
maintained this pressure throughout the century on the
Batswana tribes. Boer settlements were established both
in the eastern region of Bechuanaland along the railroad
and in the far west near the South West Africa border.
Boer demands for the incorporation of Bechuanaland into
South Africa were still heard into the early 1960's.

BOITEKO. A community venture which came into being after
a series of meetings held in one of the Serowe villages,
in 1969. Boiteko was conceived to create, through experiment, a model project capable of raising the standard
of living and promoting employment in rural areas. Its
aims have included maximizing the use of local materials
in production, providing training, encouraging cooperation,
and spontaneous capital formation. Boiteko now has a
tannery, a pottery, a brickfield, a garden, spinning and
weaving, dressmaking, food-processing, brewing, lime-
burning, building and stonemasonary, wood and water de-
livery by donkey carts, and photographic developing and
printing. In the majority of these production groups most
of the raw materials are on hand in and around Serowe.

BOJALWA. This traditional beer has long played an important part in rural life in Botswana. It is derived from
the staple food crop, sorghum. Probably it has a better
claim than most alcoholic beverages to be of nutritional
value, but beyond this it is a token that life is going well.
Its copious consumption is a sign of a good harvest in
the previous season and social relations are cemented
with its aid. At Dikgafela, the New Year celebration
now combined with Independence Day, BOJALWA is sprin-
kled over the chief by the women of the tribe, to ensure
good rains in the coming season. While these traditional
uses are still practiced today, by far the most common
forms of drinking now are those involving cash.

BOTETI RIVER. A seasonal river which drains eastward
from the Okavango-Lake Ngami region to Lake Xaw (Dow)
near the center of the country.

BOTHA, GENERAL LOUIS (1862-1919). South African statesman and soldier. The acknowledged leader of the Boer
people following the South African War, he was their
choice as the first prime minister of the Transvaal in
1907, when responsible government was granted; after the
holding of the National Convention at which he was a delegate, he was chosen the first premier of the Union of
South Africa in 1909. General Botha unsuccessfully urged
upon the British government the immediate transfer of
Bechuanaland and Swaziland to the Union.

BOTSWANA COOPERATIVE UNION (BCU). Formed in 1966
to fulfill the following functions: to serve as a wholesale
supplier, to act as an agent for the sale of crops, to
provide services to the cooperative movement, and to
provide advice and assistance for the development of the
movement. Until 1972 the Union served mainly as a
wholesale supplier for the consumer societies. However,
on January 1, 1973, the BCU took over the marketing
branch in Lobatse, which provides an agency service for
cooperatives at the BMC abattoir. By that date all consumer societies and almost all marketing societies were
members of the Union. The BCU acts as an insurance
agent for societies. See also ECONOMY, INTERNAL--
(13) Community Development.

BOTSWANA DEMOCRATIC PARTY (BDP). The BDP was
founded in late 1961 by several members of the Legislative Council. The party was established in reaction to
the anti-administration activities of the BPP. Seretse
Khama, the rightful heir to the chieftaincy of the Ngwato,
along with Mr. Quett Masire, a progressive farmer, and
several others established the BDP alliance with traditional leaders and in support of non-racialism. Although
lacking formal authority the BDP dominated the Legislative Council and enjoyed some of the benefits of a ruling
party. Although the constitutional conferences in London
disappointed traditional leaders who desired greater influence in government, the BDP remained their only outlet.
Whites and many traditional leaders were thus committed
to the BDP at an early date. Seretse Khama, although
prevented by the British from becoming chief of the
Ngwato, possessed the traditional leadership qualities--
royal origin and wealth--as well as the "modern"

criterion of a good British education. His close association with the administration in the Legislative Council,
and his being named as a member of the Order of the
British Empire assured the party of support from the administration. Close linkage with the traditional social
structure, under which most Batswana live, brought an
overwhelming victory in the country's first elections in
1965. The party secured 28 out of 31 seats and Sir
Seretse Khama became Botswana's first Prime Minister.
On independence in 1966 Sir Seretse became President.
Elections were again held in 1969, when the BDP retained
a slightly reduced majority of 24.

BOTSWANA DEVELOPMENT CORPORATION (BDC). Formed
in 1970 as a public limited liability company charged with
the task of promoting industrial development by participating in joint ventures with local or foreign entrepre-
neurs, by carrying out research in investment opportunities, by assisting with capital on loan or equity terms
where desired, and by supplementing the limited availa-
bility of local entrepreneurship. See also ECONOMY,
INTERNAL--(12) Planning.

BOTSWANA INDEPENDENCE PARTY (BIP). A breakaway
party from the BPP formed in 1964 by Mr. Motsamai
Mpho (q.v.), the former secretary general, who was accused of favoring the Communist Party of South Africa.
Although the BIP won no seats in the Legislative Assembly in 1965 it won one in the 1969 parliamentary elections.

BOTSWANA MEAT COMMISSION (BMC). Established by law
in 1965, the BMC came into existence on February 1,
1966, when it took over the assets and liabilities of the
then Bechuanaland Protectorate Abattoirs, Ltd., and the
Export and Canning Company, Ltd. The Board of the
Commission consists of a chairman and nine members
who manage its affairs. The Commission's business is
to purchase cattle from the producers and to slaughter
and process those cattle in its modern automated plant
situated in Lobatse. The plant has a capacity of approximately 1500 cattle per day. See also ECONOMY, IN-
TERNAL--(3) Cattle.

BOTSWANA NATIONAL FRONT (BNF). As a result of the
earlier splits in the BPP, the poor showing of the opposition parties in the first national elections, the allegedly

conservative domestic and foreign policies of the BDP
government, and attacks by the government on traditional
authority, a new nationalist-oriented party, the Botswana
National Front (BNF), was formed in October 1965, largely through the efforts of Dr. Kenneth Koma. Dr. Koma
returned to Botswana just before the 1965 election and
brought together the Motsete wing of the BPP, tradition-
alists led by Chief Bathoen of the Ngwaketse, civil servants and organized labor groups to form a nationalist
opposition. This was the first opposition party to attempt to unite the relatively mobilized town dwelling dis-
sidents with the rural tribesmen by promoting socialist
programs and defending the prerogatives of the traditional
authorities. By nominating Chief Bathoen as its presidential candidate, the Front hoped to win a tribal base to
supplement its anticipated victories in the towns. Although uniting with Bathoen may have cost the BNF some
support, the basic strategy appears to have had some appeal. In the 1969 parliamentary elections the BNF won
three seats.

BOTSWANA NOTES AND RECORDS. Journal of the Botswana
   Society, intended as a medium for the publication of research and articles of scholarship on Botswana. Published annually since 1968, some 50 universities and public libraries had subscribed by 1972.

BOTSWANA PEOPLE'S PARTY (BPP). The Botswana People's Party (originally Bechuanaland People's Party), was
   founded in December 1960, partly in response to the establishment of the Legislative Council and partly as an
   outgrowth of the banning of the African National Congress
   (ANC) and Pan African Congress (PAC) in South Africa.
   The three prominent party leaders, Kgaleman Motsete
   (President), Philip Matante (Vice-President) and Motsamai
   Mpho (Secretary-General) were all well educated but
   lacked the traditional status required to make a broad-
   based appeal. For the most part party support was confined to the eastern towns and villages along the rail line.
   The party demanded immediate independence, Africaniza-
   tion of the administration, an end to rule by the chiefs,
   an end to the color bar, and the nationalization of land-
   generated support, especially in the Tati and Francistown
   areas, long dominated by foreign companies. The rapid
   ascent of the BPP, however, was quickly cut short by
   internal rivalry, which, reinforced by competition between ANC and PAC elements, led to the expulsion of

Mpho and six other BPP leaders associated with the ANC. Matante and Motsete accused Mpho of attempting a "Communist" takeover of the party. Mpho in turn accused Matante of misappropriating party funds. The Mpho-led BPP faction formed the Botswana Independence Party (BIP) in 1964. Furthermore, the split caused a cut-off of funds from Ghana and Tanzania, hurting the organizational potential of both wings of the party. A further schism in the BPP resulted in the replacement by Matante of Motsete as president, with the expulsion of Motsete from the party. The fragmentation of the People's Party tended to weaken all three factions by dividing the already limited, partially mobilized constituency in the towns. In the 1965 elections the BPP won three seats in the Legislative Assembly and again three seats in the 1969 parliamentary elections.

BOTSWANA POWER CORPORATION see ECONOMY, INTERNAL--(8) Energy and Power

BOTSWANA ROAN SELECTION TRUST see ECONOMY, INTERNAL--(4) Mining

BOTSWANA SOCIETY, THE. Founded June 10, 1968, the Society undertook the encouragement of interest in and research and scholarship on subjects in the fields of the natural sciences, the social sciences, and the humanities and the arts, especially where such subjects are related to Botswana. It publishes annually a journal, Botswana Notes and Records, which is intended as a medium for research and articles of scholarship on Botswana.

BRIGADES see VAN RENSBURG, PATRICK

BRITISH BECHUANALAND. The territory south of the Molopo River was constituted as the Crown colony of British Bechuanaland in September 1885 and annexed to the Cape colony in 1895. A portion of the land was reserved for the Bechuana tribes. This action was in response to Boer attacks from Goshen upon Mafeking.

BRITISH SOUTH AFRICA COMPANY (BSAC). Following the grant, on October 29, 1888, of a concession for the mineral rights in Matabeleland by King Lobengula, a charter was issued by Queen Victoria on October 15, 1889, to Cecil John Rhodes, Alfred Beit, Albert Grey, George Cawston, the Duke of Abercorn and the Duke of Fife,

authorizing them to establish the British South Africa
Company, with a capital of £1 million and vast powers,
including those to occupy territory, enter into diplomatic
relations and carry out military expeditions.   The BSAC
nearly altered the whole course of the Bechuanaland Protectorate's history.   Even before the granting of the
charter, which described the Company's principal field of
operations as lying north of British Bechuanaland and the
Transvaal and west of the Portuguese possessions (modern Botswana), Rhodes offered to contribute £4000 a year
for the maintenance of an imperial officer in the Bechuanaland Protectorate.

From the very onset there could be no question that
it was the intention of the Colonial Office that the Company should eventually take over the control of the Protectorate and thereby relieve the British government of
the expense and responsibility of administration.   The
Botswana chiefs, however, reacted unanimously in rejecting a transfer of the Protectorate to the Chartered company and were supported by the then High Commissioner,
Sir Henry Loch.   Chiefs Sebele, Khama and Bathoen went
to London in 1895 to present their case against incorporation.   It was at last agreed that the chiefs would assist
in the plans of the Company for the extension of the railroad under construction, by ceding to it a strip of land
running along the northern road.   The Colonial Secretary,
on his part, agreed that each of the chiefs should have a
country in which to live, as before under the protection
of the Queen.   The chiefs had gained their point and were
not to come under the administration of the Company; but
this decision applied only to the areas within their own
jurisdiction and it was made clear that the tribal lands
would be further demarcated.

However, the whole question of transfering any authority to the Company was virtually rescinded in the
proclamation of March 2, 1906, which postponed "sine
die" the transfer of the Protectorate.   This decision was
a direct result of the ill-fated Jameson Raid upon Johannesburg, which was staged from the Protectorate and had
the backing of Rhodes.   It was thus made clear that the
Imperial government would exercise authority in the region, especially since the Bechuanaland colony had been
transfered to Cape Colony the previous year.   Further
delay could only give rise to the possibility of the Imperial government's losing all control over the course of
events in Southern Africa.   Following this decision, the
Protectorate's administration was moved north from

Vryburg to Mafeking, still outside the boundaries of the
Protectorate but considerably better situated for administrative purposes. Never again was the Company able to
press for the right to administer the Protectorate, despite the fact that its legal rights presumably persisted
until the termination of its charter in 1923. See also
TLOKWA; RHODES, CECIL.

BRITISH SOUTH AFRICA POLICE (BSAP). Under its charter,
    granted in 1889, the British South Africa Company had
    authority to establish its own police force, which ab-
    sorbed large numbers of the Bechuanaland Border Police,
    formed in 1885, soon after the occupation of that country.
    Units of the British South Africa Police accompanied the
    Pioneer Column in 1890 and began work immediately after
    the founding of Fort Salisbury. They did service, not
    only in normal duties but in the Matabele War, the Ma-
    shona Rebellion and in the Boer War, when 300 men
    took part.

BUSHMEN see SARWA

                              -C-

CDA [Community Development Assistant] see ECONOMY,
    INTERNAL--(13) Community Development

CDD [Community Development Department] see ECONOMY,
    INTERNAL--(13) Community Development

CAMPBELL, JOHN, THE REV. (1766-1840). Traveller and
    missionary, born in Scotland, educated with Sir Walter
    Scott. Drawn to the Church from youth, he assisted in
    founding the Religious Tract Society of Scotland at the
    age of 27, as well as other social welfare bodies. He
    became a minister of the Kingsland Independent Chapel in
    London in 1802, helped with the foundation of the British
    and Foreign Bible Society, and worked for the London
    Missionary Society. In 1812 he inspected their local sta-
    tions at Cape and travelled widely for two years. Books
    of travels, including those in the Bechuanaland country,
    appeared under the title of Journals of Travels in South
    Africa: Among the Hottentot and Other Tribes: In 1812,
    1813 and 1814, published in 1840.

CAPRIVI STRIP (Also Caprivi Zipfel, German for "Capriri
    tip"). Long narrow strip of country, extending from the

extreme northeast of South West Africa to the Zambezi
River. Measuring 300 miles in length, it is nowhere
more than 50 miles wide. Its existence is due to the
aim of the German authorities at the end of the 19th century to unite their colony in South West Africa with that
in East Africa. The name is derived from that of Count
Leo de Caprivi who succeeded Prince Bismarck as Imperial Chancellor in 1890. Under his regime the area
was ceded by Britain in 1893. The Caprivi Strip is almost dead flat, and, having several large rivers, is of
great potential importance to the possible reclamation of
the Kgalagadi Desert. Because of its isolation from
South West Africa it was joined to Bechuanaland after
World War I, but since 1939 has been administered from
Pretoria.

CATTLE   see   ECONOMY, INTERNAL--(3) Cattle

CENTRAL DISTRICT. The largest of the 12 districts, the
     Central District, with its main center of Serowe, has re-
     sponsibility over the Ngwato tribal territory with a popu-
     lation of approximately 216,000 (1972). The Central Dis-
     trict consists mainly of undulating grassy plains and
     Mophane bush, ideally suited to cattle ranching. The
     drought years during the early part of the 1970's took a
     heavy toll of the cattle herds but with good rains in 1974
     grazing improved and the Ngwato herds began to recover.
     Along the eastern border with the Republic of South Af-
     rica the Tuli Block (q. v.) with its privately owned farms
     is one of the richest farming areas in Botswana. The
     Central District is rich too in natural resources--dia-
     monds at Orapa, coal at Palapye, copper/nickel at
     Selebi-Pikwe.

CHAPMAN, JAMES (1831-1872). Explorer and hunter. Born
     in England, he went to Natal at the age of 11. In 1851
     Chapman came within 70 miles of the Victoria Falls, al-
     most discovering them before David Livingstone. Two
     years later he undertook another expedition to the north
     of Bechuanaland and the upper reaches of the Zambezi.
     He trekked overland to Walvis Bay in 1860, and was one
     of the first white men to settle in South West Africa,
     opening a cattle-breeding post at Otjimbinque. Chapman
     was a remarkable hunter and also collected natural his-
     tory specimens. Accounts of his travels in Bechuanaland
     appeared in his work entitled Travels in the Interior of
     South Africa, published in 1868.

CHARTERED COMPANY see BRITISH SOUTH AFRICA COM-
PANY

CHIEFTAINSHIP. The chief as head of the tribe occupies a
position of unique privilege and authority. Traditionally
the symbol of tribal unity, the central figure around
whom the tribal life revolved, he was at once ruler,
judge, maker and guardian of the law, repository of
wealth, dispenser of gifts, leader in war, priest and ma-
gician of the people. Under early colonial rule, the administration allowed the chief to remain the central figure of the tribal government, and without his approval
and backing no major enterprise among his people could
be initiated or successfully accomplished. Under modern
constitutional forms many of the traditional prerogatives
of the chiefs have passed to the District Councils.
The sub-chiefs are accepted leaders of subordinate
tribes within the tribal territory of the paramount chief.
The control of the allocation of land in their territory is
granted to them by the paramount chief and they in turn
are served by subordinate headmen in their own villages.
Chief's representatives are headmen or at least men of
royal birth who are members of the dominant tribe.
They are appointed by the paramount chief to rule over
subject peoples who lack the status to have their own sub-
chiefs. Their jurisdictions are usually in the more remote villages of the Kgalagadi Desert. Certain headmen
occupy positions as leaders of major sections (composed
of several wards) of the tribal capital. The paramount
chief, sub-chiefs, chief's representatives and section
headmen constitute the top leadership of the tribal political system today.
Each tribal territory is divided into a number of
wards. A ward is a patrilineal but non-exogamous body
of people forming a distinct social and administrative unit
under the leadership and authority of the hereditary headman. A ward can constitute either a distinct part of a
village or a separate village of its own. The ward headman performs the local judicial function and represents
his people before the chief. The headmen also form part
of the chief's kgotla for the hearing of major cases and
serve as advisers.

CHIEPE, GAOSITIVE KEAGAKWA TIBE, M. B. E. , B. Sc. ,
M. A. (1922-). A Botswana diplomat, she was born in
Serowe; educated in Serowe primary school, secondary
school at Tiger Kloof (South Africa) and at the Universi-

ties of Fort Hare and Bristol. Education officer, Botswana, 1948; Senior Education Officer, 1962; Deputy Director of Education, 1965; Director of Education, 1968;
High Commissioner to U.K. and Nigeria, 1970-; concur-
rently accredited as Ambassador to Sweden, Norway,
Denmark, West Germany, France and Belgium; Hon.
L. L. D. (Bristol).

CHOBE   see   NORTH WEST DISTRICT

CHOBE NATIONAL PARK.   The 4250-square-mile Chobe National Park in northern Botswana has a superb variety of
wildlife.   It takes its name from the Chobe River, one
of the main tributaries of the Zambezi River and is only
one and a half hours' drive from the Victoria Falls.   The
entrance to the reserve is at Kasane.   During the dry
season along the river bank the tourist is likely to see
elephants by the hundreds, buffalo, sable, roan, eland,
kudu, waterbuck, zebra, tsessebe, lion, leopard, impala,
reedbuck, lechwe, and the Chobe bushbuck.   Hippopotamus and crocodile live in the Chobe River.   Further inland, giraffe, gemsbok and wildebeest roam the veld.
The park contains most types of Central African birdlife,
particularly aquatic birds.   The Chobe River itself
swarms with tiger fish, often called the fresh water bar-
racuda.

CHOBE RIVER.   Flowing north and emptying into the Zem-
bezi River to the east of Kasane, the Chobe River marks
the northeast border of the country with the Caprivi Strip
(South West Africa).   The river nourishes an abundance
of aquatic and animal life.

COLONIAL DEVELOPMENT CORPORATION   see   COMMON-
WEALTH DEVELOPMENT CORPORATION

COLOREDS (EURAFRICANS).   In the southern African context
the term "Colored" is applied to the descendants of white
colonists and slave women, mostly Malays and Hottentot
and Bantu Africans, as well as those of mixed blood
through onging processes of miscegenation.   A small
Colored community has always been found in Botswana,
mostly along the rail line.   In 1971 the Colored population was set at 3500.

COMMONWEALTH DEVELOPMENT CORPORATION.   Formerly known as the Colonial Development Corporation, the

change of name was effected in 1963 when the Corporation's full powers of operation were also restored in all
those countries which had achieved independence within
the Commonwealth since 1948. The Corporation is authorized to borrow up to £225 million on long- or medi-
um-term and £10 million on short-term loan. In Botswana, before and after independence, the Corporation has
carried out a variety of activities in conjunction with the
Ngwato tribal council and other tribes. It built and
started working the Lobatse abattoir in 1954 which subsequently involved Botswana government participation. In
general, the Corporation has provided a model of cooperation between government and private enterprise and
between external capital and technology, on the one hand,
and domestic labor, land and resources, on the other.

COMMONWEALTH OF NATIONS. Botswana was recognized
as a member of the Commonwealth of Nations upon ac-
ceding to independence on September 30, 1966. High
Commissioners are accredited to the United Kingdom,
Nigeria, Zambia and Canada.

COMMUNICATIONS see ECONOMY, INTERNAL--(7) Transportation and Telecommunications

COMMUNITY DEVELOPMENT see ECONOMY, INTERNAL--
(13) Community Development.

CONCESSIONS COMMISSION. Appointed in 1893 to inquire
into the concessions that had been granted by the chiefs
to various companies, syndicates and individuals. Although the Commission was not well received by Chief
Sebele or Chief Linchwe, it cancelled most of the concessions that had been granted. Only those concessions
which had received the express consent of tribal councils
were recognized as valid according to tribal law. Except
in certain cases, any concessions granted after October
29, 1889, the date of the charter granted to the British
South Africa Company, were declared invalid. The decisions of the Commission essentially preserved the land
of the Batswana.

CONGREGATIONAL COUNCIL FOR WORLD MISSIONS see
LONDON MISSIONARY SOCIETY

CONSTITUTION. The new Constitution of Botswana came
into operation on September 30, 1966. The principal

change from the 1965 Bechuanaland Constitution concerned
the creation of the position of President, the holder of
which took over the powers and responsibilities formerly
exercised by the Prime Minister.
Executive power lies with the President of Botswana,
who is also Commander-in-Chief of the armed forces.
Election for the office of President is linked with the
General Election of members of the National Assembly.
Presidential candidates must receive at least 1000 nomi-
nations. If there is more than one candidate for the
Presidency, each candidate for office in the Assembly
must declare which Presidential candidate he supports.
The candidate for President who commands the votes of
more than half the elected members of the Assembly will
be declared President. If the Presidency falls vacant the
members of the National Assembly will themselves elect
a new President. The President will hold office for the
duration of Parliament. After the 1974 elections the
President will be an ex officio member of the Assembly.
There is also a Vice-President, whose office is
Ministerial. The Vice-President is appointed by the
President, and acts as his deputy in the absence of the
President. The Cabinet consists of the President, the
Vice-President, and eight other Ministers appointed by
the President. Every member of the Cabinet accepts responsibility before the National Assembly for the policies
of the Government.
The legislative power is vested in Parliament, consisting of the President and the National Assembly, acting after consultation in certain cases with the House of
Chiefs. The President may withhold his assent to a Bill
passed by the National Assembly, but if it is again presented to him after six months, he is required to assent
to it unless he dissolves Parliament within 21 days. The
National Assembly consists of the Speaker; the Attorney-
General, who does not have a vote; 31 elected members,
increased to 32 after the 1974 elections; and four specially elected members. There is universal adult suffrage.
The life of the Assembly is five years.
The House of Chiefs has the Chiefs of the eight principal tribes of Botswana as ex officio members, four
members elected by sub-chiefs from their own number,
and three members elected by the other 12 members of
the House. Bills and motions relating to chieftaincy matters and alterations of the Constitution must be referred
to the House, which may also deliberate and make repre-
sentations on any matter, including Bills affecting tribal
interests.

The Chief Justice is appointed by the President while puisne judges and magistrates are appointed by a Judicial Service Commission. No dual citizenship is permitted, although provision exists for easy acquisition of citizenship by residents. The Constitution also contains a code of human rights, enforceable by the High Court.

CONSTITUTIONAL COMMITTEE. Set up in 1958 by the Joint Advisory Council to frame the Protectorate's first constitution. The Committee proposed an executive council and a legislative council, the latter consisting of 31 to 35 members, with the Resident Commissioner as President. In addition to three ex officio members, there were to be seven appointed official members (white), two appointed unofficial members (white), and ten members elected by the white population. With two appointed and ten elected African members, plus one Asian, the total would come to 35, of which the Africans would comprise a third. The election of the African members was to take place through the African Council meeting as an electoral college. Consequently, the Protectorate's first Legislative Council was established in 1961 in accordance with the provisions of the Order in Council of December 21, 1960.

CONSTITUTIONAL PROPOSALS (Lobatse Conference). Constitutional consultations completed in November 1963 at Lobatse provided for the establishment of parliamentary government on the Westminister model. The legislature, constituted largely on the basis of universal adult suffrage (open to all British citizens or protected persons resident in Bechuanaland), was to consist of 38 seats, of which 32 were to be elected from single member districts on the basis of a common roll, four were to be chosen by the elected members, and two were officials. The cabinet, composed of a prime minister and five other ministers, was to be drawn from the Legislative Assembly. Local control over internal affairs was considerable, but Britain retained authority over external affairs, defense, internal security and the public service. The exercise of these reserved executive powers by the Queen's Commissioner would be with the advice of the cabinet, except in extraordinary cases. These proposals, in slightly revised form, were accepted by the British government on June 2, 1964, and it was announced that elections under the new constitution would be held in March 1965. See CONSTITUTION.

COOPERATIVES see ECONOMY, INTERNAL--(13) Community Development

COURTS see JUSTICE

CROCODILE RIVER see LIMPOPO RIVER

CROWN LAND see ORDER IN COUNCIL of May 16, 1904

CURRENCY see ECONOMY, EXTERNAL--(3) Customs and Duties; ECONOMY, INTERNAL--(9) Banking

CUSTOMARY COURTS see JUSTICE

CUSTOMS AND DUTIES see ECONOMY, EXTERNAL--(3) Customs and Duties

-D-

DAILY NEWS. Government newspaper published in Gaborone; circulation 9000 in English; 5000 in Setswana.

DAMARA see HERERO

DAMBE, A. M. (1911-). Botswana politician; born in 1911, Nswazwi, Ngwato area. He received his education at Dombodema, Mapoka, Tiger Kloof, Inyati, Tati Training Institute and Adams College. He was a teacher at Dombodem and Serowe, later headmaster. Served with High Commission Territories corps in Middle East, later Sergeant; Treasurer B. P. Teacher's Association; member of Legislative Assembly March 1965-72; Minister of Mines, Commerce and Industry 1965-66; Minister of Home Affairs April 1966; Minister of Works and Communications until 1970; then Minister of Agriculture 1970-72; Ambassador to the United States, 1972-.

DEMOGRAPHY see "Population" portion of the Introduction

DISTRICT COUNCILS. There are nine district councils in Botswana which follow very closely the tribal boundaries. See table next page.
    In addition to these districts three township areas have been defined--Francistown, Gaberone, and Lobatse. The town Councils have similar responsibilities as the district councils. These include primary education,

District	Pop. (1971)	Area (sq. mi.)	Capital
Central (Ngwato)	216,000	56,070	Serowe
Ghanzi	12,000	40,443	Ghanzi
Kgalagadi	15,000	42,552	Tshabong
Kgatleng	31,000	2,798	Mochudi
Kweneng	65,000	14,719	Molepolole
North East	26,000	2,062	Francistown
North West	53,000	50,212	Maun
Southern (Ngwaketse)	82,000	10,053	Kanye
South East	20,000	1,091	Ramoutswa

public health, supply of water, and maintenance of district roads. The major source of income for the councils comes from a nationally levied local government tax,
school fees and government grants.
    The town councils each consist of eight elected mem-
bers and a number of nominated members. The district
councils vary in size from 12 to 38 but each council has
a substantial elected majority. Chiefs and tribal authorities are ex officio members of the district councils. The
representative of the central government in the districts
is the District Commissioner, a civil servant responsible
to the Minister of Local Government and Lands. Several
important forms of authority, which in the past were regarded as the exclusive preserve of the chief, including
control over distribution of land, have been transferred
or partially transferred to the council. See also ECON-
OMY, INTERNAL--(13) Community Development.

-E-

EAC see EUROPEAN ADVISORY COUNCIL

ECONOMY, EXTERNAL (see also ECONOMY, INTERNAL)
    [containing: 1. Foreign Trade; 2. Balance of Payments;
    3. Customs and Duties; 4. Foreign Aid; 5. Tourism].
    (1) Foreign Trade. The growth in exports between 1969
    and 1972 was nearly 50 per cent per annum with exports
    rising from R13 million in 1969/70 to an estimated R43
    million in 1972/73. The two main items contributing to
    that increase were beef and diamonds. The f.o.b. value
    of beef exported rose from R7 million in 1966 to R20
    million in 1972, representing almost a three-fold in-
    crease in only seven years. Diamond production started

in mid-1971, and 1972 was, therefore, the first complete
year of production, with net (f.o.b.) sales revenue
amounting to R18 million.   For the financial year 1971-
72 Botswana had total exports of R31.00 million of which
R17 million was in livestock products, R11.7 million in
minerals and R2.3 million all others.

Imports are recorded as having grown at 30 per cent
per annum during the same period although a part of the
increase must be attributed to the improved collection of
trade statistics.   The high level of imports in 1971/72
and 1972/73 is largely due to the capital imports for the
Shashe Project.   However, the underlying trend indicates
a rapid and sustained growth of consumer imports associated with the high rate of growth of employment and
gross domestic product.   Net imports (per financial year)
were: 1969/70, R34.3 million; 1970/71, R44.8 million;
and 1971/72, R62.7 million.

Botswana is joined to Lesotho, South Africa and
Swaziland in a Customs Union Agreement, which was substantially revised in 1969.   As a result of this Agreement, goods move freely between the member countries
but until recently no precise records of the movements
of goods were kept.   All importers are required to complete customs documents for statistical purposes.   The
figures which have been collected do not indicate the origin of the goods.   Many imports are goods of South Africa manufacture that are able to compete effectively with
overseas manufacturers in the protected Southern African
market.   (See paragraph 3, Customs and Duties.)

(2) Balance of Payments.   As a consequence of not
having a separate Central Bank with power to issue currency, an overall surplus or deficit on the Balance of
Payments will be reflected as an increase or a decrease
in the holdings of foreign assets of the financial institutions and the Rand currency in circulation.   The figures
for changes in the foreign assets of financial institutions
are therefore comparable to the figures for changes in
foreign reserves of a balance of payments statement for
a country with a Central Bank.   The import of notes and
coins is comparable to the import of monetary gold in an
economy with a Central Bank, and can be considered as
a part of the overall surplus.   Under the present monetary arrangements, however, it will be impossible to
maintain the growth of the economy without a net import
of notes and coins, which from one point of view is comparable to imports of goods or services.

At the time of independence, and in the years immediately following, the structure of Botswana's balance
of payments was characterized by a relatively large deficit on visible trade and services compared with the country's Gross Domestic Product. This deficit was largely
made up by transfers and loans from the U.K. During
the previous Plan period the structure of the balance of
payments changed considerably. The deficit on the balance of goods and services increased substantially, the
composition of the imports also changed with a much
larger share consisting of capital goods. The increase
in the deficit on the balance of goods and services was
partly offset by an increase in transfers and loans but
more so by an exceptionally high inflow of private foreign
capital. In other words, the structure of the balance of
payments changed from that typical of a country at a
very low level of development, depending on external support to maintain a minimum level of public services, to
that of a rapidly expanding economy, financed through
large foreign investments mainly in the mining sector between 1971 and 1973.

(3) Customs and Duties. Before independence the
revenue received by Botswana from customs and excise
duties under the 1910 Southern African Customs Agreement amounted to about R1.2 million a year. There was
no customs and excise administration and the Government
was therefore required to rely heavily on the cooperation
of neighboring countries in the calculation of the Botswana
share of the common revenue pool, and in the enforcement of legislation that would normally fall within the responsibility of a Botswana Department of Customs and
Excise. After independence, the Government entered into
negotiations with its partners in the Customs Union (Lesotho, Swaziland, and South Africa). The negotiations
led to the signing of a new Agreement on December 11,
1969. It came into force on March 1, 1970.

Under the terms of the 1969 Agreement, the four
contracting parties agreed that legislation relating to customs, excise and sales duty similar in all respects would
be enacted in each of the countries. Botswana, Lesotho
and Swaziland undertook to establish customs and excise
administrations to collect statistics, and to assess and
collect the customs, excise and sales duties payable in
the respective countries. South Africa acts as the cus-
todian of the revenue pool, and each of the smaller countries receives its share, calculated in accordance with a
fixed formula:

$$R = \frac{i + p\ (C + E + S)}{I + P} \times 1.42$$

where

R=   revenue received by Botswana, Lesotho or
            Swaziland;
i=   total value of cost, insurance, and freight
            (c. i. f.) at border of all imports into Bots-
            wana, or Lesotho or Swaziland, inclusive
            of customs, excise and sales duties;
I=   total value c. i. f. at border of all imports
            into the Customs Area, inclusive of cus-
            toms and sales duties;
p=   total value of dutiable goods produced and
            consumed in Botswana, or Lesotho or
            Swaziland, inclusive of duties;
P=   total value of dutiable goods produced and
            consumed in the Customs Area, inclusive
            of duties;
C=   total collection of customs duties within the
            Customs Area;
E=   total collection of excise duties within the
            Customs Area;
S=   total collection of sales duties within the
            Customs Area.

The formula takes account of additional factors arising
from the existence of the Customs Union and affecting
the smaller countries, other than their share of imports
and production of dutiable goods.   The effect on Botswana
of the operation of the formula has been that about 20
per cent of the value of dutiable goods imported into or
produced in Botswana has been received as the Botswana
share of the revenue pool.   The amounts received in recent years are greatly in excess of those that would have
been received under the 1910 Agreement.
     The fixing of the tariff of duties remains the preroga-
tive of South Africa, but the new Agreement makes detailed consultation in a variety of circumstances obligatory.
To facilitate consultation, a Southern African Customs
Union Commission has been established, with representatives of the four member countries.   The Commission
meets at least once each year to review the operation of
the Agreement.   Any Botswana industry capable of supplying a substantial proportion of the total Southern African market may apply for protection in the whole Customs

Union Area on the basis of the same norms as apply to similar industry in South Africa. In the marketing of agricultural commodities Botswana has a right to participate on an equitable basis in marketing schemes operating in South Africa.

(4) Foreign Aid. Britain, the United States, Canada, Sweden, Denmark, and the Netherlands have been the most important sources of foreign aid; of these, Britain is foremost, having met government deficits until 1972. The following grants and loans have been committed:

Revenue (in sight)	Total 1970-75
U. K. Government	R 7,660,000
Netherlands Government	88,000
Danish Government	340,000
Swedish Government	734,000
IBRD and IDA	39,928,000
Others	322,000
Total	R49,072,000

For private foreign investments, see also ECONOMY, INTERNAL--(4) Mining.

(5) Tourism. At present, the bulk of foodstuffs, equipment, management skills and other items required to supply the needs of the tourist industry are imported, and the earnings of locally-based factors of production constitute only a small part of the total expenditure of tourists coming to the country. Therefore, the capacity of the tourist industry to stimulate economic growth through its secondary effects has been limited. With careful planning and control it is expected that tourism can make significant contributions to the growth of the economy. See also TOURISM.

ECONOMY, INTERNAL (see also ECONOMY, EXTERNAL) [containing: 1. National Income; 2. Agriculture; 3. Cattle; 4. Mining; 5. Housing; 6. Manpower and Employment; 7. Transportation and Telecommunications; 8. Energy and Power; 9. Banking; 10. Industry; 11. Taxes; 12. Planning; 13. Community Development]. (1) National Income. The lack of reliable economic statistics in the past makes it extremely difficult to calculate the economic growth of the country, but the Gross Domestic Product in 1971 was

estimated at Rand 87.6 showing a growth rate over the
previous five years of 10 per cent.

Estimated Gross Domestic Product and Gross National
Product for 1971-72 in Millions of Rands

	GDP	GNP
Agriculture	25.2	24.8
Hunting, Fishing, Forestry	2.2	2.2
Mining and Prospecting	12.5	5.4
Manufacturing	7.7	6.8
Construction	9.4	7.5
Water and Electricity	0.5	0.5
Trade, Hotels & Restaurants	5.9	5.3
Transport and Communications	4.2	3.4
Financial Institutions, Business Services and Real Estate	4.6	2.3
Personal and Community Services	0.8	0.8
Private, Non-Profit Services	0.9	0.9
Central Government	9.8	9.0
Local Government	2.3	2.3
Traditional Ownership and own Construction of Dwellings	2.4	2.4
Unallocated	0.8	0.8
Total	87.6	72.8

In 1971, only about 2800 families, a large proportion
of which were expatriates, had an income in excess of
R750 per annum.   Of those Batswana fortunate enough to
be employed, 77 per cent were categorized as unskilled
labor with a mean annual income of R300.   Fewer than
1.5 per cent of citizen families in salaried employment
earn more than R750 per annum.   In the rural areas
there is a greater spread in incomes, with approximately
2000 Batswana with annual incomes (again, in 1971) in
excess of R750:   a few have very high incomes.   At the
other end of the scale, in 1971/72 (a good agricultural
season) there were some 40,000 families (over one third
of the total population) falling within the R0-R250 per annum income group, equivalent to between R0 and R2 per
head per month, of whom 7000 families (10 per cent of
rural families) earned less than R50 per annum in cash,
and grew no crops.
   The above figures do not take into account the

remittances of migrant laborers working outside Botswana.
They totalled 50,000 individuals in 1971 and it may be assumed that their remittances contributed mainly to the incomes of the poorest section of the community. For the
low income categories, annual incomes are very closely
related to climatic factors that determine the size of the
cereal harvest. In a poor year large numbers may be
forced to depend on famine relief supplies. It is therefore very difficult to determine precise numbers in this
category.

(2) Agriculture. All Batswana were farmers--crop-
growers and cattlemen. Prior to independence, farming
was practiced only to subsistence level with little thought
of growing for profit. The harsh drought of 1965-66,
with its attendant starvation, brought home the need to
become self-sufficient and to produce enough to carry
over to leaner times, and even to export. In the early
1970's about 90 per cent of the population derived a living from agriculture. The main crops are sorghum,
millet, cowpeas, and groundnuts, with cotton being the
most important cash crop.

Arable production is concentrated in the east in the
Limpopo River catchment basin. Because of the erratic
rainfall, crop production varies from year to year. However, modern methods of farming are showing that even
in the worst years crops can be grown. Extensive studies are being carried out into new methods of dry land
farming and irrigation experiments are taking place using
water from the Chobe River and the Okavango. Special
efforts are being made to introduce cash crops, and to
encourage the farmer to grow enough food not only for
their own families but to produce a surplus which they
can sell.

(3) Cattle. Cattle are Botswana's principal source
of wealth.   Cattle herding employs most of the labor
force, and cattle products make up most of the country's
exports. Botswana has a total cattle population of over
1.5 million. However, because cattle are traditionally a
sign of wealth many farmers are reluctant to part with
their stock for slaughter and the annual off-take from the
National Herd is comparatively low, standing at about 8
per cent per annum. Nevertheless, this represents over
R6 million in exported beef to markets throughout the
world. It is expected that the annual off-take, depending
on climatic conditions, will continue to rise and a target

off-take of 285,000 per annum from a National Herd of
two million has been set.
     All Botswana's beef exports pass through the Bots-
wana Meat Commission (q.v.) in Lobatse, one of the big-
gest meat processing plants in Africa. The abattoir was
established with the aid and assistance of the Commonwealth Development Corporation (q.v.) and the British
Government as a first major step towards developing a
beef export industry. Early in 1966 the Botswana Meat
Commission, a statutory body, took over the administration of the abattoir and meat canning factory and is today
responsible for all cattle marketing in Botswana. Bone-
less beef, high-grade corned beef, meat extract, bone
meal, edible fats, meat meal, tallow, and hides are major products which find ready markets in South Africa,
Zambia, Zaire, and Europe. The abattoir can handle
over 1000 head of cattle per day. Botswana and the
United States have signed a grant agreement for over
R200,000 aimed at increasing the income of small stock-
holders and at improving the management of range resources essential to their livelihood. The agreement provided for an initial grant contribution of R200,000 to per-
mit the project to begin in 1974.
     A feature of cattle rearing in Botswana are the long
trek routes, where thousands of head of cattle are
trekked sometimes up to 500 miles to the abattoir. The
government has started a number of schemes, among
them a country-wide artificial insemination scheme,
aimed at increasing the numbers and improving the quality of the National Herd. Cattle owners are being shown
the advantages of modern commercial farming through
such schemes. See also BOTSWANA MEAT COMMIS-
SION.

     (4) Mining. Mining in Botswana, apart from some
ancient workings, began in the late 19th century when
gold was discovered in the North East. In the 1880's a
gold mine was opened which only finally closed down in
1964. The discovery of gold aroused interest at the time,
and for several years prospectors searched the ground
for minerals--with little success. Interest waned and
apart from occasional prospecting teams during the first
of this century little interest was shown in the country
until the establishment of the Geological Survey Department by the then Bechuanaland Protectorate government
in 1948/49.
     As more and more information about the geological

structure of the country became available, interest grew
and by the mid 1950's numerous mining and surveying
companies were prospecting for both base metals and
precious metals. Asbestos and manganese was discovered in the southeast and mines developed. By April
1969, 25 special prospecting licences were in force but
it was two major international mining companies which
made the discoveries of diamonds and large quantities of
copper/nickel that within the next ten years should make
Botswana economically independent and give hope for
rapid development.

Working in the northeast, searching mainly for base
metals, Roan Selection Trust Ltd. (R. S. T.), through
their subsidiary Bamangwato Concessions Ltd., began
prospecting in 1959. By 1973 large quantities of workable copper/nickel ore, some 37 million tons, had been
discovered in the Selebi-Pikwe area. In early 1973 the
Anglo-American Corporation-De Beers Group launched a
crash program to exploit similar nickel-copper deposits
in the Tati area. De Beers, through a locally registered
subsidiary, began mining diamonds at Orapa, where one
of the Kimberlitic pipes discovered is believed to be
among the largest in the world, likely to produce mainly
industrial diamonds. A 150-mile road built in 1973 to
the Orapa area from Francistown was financed by a loan
from De Beers to the Botswana Government. Both the
copper/nickel and the diamond mines began operation in
the early 1970's with 3.2 million carats production of diamonds expected by 1975.

Botswana RST, through its subsidiary Makarikari
Soda Ltd., is proceeding with the exploitation of the brine
deposits. In 1973 Mobil Oil began conducting explorations.
Other foreign companies are interested in gypsum and
limestone, while antimony and sulphur are known to exist.
A consortium of U. S. Steel and two South African mining
houses, Anglo-Transvaal and Middle Wits., were prospecting in western Botswana for minerals and gem stones.

An agreement was reached on royalties and taxes to
be paid by Bamangwato Concession in developing and ex-
ploiting mineral deposits in the Seleki-Pikwe Complex.
Binding for 50 years, the agreement stipulates $7\frac{1}{2}$ per
cent of profits to be paid as royalties. There will be a
basic income tax of 40 per cent, increasing by 1 per cent
for every per cent rise in the profit-to-gross revenue
ration above $48\frac{1}{2}$ with a maximum of 65 per cent. The
Botswana Government is to receive its 15 per cent share-
holding, free of charge when Bamangwato concessions

becomes a mining company, as opposed to its former
prospecting company. For the first ten years production,
which is expected to begin in 1973-74, is planned to total
2 million metric tons of ore annually, yielding approximately 100,000 tons of sulphur, 16,000 tons of refined
copper and 13,000 tons of refined nickel. Now that large
profits are in sight, the Botswana Government is finding
it easier to obtain international loan capital.

(5) Housing. According to the National Development
Plan, 1973-78, it is expected that about 75 per cent of
the R30 million required for urban investment in 1973-
78 will be raised by the public sector (Government,
Councils and Botswana Housing Corporation). The remaining 25 per cent will be raised by the private sector.
The Botswana Housing Corporation, which will carry
out most of the public sector investment in housing, will
recover its costs by sale of houses at cost, or by economic rental. Tenant purchase schemes will be available
for occupants of the Corporation's lower-cost houses.

(6) Manpower and Employment. Between 1964 and
1971 cash employment in Botswana increased from about
31,600 to 51,400 workers, an increase of 6.8 per cent
per year. Both of those figures include an estimated
6000 workers on tribal lands, many of whom may be only
seasonally employed. However, during that period, the
active labor force (defined as the economically active
resident population over the age of 10 years, excluding
housewives and subsistence hunters and gatherers), increased from an estimated 250,700 to 282,500 people.
Thus, though the proportion of the active labor force in
paid employment increased from 12.6 to 18.12 per cent
over the period, the number of workers who were exclusively engaged in the subsistence sector had been increasing by between 1600 and 1700 each year. In spite
of a fairly rapid rate of growth of cash employment, the
absolute number of people who were dependent upon subsistence activities (and therefore the numbers of unem-
ployed and underemployed workers) continued to increase.
The problem of unemployment and underemployment
is difficult to assess in quantitative terms owing to a lack
of detailed evidence. Although the numbers of people in
traditional agriculture continued to increase between 1964
and 1971, the number of males in the traditional sector
actually fell by 8 per cent. That, however, is as much
the result of a very significant emigration of males of

working age as of the growth in cash employment. Faced
with a lack of employment opportunities at home, the number of males who left the domestic labor force to search
for work abroad increased from approximately 35,700 in
1964 to 48,000 in 1971. The growth of domestic cash
employment, though significant, has not been sufficient to
absorb the growth in the labor force. If it had not been
for migration, the numbers in the traditional sector
would have been about 8 per cent higher than their 1971
level. The fall in the number of males in that sector is
therefore--somewhat unusually--itself symptomatic of a
shortage of work opportunities at home, and of the difficulty of obtaining an adequate income from the land. It
is clear then, that the numbers of absentees not only affect the numbers of cash recipients, but also crucially
affect the levels of unemployment and underemployment
within Botswana. Moreover, rural-urban migration has,
in recent years, caused open unemployment in the towns
to increase rapidly. In 1971 approximately 5000 urban
dwellers were estimated to have been out of work, but
looking for it--which compares with approximately 17,000
people who were working for cash in the towns at that
time.

(8) Transportation and Telecommunications. Communications in Botswana are steadily improving, but it is
still difficult to reach some of the more remote areas,
particularly in the north and west. Distances in Botswana are great and the small population is widely scattered which makes effective communications not only essential but also costly.

Railways: The main communication link in Botswana
is the section of the Cape Town to Rhodesia railway which
passes through the eastern part of the country. The line
enters Botswana in the South, near Mafeking, and passes
through Lobatse, Gaborone, Palapye, and Francistown before entering Rhodesia. The single-track line is 394
miles long and there are regular passenger and goods
services. See also RHODESIA RAILWAYS.

Roads: Botswana has about 5000 miles of roads.
Those in Gaborone, Lobatse and Francistown have bitumen surfaces. The main road link runs parallel to the
railway line and is an all-weather gravel and earth road.
Major construction work will be carried out on this road
in the next five years, and the section between Lobatse

and Gaborone, which carries the highest density of traffic,
will soon be bitumen surfaced. Good branches off this
road lead from Gaborone to Molepolole, Lobatse to Kanye,
Pilane to Mochudi, Mhalapye to Machaneng, Palapye to
Serowe and a 400-mile stretch of road from Francistown
to Maun. A new 311-mile road has recently been completed from Francistown to Orapa, the site of the diamond
mine. The main road west, linking Ghanzi to the eastern center runs from Kanye across the Kgalagadi Desert
and is suitable only for trucks or four-wheel-drive vehicles.

Although some of the main roads are sandy in places,
and become slippery when wet, they present no problems
under normal conditions. However away from the main
roads system, particularly in the west and north, the
roads are liable to be very heavy sand tracks and are
suitable for trucks and four-wheel-drive vehicles only.
A new American-financed, 300-mile road will replace the
present track from Nata to Kazungula. This road which
is expected to be completed in 1976, at a cost of $13.5
million, will link up with a modern ferry across the
Zambezi connecting Botswana with Zambia. It will be an
all weather gravel road.

Airways: Botswana has international air links with
South Africa and Zambia and operates an increasing number of internal services. Botswana Airways Corporation,
in which the Government has a 50-per cent interest, operates flights to Livingstone in Zambia and to Johannesburg in South Africa, the latter route in conjunction with
South African Airways. There are daily flights between
Gaborone and Francistown and regular services to Maun,
Ghanzi and Kasane. There are over 50 registered land-
ing strips in the country and some of the remote areas
are more easily accessible by air than by road. The
main airfields are at Gaborone, Francistown, Maun and
Kasane. A new airfield has been built at Selebi-Pikwe.

Telecommunications: At the end of March 1973
there were 85 post offices (about one for every 7500 people and every 6900 km.) and 35 telephone exchanges with
3500 lines connected to 5500 telephones (one telephone
for every 114 people). Postal, telephonic and telegraphic
services are the responsibility of the Department of Posts
and Telecommunications, which also runs the Post Office
Savings Bank. The average rate of growth in the number of telephones has been 16 per cent over the previous

eight years. The number of post offices has grown by 7 per cent a year. The growth in the number of telephones has been determined by the supply, as is shown by the numbers on the waiting list, and therefore does not accurately reflect the growth in demand that has occurred during the period.

(8) Energy and Power. The Botswana Power Corporation, the Francistown Town Council, the Botswana Meat Commission and the Government itself are the most important public-sector producers of power in Botswana. Bamangwato Concessions Ltd. (temporary power at Selebi-Pikwe) and De Beers Botswana Mining Company (at Orapa) are the main private producers. Power is also produced, but on a small scale, by a number of concerns such as Rhodesia Railways, mission hospitals, certain schools and domestic users that live away from public supplies. It is difficult to obtain an accurate figure for the total amount of power produced in Botswana since detailed records have not been kept for the whole system. However, excluding supplies from small private producers, it is estimated that about 64. 4 billion watt-hours of electricity were generated in Botswana in 1972/73 with a maximum demand of 14. 9 megawatts; the same figures for 1966/67 were estimated at 10. 7 GWh and 2. 3 MW respectively, giving an average annual growth rate of 25 per cent for both units generated and for maximum demand.

The Botswana Power Corporation was established on January 1, 1971 with the functions of generating, transmitting, supplying and distributing electricity in prescribed areas. Its operations were initially confined to generating and supplying power in the Gaborone-Lobatse area (where there were in 1972 some 1780 domestic and 235 commercial users), using the assets that were transferred from the Electricity Branch of the Gaborone Water and Electricity Unit. The installed capacity of its power station at Gaborone, which also serves the Lobatse area by way of a 33-kilovolt (kv) transmission line, is 12 MW, made up of three steam generators with a combined capacity of some 4 MW, and five diesel generators with a combined capacity of 8 MW. Both Lobatse and Gaborone are served by 11 kv distribution systems.

(9) Banking. Two long-established South African banks operate in Botswana--Barclays Bank (D. C. O.) and the Standard Bank, Ltd. Each bank has branches in

Gaborone, Lobatse, Francistown, Selebi-Pikwe and Mahalapye and in addition weekly agencies and a mobile
service are operated in the smaller centers.   Full facilities are available from the two commercial banks, whose
rates are related to those ruling in South Africa.
In 1963 a National Development Bank was established
for the purpose of promoting the economic development
of the country.   Priority has been accorded agricultural
credit, cooperative credit and loans for local business
ventures.   Impact of the Bank has been limited due to a
shortage of capital.   There is presently no general legislation governing the operations of banking and other similar institutions in Botswana.   The government proposes
to exert greater influence than is now possible over the
disposition of domestic savings that are deposited with
banks operating in Botswana, and to ensure that any new
financial institutions that may be established in the future
will be soundly managed.   The enactment of this legislation will also provide a logical basis for the evolution of
an enlarged financial structure in which the use of modern techniques for influencing local credit conditions will
eventually become possible.   The volume of deposits with
the Post Office Savings Bank grew to some R700,000 by
1974 and remains relatively stable.

Botswana, in common with Lesotho and Swaziland,
participates in a joint monetary system with South Africa,
their Rand being legal tender in the country.   This arrangement, through automatic changes in the money supply,
eliminates any international payments disequilibria in the
conventional sense, and provides the country with a strong
and internationally accepted currency.   However, it has
the serious disadvantage of making Botswana subject to
monetary and credit policies over which it has only limited effective control.   Botswana is deprived of the normal services of a central bank, and has no scope what-
soever for influencing the money supply.   There is no
formal agreement with South Africa governing the use of
the Rand in Botswana, and lack of precision concerning
the arrangements has in some instances hindered foreign
investment.

Botswana has never received any income from the
foreign exchange reserves backing the currency in circulation within the country.   Consequently Botswana has for
years made to South Africa what is effectively a substantial, indefinite-period, interest-free loan.   At present it
is estimated that currency in circulation in Botswana
amounts to about R12 million.   See also ECONOMY, EX-
TERNAL--(3) Customs and Duties.

(10) <u>Industry</u>. The country's secondary and tertiary
sectors are quite undeveloped. Only 1 per cent of the
work force is currently engaged in secondary activities,
which are all located in the southeast, so that there is
a regional imbalance. Also, ownership of almost all industries, with the important exception of the Lobatse
abattoir, is nonindigenous.

Lobatse might be called the industrial "nucleus," for
located there is the most important industry, the abattoir
and related canning plant, which are operated by the
Botswana Meat Commission. A small mill, a cap and
helmet company, a small garment manufacturer, and a
crafts shop are also located in Lobatse. The only other
manufacturing establishments in the country are a brew-
ery, a tannery, a furniture factory, and two light engineering works in Gaborone; the Botswana Game Industries
which prepares skins and trophies, a garment maker, a
tannery, and a small abattoir for locally eaten meat in
Francistown; a small garments and crafts enterprise run
by Swaneng Hill School in Serowe; and a one-man garment-
making shop in Palapye. Village handicrafts, which include production of pottery, basketwork, wood carvings,
knives, and spears, and practiced, but they have little
economic importance.

(11) <u>Taxes</u>. The income-tax year covers the period
from July 1st to June 30th of each year. A graduated
pay-as-you-earn system of collection is in force.

The most significant tax legislation was the Mineral
Rights Tax Bill of 1972. Its aim was to tax private
owners of mineral rights, i. e., the white-owned companies, like the Tati Concession and those in the Tuli,
Gaborone and Lobatse Blocks, and others with mining
rights and concessions. All the tribal authorities have
transferred their mining rights to the State. The government does not intend to expropriate these private rights,
but seeks to force landowners and companies to carry
out intensive prospecting as an alternative to paying high
taxes.

(12) <u>Planning</u>. In 1963, the Bechuanaland Protectorate Government published a five-year public expenditure
program based on the limited development finance thought
likely to be available from the colonial power. At independence, the Botswana Government published a <u>Transi-
tional Plan for Economic and Social Development</u>, outlin-
ing national policies and development objectives to be

adopted in the initial period of independence and listing
the projects to be undertaken by Government in the first
three years.
When the Democratic Party Government came to
power in early 1965, an Economic Planning Unit was established within the Ministry of Finance. This arrangement proved inadequate to meet the challenge of independence. To meet this need a Ministry of Development
Planning was created. The first task of the new Ministry
was to review the immediate policies and objectives of
Government, and hence to revise the Transitional Plan
and bring it up to date. In 1968 a five-year (1968-1973)
National Development Plan (q. v.) was advanced. Almost
all the expenditure proposed in this plan was dependent
on finance being raised from friendly governments and
agencies abroad. The 1973-78 Plan called for the following economic objectives:

1. To secure the fastest possible rate of economic
   growth in a manner designed to raise the living
   standards of the great mass of the inhabitants of
   Botswana;
2. To achieve budgetary self-sufficiency in the shortest
   possible time consistent with rapid economic
   growth;
3. To maximize the number of new job opportunities;
   and
4. To promote an equitable distribution of income; in
   particular, by reducing income differentials between the urban and the rural sectors through
   rural development.

The government exceeded its 15 per cent per annum
target rate of economic growth in real terms; achieved
budgetary self-sufficiency in 1972/73; and reached the
1975 employment target in 1972. The critical problem
to be faced in the rural areas remains that of overgrazing; a major effort will be made during the Plan period
to modify land tenure and to improve livestock management practices in order to prevent the ruination of the
nation's ranch land.

(13) Community Development. Community Development in Botswana refers essentially to rural development
and major emphasis is placed upon it. Considerable

efforts were made in 1972-73 to analyze the special problems associated with rural development and to formulate
a comprehensive program of policies and projects aimed
at improving living standards in the rural areas. As a
result of this work the government published Government
Paper No. 1 of 1972, Rural Development In Botswana,
followed by Government Paper No. 2 of 1973, National
Policy for Rural Development. In 1972 a Rural Development Council was established.

Development plans of each district must be finally
approved by the Ministry of Local Government and Lands
in consultation with the Ministry of Finance and Development Planning. The focal point of development planning
at district level is the District Development Committee
(DDC). The DDCs, located in the administrative center
of each district, are also responsible for follow-up action
on approved plans. The development programs of the
district council constitute the major part of the nine District Development Plans which in turn constitute a portion
of the National Development Plan. Taken together, the
district development programs involve a total estimated
expenditure of R9.62 million over the Plan period, 1973-
1978.

Community development has also meant the expansion
of the cooperative movement. From two cooperative societies registered in 1964, the total had grown to 79 by
mid-1972. Three main types of cooperative have been
encouraged--agricultural marketing, thrift and loan, and
consumer cooperatives. At the end of 1972 there were
32 marketing cooperatives with a total turnover of about
R1 million. Some societies deal solely with livestock
but others handle crops and farmers' requisites. By
1972 the proportion of the total throughput of the BMC
supplied by cooperatives had increased 9 per cent. Thrift
and loan societies are simply savings clubs. Since the
first such cooperative was established in Serowe in 1964,
16 were in existence in 1972 with an annual turnover of
about R1 million.

The Cooperative Development Trust was established
at the beginning of 1966 to administer a grant of R60,000
from the British Co-operative Movement and Oxfam, for
the promotion of consumer societies. At the end of 1972
the Trust had made loans to cooperatives to a value of
R116,000 and during the same year it paid out R3000 in
interest on deposits. See also BOTSWANA COOPERA-
TIVE UNION.

The Community Development Department (CDD) was

created in 1965 out of the former Social Welfare Department, itself created in 1962. While the work of the CDD
has embraced social welfare, women's activities, youth
affairs and home economics, the Community Development
Assistant (CDA) scheme has been the dominant feature of
the Department's work. The role of CDAs has been to
supervise famine relief, to promote and supervise self-
help community development projects and to coordinate
sources of assistance. In this way about 100 primary
school classrooms and some 200 ancillary school buildings had been completed by 1970.

EDUCATION. The first schools in Botswana were established
by the London Missionary Society during the early part of
the 19th century. One of the first was in the present
Kwena reserve. Subsequently, additional schools were
established and developed by the Hermannsburg Mission
and by the Dutch Reformed and Catholic churches. Although a tribal pattern of schools has persisted the tribal
school committees which run the schools, the syllabuses,
etc., are under the control of the Education Department.
While tribal management ensured a very large degree of
genuine local interest in education and afforded invaluable
opportunities for training in committee work and in financial management, the system also allowed for financial
mismanagement, loss in planning efficiency and unequal
facilities. Prior to 1965, out of some 218 primary
schools, the government directly administered 25 and the
missions, nine. In 1972 there were 294 registered primary schools with a total enrollment of 81,662. During
the period 1964-72, the number of registered schools
rose steadily, as they were established in the less dense-
ly populated areas. Private schools were registered
usually after being taken over by District Councils. Between 1964 and 1972 the number of registered secondary
schools in Botswana almost doubled, rising from eight to
fifteen, chiefly between 1969 and 1972. Although the
Ministry of Education has overall responsibility for secondary education, the schools, registered under the Education Law, 1966, and subject to regulations formulated
by the Ministry, are administered and financed by a number of different bodies. The Ministry of Education itself
runs seven schools, including four former tribal schools
at Kanye, Mochudi, Moeng and Molepolole, which were
taken over after 1967, and Tutume Community College,
responsibility for which was assumed in 1971. Four are
controlled by mission bodies. Five of the seven "non-

Government" schools receive an annual deficit grant from
the government to balance their recurrent budgets.   Secondary school enrollments have expanded rapidly since
independence, from 1036 in 1964 to 5564 in 1973.   Botswana continues to depend heavily upon expatriate teachers
in the secondary schools.

Rapid growth has also taken place in teacher training, and in 1970, the two initial teachers training colleges had an enrollment of over 300 student teachers.
The third of the colleges, opened in 1968 in Francistown,
has embarked on an intensive programe of in-service
training upgrading the standard of existing primary school
teachers, and over 600 teachers have been involved in
this program.

Radical changes are also taking place in both the primary and secondary school syllabuses to make them
more relevant to the type of life the students will live
after leaving school.   Agricultural and handicraft subjects
are gradually being introduced throughout the school system.

Botswana is a partner with Lesotho and Swaziland in
a regional university: the University of Botswana, Lesotho and Swaziland (UBLS).   The University, with headquarters in Roma, Lesotho, took over the buildings previously owned by Pius XII College.   It was established
by royal charter in 1964 but it is now planned to bring
the University into line with modern circumstances.   The
University is controlled by a tri-national Council on which
sit representatives from the three governments, the University Senate and Administration and a small number of
representatives from outside Southern Africa.

Although between 1964 and 1970 the University's impact upon Botswana in terms of enrollments was small,
the government has always seen UBLS as an institution
which could provide the major part of the graduate manpower requirements of the three countries.   A series of
planning reports were produced, culminating in 1970 in
the Report of the Academic Planning Mission.   Following
the acceptance of the Report by the University and the
three governments, plans for campuses in Botswana and
Swaziland were prepared, and financed by grants from
the Canadian, American and British Governments.   In
July 1971, degree teaching began in temporary facilities
at the Gaborone Secondary School and the Botswana Training Center.   In 1972 a total of 198 Batswana students
were enrolled with UBLS.

Vocational training in commercial and artisan skills

is carried out in the Botswana Training Center. A new
vocational training center at Gaborone will concentrate on
technical training. A unique feature of the educational
system in Botswana is brigade training. This is a system of "on-the-job" training and the work the trainees
produce cover most of the running costs of their training.
Such skills as carpentry, bricklaying, farming, weaving,
tanning, motor mechanics, and textile manufacture are
taught in brigades throughout the country. In origin the
system is largely attributable to Patrick Van Rensburg
(q.v.), principal of Serowe's Swaneng Hill School.

EDWARDS, SAMUEL HOWARD (1827-1922). Trader and explorer. Accompanied David Livingstone on some of his
earlier journeys into Bechuana country. With his friend,
J. H. Wilson, he made one of the earliest journeys to
Lake Ngami. He followed this with numerous other expeditions and entered Matabeleland, where he gained the
friendship of Mzilikazi. Accompanying Sir John Swinburne on his early expedition to Matabeleland in 1869, he
was one of the earliest white men to work for gold in
that country, particularly on the Umfuli and Wunyani Rivers. He became a digger in the 1870's on the Diamond
Fields, and then Managing Director of the Monarch Gold
Mine in Tati.

EUROPEAN ADVISORY COUNCIL (EAC). The dichotomous
racial and cultural differences which permeated the legal
system of Bechuanaland provided the rationale for the
British to create a separate European Advisory Council
in 1921. Unlike its African counterpart, membership on
the European Advisory Council was determined by popular
elections every third year. Initially, six single-member
constituencies were delineated to encompass the widely
scattered European settlers. In 1927 the number was increased to seven. In 1947 it was established on a statutory basis and consisted of eight elected members and
seven official members. The Council's function was to
advise the Resident Commissioner on matters directly affecting the European residents of the territory. However,
neither the High Commissioner nor the Resident Commissioner was obligated to accept its advice. Since the
Council's scope did not extend to matters concerning African affairs, there was always a section of the council
which strongly advocated closer association with the
Union of South Africa if not actual incorporation.
     In order to prevent an influx of Boers from gaining

control over the Council, qualifications for the franchise
were made restrictive. To vote, an individual had to
own property valued at at least $200, or a general li-
cense, and be a British subject of European descent.
Other Europeans, meeting the property qualifications,
were eligible if they had resided in the Protectorate at
least five years.

The European Advisory Council was created for the
purpose of providing a forum for the discussion of matters directly affecting European interests. From the beginning it was clear that the "whites only" Council was
to be more influential than the African Council. Since
the administration consisted entirely of Europeans, social
relations were centered on the European community. Access to administration was more readily available for
settlers and merchants than for Africans. The European
Council met semi-annually (twice as often as the African
Council). Budget estimates for the Protectorate were
presented to the European, but not the African Council
for consideration. Europeans alone were able to make
an input in the vital area of government expenditures.

The main formal purpose of the European Council
was to review legislation involving only the European community (i. e. , income tax legislation). Needless to say,
matters of concern to Europeans, quite often were directly related to African affairs. Demands initiated in the
European Council were presented to the African Council
by the administration. Rather than bringing the two
groups into direct conflict, the administration suggested
that the chiefs implement policies which would satisfy
European complaints. This formal communication channel between Africans and Europeans worked to the advan-
tage of the Europeans while leaving the administration in
the position of arbitrator.

Relations between the European Council and administration were not all purely harmonious. Members of the
European Advisory Council gradually came to recognize
that their interests might better be served through direct
contact with the African chiefs. Partly as a means of
forestalling growing demands for the creation of a legislative council, and partly as a reward for extensive African service with the Allies during World War II, the administration agreed (1950) to establish a Joint Advisory
Council. While the new council was to supplement rather
than replace the existing African and European Councils,
all of these bodies ceased to exist with the creation of
the Legislative Council in 1961.

EUROPEAN FARM LANDS. A strip of land along the southeast border of the Protectorate ceded by the Rolong and
Malete to the British South Africa Company in 1895.
Subsequently, the Company sold the land to private owners.

-F-

FAUNA   see ANIMAL LIFE; CHOBE NATIONAL PARK;
MOREMI WILDLIFE RESERVE

FAWCUS, SIR R. PETER (1951-). Officer, civil servant
and Resident Commissioner and Queen's Commissioner.
From 1939 to 1946 he served as a Lt. Commander. In
1946 he was appointed assistant District Officer in Basutoland. Seconded to the High Commissioner's staff from
1950 to 1953, he was appointed Government Secretary of
Bechuanaland Protectorate in 1954. In 1959 he was appointed Resident Commissioner. Following new constitutional arrangements in 1963 his title was changed to Her
Majesty's Commissioner, 1963-65.

FINANCE   see ECONOMY, EXTERNAL; ECONOMY, IN-
TERNAL

FLAG. The Botswana flag consists of a central horizontal
band of black, one-sixth of the width of the flag. It is
edged by two horizontal strips of white, each 1/24th of
the width of the flag. At the top and bottom of the flag
are horizontal bands of azure blue each three-eighths of
the width of the flag. The length of the flag is one and
one-half times its width. The two large blue stripes
represent water and sky, the black band represents the
majority of the racial group in the country, while the two
thin white bands on either side represent the white group.
This flag replaced the British flag on Independence Day,
September 30, 1966.

FLOGGING CASE. In 1933, Chief Tshekedi Khama ordered
a European, Phineas Macintosh, previously involved in a
morals case, to be flogged in the kgotla. The misconduct of Macintosh and other Europeans had been frequently brought to the notice of the Administration but the Administration had ignored Tshekedi's appeals to have them
punished. Tshekedi then took it upon himself in the interests of just administration and the good of the Ngwato

people to order the punishment of Macintosh. This action, the punishment of a white man, brought international attention to Bechuanaland when Vice-Admiral Edward
Evans, the Acting High Commissioner, backed by marines
and fieldguns, marched overland to depose Tshekedi. At
the official inquiry held in Palapye the Chief was refused
legal representation on the ground that the inquiry was an
administrative one. But he was suspended from the chieftainship for violating the proclamation of June 10, 1891,
which forbade the chiefs to exercise jurisdiction over
Europeans except with their consent. Tshekedi was banished from the Ngwato Reserve and ordered to reside in
the Tati district excluding the native reserve. Several
weeks later, however, following protests of Europeans
and a letter from Tshekedi withdrawing any claim to try
any European in the future, he was reinstated as Chief.

FOREIGN AID   see   ECONOMY, EXTERNAL--(4) Foreign Aid

FOREIGN RELATIONS. Botswana's foreign policy is essentially determined by the fact that her neighbors are the
white-controlled, or segregated countries of South Africa,
South West Africa and Rhodesia. In these circumstances,
Botswana's foreign policy has reflected pragmatic concessions to economic-political realities without compromise
on basic principles. Thus, Botswana has become a member of the Commonwealth, the Organization of African
Unity and the United Nations, and has extended asylum to
refugees from South Africa, South West Africa, Angola
and Rhodesia. While not rejecting diplomatic ties with
South Africa, Botswana has firmly indicated that no exchange of diplomatic representatives can be considered
until all Batswana visiting South Africa are assured of
non-discriminatory treatment. While condemning apartheid, Botswana has, however, clearly indicated that no
subversive operations would be tolerated against neighboring governments. At the same time, Botswana cooperates
with South Africa in the Southern African Customs Union
and the Rand Currency Area. It also cooperates with
South Africa in the control of disease and pests. While
Botswana has declined any official South African aid, private investment from any country has been welcome.
    In his foreign policy statements President Seretse
Khama has indicated his government's preference for
democratic, representative states. Special relations of
friendship exist with Zambia and Tanzania and heavy reliance has been placed upon the United Nations. Lacking

any military strength to defend its territorial integrity, Botswana must look to the United Nations for moral and technical support.

Although Botswana has pursued a non-aligned position in world politics, it has been made clear that traditional ties of friendship would be maintained with Britain. According to President Khama, Britain provided valuable aid designed to sustain the country at a critical stage of development. Nevertheless, diplomatic relations have also been established with several Communist states, including the USSR, Czechoslovakia, Rumania and Yugoslavia.

The unilateral declaration of independence (U. D. I.) by Rhodesia placed Botswana in a difficult position. The railway on which Botswana itself depends and which in 1974 was the only rail link between South Africa and Rhodesia, is owned and operated by Rhodesia Railways. For reasons simply of economic survival, Botswana was in no position to take part in economic sanctions against Rhodesia. Nevertheless, President Khama has spoken out strongly against both the rebel Rhodesian regime and against apartheid and the sale of arms to South Africa, with whose economy Botswana is intimately linked. Strong opposition was expressed to Portugal's former control of Angola, Guinea and Mozambique.

In an effort to reduce dependence on its racist neighbors, Botswana has also established an embassy in Washington, a U. N. Mission in New York, a High Commission in London and Lusaka. These missions are accredited to various states which have formal diplomatic ties with Botswana, including Japan, Belgium, Netherlands, France, Switzerland, Czechoslovakia, Austria, Canada, Denmark, German Federal Republic, Korea, Nigeria, Rumania, Sweden, Tanzania and Yugoslavia.

FOREIGN TRADE   see   ECONOMY, EXTERNAL--(1) Foreign
    Trade

FOURTEEN STREAMS   see   WARREN, SIR CHARLES

FRANCISTOWN.   Situated in the north of the country, Francistown is the traditional industrial center and with the advent of large scale mining in the area it is likely to assume even greater industrial importance over the next five years.   Its population is expected to jump from the present 19,000 to over 25,000 in the next ten years and perhaps even to 50,000 by 1990.

Industries located in the town include engineering,
textile work, brewing, tanning and a game skin industry.
Three hundred miles separate Francistown from the capital along the line of rail. Francistown has two hotels
and numerous sporting facilities. These facilities will
increase when Botswana's tourist industry expands and
Francistown becomes the major staging point for the
game parks in the north.

-G-

GABORONE. Gaborone is the capital of Botswana and the
seat of government, as well as the seat of the Tlokwa
tribe. Named after Chief Gaborone Matlapin, who reigned
there when the place was founded in the 1890's, it has a
population of about 18,000 (1971) and is situated on the
line of rail in the southeast of the country close to the
South African border. Gaborone is a completely new
town. Until 1965, Bechuanaland was governed from Mafeking in South Africa, 16 miles south of the Bechuanaland
border. When it became apparent that the country would
soon attain its independence it became necessary to find
a site for the country's capital. The dominant factor in
choosing the site for the country's capital was the avail-
ability of water and Gaborone was chosen because a suitable dam site could be found on the nearby Notwane River.
Work started on the Capital in late 1963 and by March
1965, when Botswana was granted internal self-government, the first phase was completed and the capital was
moved into Botswana.

Post-independence Gaborone is growing fast and a
modern traffic-free shopping precinct is in the center of
the city. Gaborone has two hotels plus another first-
class hotel and casino complex. Amenities include a
wide range of shops, a cinema, museum, and library,
and sports and recreational facilities. Gaborone Dam,
three miles from the town center, offers a site for water
sports such as boating and water skiing and there is an
outdoor activities center next to the lake. The major
buildings include the National Assembly, a 140-foot water
tower, which dominates the town, and the Catholic Cathe-
dral. A fast growing industrial site is located near the
railway station with such industries as brewing, light
engineering and furniture manufacturing. See also TOUR-
ISM.

GABORONE, Chief see TLOKWA

GABORONE, CHIEF KGOSI (1905-1973). He assumed the office of paramount chief of the Tlokwa in 1949 and was gazetted as Native Authority in 1950 succeeding his father Matlala Gaborone. Kgosi Gaborone, who received his early education at the Batlokwa National School, served as a policeman in South Africa before he was appointed to the chieftainship office. During his rule he was a member of both the Botswana House of Chiefs and the Southern East District Council. He died July 28, 1973 at the Bamalete Lutheran Hospital in Ramotswa.

GASEITSIWE, Chief see NGWAKETSE

GHANZI. The village of Ghanzi in the Kgalagadi Desert, is an important cattle center. It marks the beginning of one of the longest cattle trek routes left in the world. Cattle are trekked nearly 500 miles across the desert to the Lobatse abattoir.

GHANZI DISTRICT. Covering an area of 40,443 square miles, Ghanzi District has only 12,000 people (1971). The bushmen of the Kgalagadi make up the majority of the sparse population which, from the village of Ghanzi, administers most of the region. Surrounding Ghanzi and stretching towards the South West Africa border there are a number of large white-owned ranches called the Ghanzi farms and under a resettlement scheme vast acres of State Land are being divided up and sold to Batswana.

GOOLD-ADAMS, COL. HAMILTON (1858-1920). Lieutenant-Governor of the Orange River Colony. In 1878 was commissioned a lieutenant. First served in South Africa with General Sir Charles Warren's expedition against the Bechuana in 1884, and as a major commanded the Field Force in the Matabele War of 1893. In 1895 he became a major in the 1st Batallion of the Royal Scots and Resident Commissioner for Bechuanaland. There he was respected by all races for his ability and tact in carrying out numerous demarcations of tribal boundaries. During the siege of Mafeking in the South African War he further distinguished himself, and thus in 1901 became Lieutenant-Governor of the newly-annexed Orange River Colony. He remained there till 1910, seeing the introduction of responsible government and the preliminaries to the National Convention and Union.

GOSHEN (more correctly, "Het Land Goosen"). Miniature
Boer Republic, set up by a group of Transvaal burgers
under N. C. Gey van Pittius on October 24, 1882.
Founded on land ceded to them by the Bechuana chief
Moshete, as a reward for their help in an inter-tribal
war. Name is derived from the Bible, the area previously being called the Rooigrond (Red Ground). The republic attempted to unite with Stellaland. President
Kruger placed both states under Transvaal protection,
but they ceased to exist after the British occupation of
Bechuanaland in 1884.

GOVERNMENT see CONSTITUTION

GROBLER AFFAIR see KHAMA III

GROSS DOMESTIC PRODUCT see ECONOMY, INTERNAL--
(1) National Income

GROSS NATIONAL PRODUCT see ECONOMY, INTERNAL--
(1) National Income

-H-

HASKINS, JAMES GEORGE, O. B. E., J. P. (1914-). Botswana politician, born in Bulawayo, Rhodesia; he received his education at Plumtree School. Worked as business trainee, J. W. Jagger and Co., Ltd., 1935-42;
served with South African Service Corps and 4th Battalion
(Wits.) Reserve Brigade, 1942-46; Vice-Chairman European and member Joint Advisory Councils, 1948-61; Member of Legislative Council, 1961-64 (Botswana-Chobe constituency); former member of Executive Council, Constitutional Committee of Self-Government, Rhodesia Railways
Central Consultative Committee; later Botswana Representative and member of Rhodesia Railways Board, 1957-61;
former chairman of Finance and Public Accounts Committee, Francistown Agricultural Society; delegate to Commonwealth Parliamentary Association, U. K. 1963; Trustee,
Botswana National Sports Appeal Fund; specially elected
member of National Assembly, March 1966- ; Minister of
Commerce, Industry and Water Affairs, 1966-69; Minister of Finance, Oct. 1969-June 1970; Minister of Agriculture, June 1970; then Minister of Works and Communications; Treasurer of Botswana Democratic Party.

HEADMEN see CHIEFTAINSHIP

HEALTH. Because of its clear, dry air and temperate climate Botswana is generally a healthy country. The prevalent sicknesses are tuberculosis, gastroenteritis, pneumonia, and food deficiency diseases. Malaria is endemic in Chobe and Ngamiland, which is also infected by sleeping sickness. Bilharzia (schistosomiasis, a parasitic disease) occurs in the eastern area and in the Okavango Basin. While the country has 36 doctors (1972)-- giving an average ratio of one doctor to 17,475 persons-- in some areas the ratio is as low as one doctor to 67,000 people. Registered nurses and midwives number about 500. There are 12 hospitals and several health centers, dispensaries, and clinics.

HEPBURN, JAMES DAVIDSON (1840-93). Missionary; he joined the LMS and, after ordination, sailed for South Africa in 1870. His destination was Shoshong, capital of the Ngwato where he arrived in 1871. There his colleague was John Mackenzie (q.v.). When Mackenzie was transferred to Kuruman, he continued the work of the station alone until 1885, when he was joined by Edwin Lloyd. Like his predecessor he identified himself closely with the Ngwato and became a firm friend of their Christian Chief, Khama III.

He had long cherished a desire to found a church in Ngamiland. In 1877 the results of his first visit to this new field were promising, but defections resulted from the chaos caused by Matebele raids, and the hostility of Moremi, the local chief. The first Christian church in Ngamiland foundered in 1886, when Hepburn, on his last visit to that part of the country, was driven out by Moremi.

When the Ngwato moved from Shoshong to Palapye in 1889, Hepburn devoted himself to building a church at the new capital. The strain was too much for him and in a state of mental and physical exhaustion, he disagreed with Khama on various church matters. Believing himself deliberately thwarted, he precipitately left the country in 1891 and, on his return from London, Khama refused to see him or to have him back.

HERERO (DAMARA). A Bantu-speaking people who inhabit parts of South West Africa, Angola and Botswana. Many Herero in Botswana are descended from the followers of Chief Frederick Samuel Maherero, who took refuge from

the German extermination campaign in South West Africa
during the period 1904 to 1905. At that time their number was 1175. However, a considerable number of Herero appear to have come into Botswana at an earlier
date.
The Herero are primarily a cattle-owing people.
Each person belongs both to an exogamous patrilineal
clan (oruzo) and to an exogamous matrilineal clan (eanda).
There is evidence to show that a number of the Herero,
under the leadership of Kahaka, and of the Mbanderu,
under the leadership of Koneha, entered western Ngamiland about 1891, settling first at Makakung. The Herero
refugees under Samuel Maherero were allowed by the
Protectorate Government to settle at Tsau in 1905 and a
number of Mbanderu, under their headman Nicodemus,
settled near Nokaheng a year or two afterwards. There
were a number of subsequent movements: Samuel with
some of his followers went to the Transvaal; Nicodemus
moved first to the Chobe and subsequently to the Boteti
riverain; one small group of Mbanderu broke away and
left Ngamiland for Ghanzi District. There are now a
considerable number of these immigrants living at various places in the Tawana and Ngwato Reserves.

HERTZOG, JAMES (1866-1942). Prime Minister of the Union
of South Africa. He took part in the National Convention
(1908-09) where for financial and security reasons he
initially opposed the transfer to the proposed Union of
Bechuanaland, Basutoland and Swaziland. He argued that
if the Union took over the administration of the protectorates, Britain would then have no commitment to defend
South Africa against external foes or internal disorder.
Moreover, he felt that since Britain would insist upon en-
forcing the conditions of transfer, the imperial factor
would not be removed from South Africa. Almost immediately after becoming Prime Minister in 1924 he re-
opened the question of the transfer of Bechuanaland and
Swaziland by requesting the High Commissioner in Pretoria to ascertain the feelings of the British government
on the subject. British coolness toward Prime Minister
Hertzog's suggestion, again advanced in the 1930's, added
to the growing Anglo-South African estrangement.

HIGH COMMISSION TERRITORIES. Three territories in
southern Africa which came under British protection during the latter part of the 19th century and the beginning
of the 20th during the course of the struggle between the

Boers and the British for dominance were Basutoland in 1884, Bechuanaland in 1885 and Swaziland in 1906. In each of the Territories the High Commissioner, acting through a Resident Commissioner, was proclaimed sole legislative authority in a system known as indirect rule. The administrative responsibility for internal affairs was left on the whole to the chiefs, who continued to exercise their traditional political and judicial authority and in addition regulated the economic life of their people. If the inhabitants were not entirely satisfied with this arrangement, fear of their South African neighbor deflected the force of their protests. As British Protectorates they were afforded security with stagnation. But traditional leaders, unaware of the economic forces which were transforming their lives, and without real decision-making power, could not respond to this new challenge without major institutional changes. However, any fundamental change in the traditional structure of society--a condition for political advancement or constitutional evolution --seemed to invite the loosening of British protection and, conversely, the encroachment of the historic enemy.

HIGH COMMISSIONER. The office of High Commissioner was originally attached in 1846 to that of the Governor of Cape Colony in recognition of the fact that negotiations had to be carried on with various tribes living beyond the Cape Colony boundaries. But it was the Order in Council of May 9, 1891, which constituted the fundamental law providing for the administration of the Bechuanaland Protectorate until 1960. This gave the High Commissioner authority to legislate by Proclamation, subject to the condition that his Proclamations must "respect any Native Laws or customs by which the civil relations of any Native Chiefs, tribes or populations under Her Majesty's power and jurisdiction are now regulated, except so far as the same may be incompatible with the due exercise of Her Majesty's power and jurisdiction." The Order further provided that the High Commissioner was to have authority to appoint officers for the Protectorate who might be Deputy Commissioners or Assistant Commissioners or Judges or Magistrates.

From 1897 to 1910 the office of High Commissioner was separate from that of Governor of Cape Colony. However, the Statute of Westminister of 1931, which defined a new relationship between the various Commonwealth or Dominion governments on the one hand and the British government on the other, necessitated the

separation of the office of High Commissioner from that
of Governor-General, the latter now representing merely
the Crown and not the British government. Only in this
way could the three protectorates remain as Britain's responsibility. This move also emphasized the differences
of policy between the two governments and left the inhabitants, as they preferred, outside the Union of South
Africa. It did not, however, gove them the advantages
of the regular British colonial service. For now, in addition to his usual functions, His Majesty's High Commissioner to South Africa remained responsible for the
administration of Basutoland, Bechuanaland and Swaziland.
Since the office of High Commissioner fell not under the
Colonial Office but under the Commonwealth Relations
Office, the Territories were placed in the anomalous position of being worse off than other British colonies and
protectorates inasmuch as these could theoretically evolve
towards independence. The High Commission Territories
remained in a political limbo without prospect of change
except in the direction of incorporation into South Africa.

The history of the legal and constitutional developments of these countries was greatly influenced by the
fact that the High Commissioner had his seat at the same
place as the seat of the Government of the Union (now
the Republic) of South Africa, either in Cape Town or
Pretoria. It was from those cities that he legislated for
Bechuanaland by Proclamations which only required being
put in the Gazette--even then, this was unnecessary for
their validity until 1959. The close proximity of the seat
of the High Commissioner to the seat of the Government
of the Union led to a large number of proclamations designed to create segregated communities on the pattern
of that in the Republic of South Africa.

The abolition in late 1964 of the office of High Com-
missioner--combined since 1961 with that of British Ambassador to South Africa--reflected the changed political
status of the Territories as each advanced towards independence under its respective constitution. Already,
by terms of the Order in Council of September 29, 1963,
the post of Resident Commissioner was upgraded to Her
Majesty's Commissioner (Queen's Commissioner) in
Bechuanaland and Swaziland. A similar step was taken
for Basutoland in August 1964 and thus each territory received the equivalent of a Governor responsible directly
to the Secretary of State for the Colonies. Henceforth,
the British Ambassador to South Africa was informed
about aspects of the three territories' affairs affecting

foreign relations or defence, but he had no further re-
sponsibility for purely territorial matters. See also
ROBINSON; LOCH; MILNER; SELBORNE; RESIDENT
COMMISSIONER.

HIGH COURT. see JUSTICE

HOLIDAYS. New Year's Day, Good Friday, Saturday before
Easter, Easter Monday, Ascension Day, President's Day
(May 24), Whit-Monday, Commonwealth Day, First Mon-
day in August, Botswana Day (September 30), Christmas,
Boxing Day.

HOUSE OF CHIEFS see CONSTITUTION

HOUSING see ECONOMY, INTERNAL--(5) Housing

HUME, DAVID (1796-1863). Early Cape traveler, arriving
there in 1817. As a trader, he found his way to Bechuanaland in 1825 and made his headquarters in the present
village of Kuruman (S.A.). He enjoyed the high respect
of the Africans and when in 1829 the Rev. J. Archbell
arrived, intending to call on Mzilikazi, it was Hume who
brought him there safely. Inspired by reports of gold
inland, Hume trekked on beyond the Limpopo into what is
now Rhodesia. Occasionally he went down to the Cape
and in 1854 brought a consignment of ivory to Grahamstown. Upon his return he acted as guide to Sir Andrew
Smith when he went into the country of Mzilikazi.

-I-

IMPERIAL FACTOR see RHODES; HERTZOG; SMUTS

INDEPENDENCE. Achieved September 30, 1966, exactly 81
years after the declaration of a British Protectorate over
Bechuanaland.

INDEPENDENCE CONFERENCE. The final steps toward independence were taken in February 1966 during the Independence Conference held in London. The only major
objections to the new constitution were expressed by
Philip Matante, leader of the opposition BPP. His main
demand was that new elections be held before independence.
These objections being rejected by Britain, the Republic
of Botswana was officially allowed to come into existence
on September 30, 1966.

INDIRECT RULE   see   HIGH COMMISSIONER; RESIDENT
COMMISSIONER

INDUSTRY   see   ECONOMY, INTERNAL--(10) Industry

IRONSTONE KOPJE MOUNTAIN.   Located in southeast Kgala-
    gadi about 40 kilometers from the Molopo River.   Eleva-
    tion, 1075 meters.   Noted for its unusual outcroppings.

ISANG, CHIEF (1884-1941).   Born at Mochudi, the capital
    town of the Kgatla, hie early education began with the
    Rev.   Thomas Phiri at Malolwane village where a small
    Dutch Reformed Church Mission was established by his
    father, Chief Linchwe.   Through his father's influence he
    was later sent to Zonneblom College at Cape Town, where
    he took a special interest in the study of Latin.   In 1920
    Isang became Regent.   While imperious and arbitrary in
    conduct, he strove to advance the Kgatla tribe.   Isang's
    succession to the chieftainship after the death of his fa-
    ther, Linchwe in 1924, was challenged by his uncle,
    Segale and supported by Ramorotong.   Segale claimed
    that the chieftainship could have been occupied either by
    himself or by Ramorotong, the son of Maganelo.   A furi-
    ous discussion on the matter took place in the kgotla,
    where Ramorotong, Segale's supporter, even insulted
    Chief Isang.   Chief Isang took serious exception to this
    insult and consequently Ramorotong was banished to the
    Kwena Reserve.
        Despite his severity, Chief Isang took a deep interest
    in education.   His views on this important aspect were
    implemented in the establishment of a modern school known
    as the Bakgatla National School erected on the revered
    Phutha-dikobo Hill.   The funds for this project were
    raised from special levies.   The new school gradually de-
    veloped to a junior secondary school, the first such
    school to be established in the Bechuanaland Protectorate
    under tribal administration.   Because of his interest in
    education he was appointed supervisor of schools for the
    Kgatla and the Tlokwa areas.   He was also a member of
    the Advisory Board on African Education.
        Like Chief Kgama III of the Ngwato tribe, he intro-
    duced a system of controlling beer drinking among his
    people.   He asked the government to undertake water bor-
    ing operations in the reserve, and the funds for these
    were collected from every taxpayer.   He discouraged beg-
    ging and idleness.   When the Bechuanaland Protectorate
    government established the African Advisory Council in
    1920, Chief Isang became one of its first members.

Chief Isang knew African law and custom very well. As
an enlightened chief, he retained what he considered to
be good tribal laws and customs while striving to improve
the general administration of the kgatla. In 1929 Chief
Isang gave way to his nephew to be installed as the rightful chief of the tribe. It was not long after this that
tribal disputes arose between Isang and Molefi. Chiefs
Bathoen II and Tshekedi Khama intervened as arbitrators.
See also KGATLA.

-J-

JAMESON, SIR LEANDER STARR (1853-1917). South African
and Rhodesian statesman, born in Edinburgh; studied medicine at University College, London, and went to South
Africa in 1878. He gained the close friendship of Cecil
John Rhodes and from a common interest in finance they
turned to the development of Mashonaland and Matabeleland. On Rhodes' behalf Jameson undertook three successive missions to Lobengula in 1889 and 1890, the out-
come of which was the confirmation by the Ndebele King
of the concession to the British South Africa Company.
In 1891 he became Administrator of Mashonaland, further
establishing his popularity with the settlers. Under his
regime Lobengula was eventually defeated and Matabeleland also came under his administration in 1894. The
following year he assembled a force of police and volun-
teers at Pitsani, on the frontier of Bechuanaland and the
Transvaal and, on December 29, 1895, without the approval of Rhodes, marched on Johannesburg. Although
the raid was driven off and Jameson imprisoned, the increased political friction which resulted made the South
African War (Boer War) almost inevitable.

JOINT ADVISORY COUNCIL. Consistent demands by members of the African Advisory Council, most notably Tshekedi Khama and Bathoen II, for the creation of a unified,
non-racial legislative body resulted in the establishment
of a Joint Advisory Council in 1950. The Council was
composed of all eight members of the European Advisory
Council, eight members elected by the African Council
and four official members.
    The prime importance of the Joint Advisory Council
was not its success as an advisory body, but its utility
as a transitional organization. Important relationships
were established between some of the European and African representatives, and demands for the creation of a

legislative council and increased self-rule were pressed.
The creation of legislative assemblies in Northern Rhodesia (Zambia) and Nyasaland (Malawi) added weight to
calls, in the Joint Council, for the setting up of a similar body for Bechuanaland. Charges were made that the
progress of Bechuanaland was being unduly delayed because of pressure from the South African government.
The consolidation of nationalist power in the Union, exemplified by the removal of the Colored population from
the common voter rolls of the Cape in 1956, strengthened
the position of those seeking self-rule for Bechuanaland.

JUSTICE. The Botswana Court of Appeal succeeded the
Court of Appeal for Basutoland, Bechuanaland and Swaziland, which was established in 1954. It has jurisdiction
over criminal and civil appeals emanating from the High
Court of Botswana. In certain circumstances further appeal can be made to the Judicial Committee of the Privy
Council. The High Court of Botswana succeeded the High
Court for Bechuanaland, which was established in 1938
and given unlimited jurisdiction in criminal and civil
cases. In general, all the jurisdiction, power and authority vested in the Supreme Court of South Africa were
also given to the (Botswana) High Court. The 1966 Constitution created the judicial service commission which
was made responsible for advising the President on matters relating to the appointment, discipline and removal
of judges, magistrates and other officers holding judicial
offices.

The High Court consists of the Chief Justice and such
number, if any, of puisne judges as may be prescribed
from time to time. In criminal matters the Court of Appeal, High Court and Subordinate Courts are governed by
the Criminal Procedure and Evidence Proclamation and
the Penal Code brought into force on June 10, 1964.
From that date the unwritten substantive criminal law in
force in the Cape Colony on June 10, 1891, hitherto of
force and effect in Botswana, ceased to apply.

There are Subordinate Courts and African Courts with
limited jurisdiction in each of the districts of the country.
Until 1943, trials in native or customary courts were not
regulated by any statutory enactments and the chiefs administered justice in their kgotla as they had been doing
more or less before 1891. However, by the Native
Courts Proclamation of 1943, provisions were made for
the first time for the recognition, constitution, powers
and jurisdictions of these courts, and generally for the

administration of justice in them. These courts were
given limited jurisdiction in both criminal and civil cases.
They were confined to applying (1) native law and custom
prevailing in their areas of jurisdiction, (2) the provisions of all rules and orders made by the Resident Commissioner, etc., under the Native Administration Proclamation, and (3) the provisions of any proclamation or any
other laws which they were specially authorized to administer.

The Native Courts Proclamation was repealed; sub-
stituted for it was what was called the African Courts
Proclamation, 1961, possibly in consonance with the
scheme of the government at the time to create an administration for Africans different from the general one
mainly for Europeans, on the pattern of that in the Republic of South Africa. As its name implied, the African Courts were open only to Africans and they had no
jurisdiction over non-Africans.

-K-

KALAHARI see KGALAGADI

KANYE. The capital of the Ngwaketse tribe has a seasonal
    population approaching 40,000. The second largest tribal
    village in Botswana, Kanye is situated on top of a range
    of hills. It is the last main village on the road into the
    Kgalagadi (Kalahari).

KASANE. North of Maun on the Chobe River, Kasane is the
    entry point for the Chobe National Park (q.v.). It is
    situated near the confluence of the Chobe River and the
    Zambezi and where the borders of Botswana, Caprivi
    (South West Africa) Zambia and Rhodesia meet. Hotel
    accommodation is available. See also TOURISM.

KAZUNGULA. A small village in the extreme northeast of
    North West District (Chobe) that is the terminus of the
    Nata-Kazungula road, projected for completion in 1975.
    A ferry boat from Kazungula to the Zambian side of the
    Zambezi River is Botswana's sole link to the north that
    lies outside of white, minority-controlled territory.

KGABO, E. M. K. (1925-). Botswana politician, born at
    Lientsweng and educated in Kanye. Secretary of School
    Committee, Bakwena Administration, later Treasurer,

Councillor and member of Licensing Board, J. P., 1964;
Member of Legislative Assembly, March 1965- ; Parliamentary Secretary, March 1965 to October 1966; Minister
of Local Government and Lands, 1966-73; Minister of Information and Broadcasting, 1973- .

KGALAGADI DESERT (also known as Kalahari). A region of
southern Africa and covering more than 100,000 square
miles (259,000 sq. km.), the Kgalagadi Desert consists
of large sand belts and areas that are covered with grass
and acacia--thorn scrub much of the year. The name is
applied mainly to the western part of Botswana but also
to parts of South West Africa and the Cape Province of
South Africa. Very little of it is desert in the full sense,
the annual rainfall varying from 20 inches in the northeast to five inches in the southwest. Active dunes are
found only in the dry part. Its elevation is fairly uniform
at about 3000 feet, the lowest part being the large Makgadikgadi Pan which is salt and receives the overflow from
the Okovango River to the North. An almost universal
covering of reddish sand overlying very old rocks quickly
absorbs any rain, so there are practically no surface
streams lasting for more than a day. The vegetation
varies with the rainfall from forest to low thorn scrub,
but grass grows everywhere in the rainy season. Much
of the grass is good feed for animals, and consequently
most of the game animals of southern Africa, including
elephant, may be found in the Kgalagadi, especially in the
rainy season. In the southwest the Kgalagadi Gemsbok
National Park (see entry after next), partly in Cape Province (South Africa) and partly in Botswana, covers about
8000 square miles total in the two countries. Small
bands of nomadic Sarwa still roam the central Kgalagadi
living much as they have done for generations. See also
TOURISM.

KGALAGADI DISTRICT. An administrative district of 42,552
square miles in southwest Botswana bounded by South Africa and South West Africa on the south and west respectively. Population in 1971 was estimated at 15,000.
The administrative center is Tshabong.

KGALAGADI GEMSBOK NATIONAL PARK. A remote wildlife
reserve comprising some 3650 square miles in southwest
Botswana where the boundaries of South Africa, South
West Africa and Botswana meet. The reserve is in the
shape of a triangle and lies between the dry Auob and

Nossop rivers. It is a region of sand and orange-col-
ored sand-dunes; dry, hot and sparsely covered with
thorn-scrub, quickgrass and camelthorns.

KGAMANE, RASEBOLAI (1907-1973). Kgamane was appointed
in May 1953 as African Authority in the place of the District Commissioner, for the Ngwato tribe. In September
1956, a tribal council of an advisory nature was announced
with Rasebolai Kgamane as Chairman. In late 1963 it was
announced that Rasebolai wished to retire after ten years
of service. It was agreed that the eldest son of Tshekedi
Khama, Leapetswe Tshekedi Khama, should be appointed
head of the African Authority replacing Rasebolai Kgamane,
and the change was made at a kgotla in January 1964.

KGATLA (BAKGATLA). The Kgatla claim to be an early offshoot of the Hurutshe, but little is actually known of the
reasons for their secession or of the date at which it
took place. It is possible that the section of the Kgatla
which now occupies the reserve in Botswana left the main
body in the Transvaal early in the 18th century. For
nearly a century after that the history of the Kgatla is a
confused record of fights with their neighbors, but there
was a period at the end of the 18th century when the
Kgatla, under the leadership (1790?-1805?) of their Chief
Pheto II, succeeded in winning a prominent position
among the tribes living in the triangle of land formed by
the Crocodile, Marico and Eland's Rivers. Scattered for
a time, part of them became subject to the Kwena, but
again became united under Pilane (Chief 1825?-1850?),
though they suffered severely from the depredations of
Mzilikazi's raiding parties. As the result of the Sand
River Convention of 1852 between the British and the
Boers, the latter claimed the right to tax the Africans in
the Transvaal and the climax came when Paul Kruger
publicly flogged the Kgatla Chief Kgamanyane (chief 1850?-
74) for failing to provide labor for work on the Boer
farms. The Kwena tribe then invited the Kgatla to take
refuge in their country, and in 1871 they established
themselves at Mochudi, about 50 miles from the Kwena
headquarters at Molepolole. They were joined by a small
body of Kgatla under Letsebe, the younger brother of
Kgamanyane, who had previously seceded and taken up his
residence at Molepolole, but now came back to the main
group. Both the Boers and the Kwena Chief claimed the
Kgatla as their subjects.
    When, in 1895, the British South Africa Company was

encouraged to deal directly with certain of the tribes in
regard to the acquisition of land for the railway and
other purposes, Linchwe (1875-1924) showed himself ready
to join the Rolong and Malete in accepting the Company's
jurisdiction. This fact apparently determined the attitude
of the Protectorate Administration in regard to the disputed paramountcy over the Kgatla lands. Sebele I, who
had succeeded Sechele I in 1892, was told that in the
pending demarcation of areas to form the new tribal reserves a line would be laid down separating his area from
that of the Kgatla. This was effected in 1896, in spite
of Sebele's protests, and Linchwe, like other Chiefs,
granted the Bechuanaland Railway Company a strip of land
passing through his territory. The boundary thus fixed
was finally confirmed by the issue of Proclamation No. 9
of 1899 which constituted the Kgatla Reserve.

In the years following there were many signs of progress in the Reserve. By 1905 for example there were
1600 children at school. There was a steady growth in
the area of cultivation and the use of the plough. But
during World War I there were signs of a growing debili-
ty in Linchwe, to whom the progress made by the tribe
had been largely due, and in 1920 the control of tribal
affairs was taken over by his second son, Isang, his
eldest son, Kgafela, having died in 1914 and Molefi, Kgafela's son, being still a minor. Linchwe lingered on for
four years, and on his death in 1924 was mourned by the
tribe as the "founder of the nation. "

During the nine years (1920-29) that Isang (q. v.) held
charge as Acting Chief, the tribe continued to make progress, and the Government Reports of the period frequently spoke of the Kgatla as the most advanced community in
the Protectorate, particularly in respect of its agricultural production.

After Molefi had assumed the chieftainship in 1929 a
serious quarrel developed with Isang over Chief Linchwe's
estate. It was resolved in 1935 and Isang was welcomed
back after a brief exile, remaining, though still influential, in the background until his death in 1941. In 1936
Molefi was himself suspended from exercising the chieftainship and in 1937 was banned from the reserve. His
younger brother, Mmusi, was appointed to act in his absence. Molefi's supporters, meanwhile, formed themselves into a society called the Ipelegeng and later took
on the characteristics of a religious sect generally known
as Zionists.

In spite of the existence of domestic differences

within the tribe, the Protectorate Administration continued
the efforts to improve the condition of the Reserve. A
formal Tribal Council was instituted in 1935, following on
the issue of the Native Administration Proclamation of
1934, and the judicial system was reorganized in 1937 by
the constitution of "sectional" and village courts. Post
primary education was introduced in 1937. One of the
first results of the grant of a sum of £25,000 to the Protectorate from the Colonial Development and Welfare Fund
was the provision made for the construction of a number
of bore-holes in the Kgatla Reserve, and it appears that
the Kgatla were the first to initiate the system of "syndicates" for their maintenance. The tribe has contained
some of the more active of the agriculturists in the country. It is noteworthy that the Reserve was chosen in
1949 as the area in which most of the Agricultural Dem-
onstrators were concentrated as part of the intensive
campaign undertaken for the improvement of subsistence
production, and the results were described as very encouraging.

Both Molefi and Mmusi served with the African Pioneer Corps during World War II, the former with the
rank of Regimental Sergeant Major. A council of regency
meanwhile carried on the affairs of the tribe. Molefi
was joined by a number of his Ipelegeng followers at the
front who continued to champion his chieftaincy. On
Molefi's return from the war in 1945 he was reinstated
as chief and his wartime Ipelegeng followers, with Molefi's
encouragement, disowned the Zionist cult. But dissension
between Zionists and non-Zionists continued to agitate the
tribe. Molefi was succeeded in the chieftaincy by Mmusi.

Kgatla Chiefs, with dates of chieftaincy
(early dates not known)

Malekeleke	Makgotso c. 1780-1790
Masilo	Pheto II c. 1790-c. 1805
Legabo	Senwelo c. 1805-c. 1810; c. 1817
Pogopi	Letsebe c. 1810-c. 1817
Botlolo	Motlotle c. 1817-1823
Mogale	Pilane c. 1825-1850
Matshego	Kgamanyane c. 1850-1874
Kgafela	Bogatsu 1874-75
Tebele	Linchwe 1875-1924
Masellane (Pheto I)	Isang 1920-29 (acting)
Kgwefane	Molefi Kgafela Pilane 1929-
Molefe c. 1780	36; 1945-58

Mmusi Kgafela Pilane   Bakgatla 1942-45
1936-42; 1958-63   Linchwe Kgafela II 1963-

KGATLENG DISTRICT. The Kgatleng District which borders
the Transvaal in South Africa is populated by the Kgatla
tribe. In this 2798-square-mile area of undulating grass-
lands with isolated rocky hills, water is the main problem; the Kgatla lost over 60,000 head of cattle during the
mid-1960's drought--one of the hardest hit tribes. There
is little or no industry and the land is not good for farming but the good rains of 1967 and to a certain extent
1968 helped to increase the amount of grazing. The main
village is Mochudi, with 19,000 people. The population
of the district is 31,000 (1971).

KGOTLA. The prime source of "formal" authority remaining
in the hands of the tribal leaders is control over the
kgotla. It is the kgotla in which the main local judicial
function is performed. The kgotla also remains the only
legitimate means of government communication with the
populace. All meetings, except political rallies, must
be held in the kgotla and sanctioned by the appropriate
chief or headman. A meeting in kgotla may be called
only by a headman. He must be consulted by the central
government or council leader who wishes to address such
a meeting. In fact, meetings requested by central government authorities are always held, but there have been
several cases of headmen refusing to call meetings for
councillors whom they dislike.
    The main importance of the kgotla lies in the fact
that it represents the point of intersection of the traditional political system and the organizations of the central government and district council. It acts as the
means of offering traditional legitimacy to the introduction
of new ideas, ways of doing things, and regulations issued by the new elites at the central and local level.

KHAMA III (1837-1923). Chief of the Ngwato (Bamangwato),
was the eldest of the 16 sons of Sekgoma I. In 1857 he
fell under the influence of missionaries of the Hermansburg (Lutheran) mission society and both he and his
brother, Kgamane, became devout Christians, Kgamane
being baptized in 1860 and marrying a Christian. Sekgoma I, a strong traditionalist deeply rooted in the old
ways, viewed his sons' conversion to Christianity with
bitter disapproval, resenting especially their rejection of
ancient tribal rites and ceremonies. Differences between

the chief and his Christian sons, arising from his disapproval of Christian influences, caused violent dissension
within the tribe and culminated in 1875 in Khama's forci-
ble assumption of the chieftainship upon his father's
flight into exile.
    Khama settled at Shoshong, where he was to remain
until 1889, when he moved to Palapye, and later to Serowe. Upon his accession Khama set about reforming
his tribe. One of his first acts was to prohibit liquor,
while he progressively discouraged most of the traditional
customs that had been so dear to his father. He collabo-
rated wholeheartedly with the missionaries of the LMS
who had replaced the Hermansburg Lutherans. He fos-
tered education and set himself purposefully to strengthen
the unity of his tribe and to preserve the tribal lands
against encroachment and agression. The tribe had already suffered severely from warfare; only one fifth were
Ngwato proper, the rest being other Tswana groups or
Sarwa.
    As early as 1876 concern about his eastern boundary
and relations with the Transvaal republic prompted him
to ask for British protection. His attitude towards the
Transvaal was consistently apprehensive and mistrustful.
When, therefore, in the early months of 1885, Sir Charles
Warren, accompanied by Khama's former missionary,
John Mackenzie, arrived at the tribal capital, Shoshong,
to announce the establishment of a British protectorate,
Khama was delighted, protesting only that the proposed
northern limit of the protectorate, latitude 22°S, cut his
country in two. He then provided a large area of land
for British settlement, first setting aside adequate territory for the use of his own people. Not wishing to under-
take heavier responsibilities in the new protectorate, the
British Government declined the offer. In July 1888
Khama sent a regiment to intercept P. D. C. J. Grobler,
who, on his return from Lobengula, was following a route
which Khama considered passed through Ngwato territory.
Grobler was wounded and died. Sir Sidney Shippard,
commissioner of the Bechuanaland Protectorate, was in-
structed to hold an inquiry. Khama was exonerated by
him from what the Transvaal termed the Grobler murder.
    The charter granted in 1889 to the British South Af-
rica Company placed the Protectorate within the Company's sphere. Although Khama gave valuable help to the
forces advancing on Matebeleland in 1893, he subsequently
was disturbed by the Company's attitude to the Protectorate. In 1895 he heard that the British government

proposed to transfer the administration of his country to
the Company. He therefore sailed for England with Chief
Sebele of the Kwena, and Chief Bathoen I of the Ngwaketse, to oppose the intended transfer. As he already
enjoyed a reputation for being an enlightened chief, his
visit aroused considerable public interest and sympathy.
It proved successful, for Joseph Chamberlain, the Colonial Secretary, promised that the Queen's protection would
continue. In return the chiefs ceded to the British South
African Company a narrow strip of territory on their
eastern boundaries so that the Company could build a railway to the north. Khama's relations with the Protectorate's administration remained harmonious, though marked
on his side by unceasing watchfulness against any in-
fringement of tribal rights or of his own prerogative as
chief.

His tribal and domestic affairs were on the whole
less happy than his relations with the protecting power.
He twice felt called upon to send armed expeditions
against subordinate tribes, in 1887 and in 1922. In the
latter case, the uprooting of the Birwa led to international protests. Quarrels in his own family led to estrange-
ments with most of his senior relatives, also his son,
Sekgoma II, with whom, however, he was reconciled by
1920. Khama, called "the Good," died at Serowe and
was buried there in 1923.

KHAMA, SIR SERETSE, K.B.E. (1921-). President of
Botswana. Born July 1921, the son of Sekgoma II (died
1925), Chief of the Ngwato, he was educated at Lovedale,
Tiger Kloof, Fort Hare, and the University of Witwatersrand, South Africa. His uncle, Tshekedi Khama was appointed Regent of the Ngwato during his minority. Wishing to continue his education, Seretse secured a postpone-
ment of his official accession so that he might study at
Oxford where he went to Balliol College in 1945. Subsequently he left Oxford to pursue legal studies in London
at the Inner Temple. In London he met and became engaged to Ruth Williams. In spite of opposition from
Pretoria, Salisbury, Whitehall and his uncle the Regent,
Seretse was married in September 1948.

In June 1949, a kgotla endorsed Seretse as their
rightful chief and accepted "the white queen" rather than
suffer further inroads upon the tribal system. By this
time, however, the British government was inclined to
bow to pressure from the South African government which
feared the unsettling example on the borders of the

country of a white woman married to an African chief.
While strongly opposing Seretse's action as a serious violation of tribal custom, Tshekedi also feared that the government might act arbitrarily to prevent Seretse from
ever becoming chief and so resigned the regency. Meanwhile, Ruth Khama had arrived in August 1949 to settle
down while a government commission, sitting in Bechuanaland, unsuccessfully tried to come to a decision on
whether Seretse would be recognized as chief.

Seretse was officially invited back to London in February 1950 for conversations with the Secretary of State
for Commonwealth Relations to discuss "the future administration of the Bamangwato." Although his wife was
also invited, Seretse correctly suspected a plan to prevent her return to the Territory, and, as a precaution,
Ruth remained in Serowe. The Secretary offered Seretse
£1000 a year tax free if he would live in England and
renounce all claim to the chieftainship. But Seretse refused to give in to this pressure and was therefore exiled from the Protectorate and then deprived of the chieftainship in 1952. The Ngwato refusal in 1955 to discuss
a mining agreement unless both Khamas were present
undoubtedly influenced the British government to review
the bans imposed. The British government announced on
September 26, 1956, that both Khamas were free to return as private citizens and participate in the affairs of
their tribe. Simultaneously, a tribal council of an advisory nature was announced for the Ngwato, with Rasebolai
Kgamane as Chairman. But the major political objective
was the establishment of a legislative council for the
Protectorate. In 1958, Seretse and Tshekedi, supported
by the Chairman of the European Advisory Council, Russell England, initiated a motion in the Joint Advisory
Council calling for the establishment of a legislative
council.

During the years of Seretse's banishment, the Ngwato
had refused time and again to elect another chief in his
place. After his return in 1956, Seretse worked quietly
with Rasebolai Kgamane and Tshekedi in the administration of the tribe. But after Tshekedi's death in June
1959, Seretse began to play a more active political role.
Already, as Secretary of the Tribal Council and then as
Ngwato representative to the African Council, Seretse had
made his mark on the modern political scene.

Under the constitution of 1961, Seretse was elected
to the country's first Legislative Council. Having been
brought fully into the Territory's political structure,

Seretse's good relations with the government were sealed
when he was named in 1961 as the senior of two Africans
on the governing Executive Council. He was also made
a member of the Order of the British Empire. The
wheel of fortune had thus turned full circle for Seretse,
inasmuch as the deposed chief was once more a considerable power as plain Mr. Khama. While enjoying all the
charismatic attractions of chieftainship, he had all the
political advantages of being free from ceremony and un-
involved in the usual petty disputes which so complicate
the life of a chief. Indeed, his removal from the succession facilitated his acceptance as a modern political
leader of a country-wide party. Moreover, he could dis-
avow rigidly traditionalist decisions by chiefs without being disloyal to the institution of chieftainship, and could
thus compete with the growing BPP.

Seretse Khama's BDP, as generally predicted, scored
an overwhelming electoral victory by capturing 28 of the
31 parliamentary seats. Following the election, Seretse
Khama was asked to form Bechuanaland's first African
government. Final constitutional talks were held in London in 1966 and, under the leadership of President (now
Sir) Seretse Khama, the newly named Republic of Botswana came into being. In 1969 the BDP was again returned to power in general elections and Sir Seretse
Khama was sworn in for a second term as president.

KHAMA, TSHEKEDI (1905-1959). Born in 1905, the son of
Khama III. After finishing his schooling in Bechuanaland
and at Lovedale, South Africa, he went on to the University College of Fort Hare. Although he had intended to
study overseas for a degree in arts or law, in 1926, at
age 21, and before he had completed his matriculation,
Tshekedi was recalled to become Regent. His brother,
Chief Sekgoma II died in 1925, while his nephew (Segoma
II's son) Seretse Khama was still a minor.

His period of regency, which lasted until 1949, was
marked by many developments. Transport facilities were
improved, a livestock center called Leupane was established, granaries were constructed and education grew.
In 1930 he visited England to discuss with Lord Passfield,
Secretary of State for the Colonies, some of the concessions for mineral rights. In addition to disputes with the
Administration on mineral rights and chieftainship reform,
he also incurred official disfavor, and was briefly suspended in 1933 by the Acting High Commissioner, Admiral
Evans, for sentencing a white youth to be whipped (see
FLOGGING CASE, 1933).

In the Second World War Tshekedi appealed to his
people to join the armed services with Great Britain
against the Nazis. Ten thousand men joined from the
whole of Bechuanaland. In 1942, Regent Tshekedi Khama,
along with other territorial representatives, went to the
Middle East to see their forces in the African Pioneer
Corps.

In 1945 Tshekedi Khama sent his nephew, Seretse,
to England for law studies. But the 1948 marriage of his
nephew to an English woman precipated a serious conflict
involving himself, Seretse, the British government, and,
in the background, the government of South Africa. In
Tshekedi's view, his nephew's marriage spelled doom for
the tribe. The marriage of a sovereign, he contended,
was the concern of the people, who must be consulted if
feuds were to be averted. This seemed doubly dangerous,
since the Union government might seize upon disturbances
in Bechuanaland as an excuse for intervention. Tshekedi
therefore informed Seretse, who had returned in October
1948 to press his case, that if the tribe were not unani-
mous in any of its decisions, he himself would leave the
Ngwato country. However, even before Seretse returned
to England in early January 1949 to rejoin his wife and
resume his studies, there were strong signs that the sen-
timent of the tribe was turning in favor of Seretse. At
the same time, it was rumored that Tshekedi was himself seeking the chieftainship--an unlikely proposition but
indicative of the tribe's concern for their rightful chief.
Tshekedi was banished in 1950 from the Ngwato reserve,
but even in exile he continued to press the administration
to set up tribal councils which would give the people a
greater understanding of the aims of the government. All
these suggestions, however, were ignored, even though
official attempts to introduce reforms were not particularly successful. The government unconvincingly explained
that Seretse and Tshekedi had been exiled so that local
councils could be formed, an assertion contradicted by
the fact that not only was Tshekedi the leading spirit seeking administrative reform, including the establishment of
Legislative Council for the Protectorate, but he was the
first person to submit a scheme to implement local councils.

In the absence of a properly constituted tribal authority, disorders among the Ngwato continued to plague
the administration. Although the exile order against
Tshekedi was revoked in August 1952 (though he remained
banned from participating in politics inside the Ngwato
reserve), it was not until the appointment in May 1953 of

Rasebolai Kgamane, third in line of succession and an
uncle to Seretse, as African Authority in place of the
District Commissioner, that a gradual restoration of orderly tribal life was brought about.

As a member of the African Advisory Council, having been appointed one of the regular representatives of
the Kwena by Chief Kgari Sechele, Tshekedi was joined
by Chief Bathoen II, another long-time supporter, in
arguing for the political advancement of the Protectorate.
The government's argument that the time was not ripe
for the creation of a legislative council was attacked as
a concession to South Africa, which feared such development for Africans. Whereas the guiding principle of
British policy in colonial areas was said to be the aspirations of the people, the chiefs contended that in Bechuanaland the government seemed concerned only with the aspirations of official bodies which did not confide in the
people, such as the Colonial Development Corporation.
Despite the opposition of the Resident Commissioner,
Tshekedi continued his fight in the Joint Advisory Council
for a legislative council. Meanwhile, Tshekedi became,
on Seretse's nomination, the council's secretary, despite
opposition from the Bechuanaland Administration.

KOMA, DR. KENNETH. Koma was educated at Cape Town
University, Nottingham (United Kingdom) and Charles University in Prague, and he completed his academic work
at the University of Moscow. He returned to Botswana
in 1965. While disclaiming any such affiliation, it was
generally rumored, with official concurrence, that he was
a Communist. (He was banned from South Africa as
such.) Koma was named Secretary for External Affairs
of the Botswana National Front upon its formation in 1965.

KOPONG CONFERENCE see SHIPPARD

KRAAL. Afrikaans word used in Botswana to mean a group
of houses surrounding an enclosure for livestock or the
social unit inhabitating these structures. The term has
been broadly used to describe the way of life associated
with the kraal found among Batswana's various tribes.
The inhabitants of a kraal are generally members of an
extended family.

KRUGER, OOM PAUL (1825-1904). Last President of the
South African Republic. In 1884 Kruger signed the Convention of London, the effect of which on Bechuanaland

was a small amendment to the frontier established by the
Pretoria Convention so as to include in the Transvaal a
small part of the Stellaland and Goshen Republics.
Though Kruger tried very hard, he did not get the "missionaries" road in Bechuana country, and the southwestern boundary of the Transvaal was fixed to the east of
that road. In 1895 the Jameson Raid was staged upon
the Republic from Bechuanaland, then under the control
of Rhodes' British South Africa Company. (See also
KGATLA).

KUTLWANO ("MUTUAL UNDERSTANDING"). The monthly
      journal published by the Information Office in Gaborone.

KWELE, DANIEL K. Elected first president of the Botswana
      National Front in 1967. Born in the northern region of
      the Ngwato territory, he completed his secondary educa-
      tion with the University of South Africa. After training
      as a teacher in the Government Teachers College in
      Lobatse, he went to Nottingham University in the United
      Kingdom in 1963. He served as a teacher and head-
      master at various schools in Botswana from 1957.

KWENA (BAKWENA). The main body of the Hurutshe from
      which the Batswana tribes trace their descent appears to
      have been resident in the southwestern Transvaal, and
      the breakaway to which the tribes in the Protectorate owe
      their origin is ascribed to the lifetime of a chieftain
      known to legend as Malope. According to this tradition
      he had three sons, Kwena, Ngwato and Ngwaketse, and
      the first to break away were the followers of Kwena.
      For some time they remained a united body under Kwena
      and his successors in the Western Transvaal. During
      the chieftainship of Mogopa, who was credited with being
      a direct descendant of Kwena, and who reigned from about
      1720 to 1730, the greater part of the tribe were driven
      by famine to move to Rathateng, on the east bank of the
      Crocodile River, near its junction with the Marico. Mo-
      gopa and his own adherents afterwards returned to their
      home in the Western Transvaal, but he left behind his
      half-brother Kgabo, then the head of a separate ward or
      village. The modern Kwena of Botswana, considered the
      country's senior tribe, living in the Kwena Reserve, are
      the tribe then established by Kgabo.
      Tradition asserts that when the Ngwaketse and Ngwato
      groups broke away from the Kwena, the latter were still
      in the neighborhood of the Ditheywane Hills, though they

afterwards moved to Sokwane, northeast of the present
Molepolole, and in the period which followed they had
conflicts both with the Ngwaketse and the Kgatla. At the
beginning of the 19th century, when Motswasele II was
the Chief of the Kwena, they were visited by the explorers Cowan and Donovan, but the tribe was then weak, and
soon afterwards was only saved from conquest by the
Ngwaketse through the aid of the Kgatla. It was to this
incident that the Kgatla owed the offer made by Sechele I
at a later date to receive them in the Kwena country in
order to provide them with a refuge from the Boers in
the Transvaal.

When Motswasele was assassinated by a disaffected
tribesman about 1821 or 1822 there was a period of tribal disruption, aggravated by attacks from Sebetwane and
the Makalolo. Part of the tribe, accompanied by Sechele
(Setshele), the elder son of Motswasele, accepted the protection of the Ngwato, and Sechele allied himself by marriage with the family of Khama. It is to this connection
that Sechele owed the fact that he was ransomed by
Khama when captured by one of Sebetwane's raiding parties, though he owed his return to the main body of the
Kwena in 1839 to assistance given not by the Ngwato but
by the Hurutshe.

Harried by the Matebele, Sechele and his followers
took refuge in the Kgalagadi, going as far west as the
Kgakgalane Pan, and it was not until 1837, when the
Ndebele had been defeated by the Boers and had moved to
the north, that Sechele was able to move his group back
to Sokwane. It was here that he was visited by Livingstone in 1841. Owing to subsequent raids by the Ndebele,
the tribe moved successively to Mogodimo, to Thamaga,
to Kolobeng, and then to Tshonwane (in the Western Transvaal), but in 1847 Livingstone persuaded Sechele to move
back to Kolobeng, where he baptized him in 1848. In
1849 Sechele was joined by the Kaa of Shoshong, who had
separated from the Ngwato, then under Chief Sekgoma.
In 1850 he moved his capital upstream to Dimawe, and it
was there, in 1852, that a Boer raid took place which acquired very considerable notoriety in England owing to the
fact that Livingstone's house was ransacked in his absence
by a party of the Boers. Sechele himself attempted to
visit England in order to appeal to Queen Victoria for support against the Transvaalers, but he did not get further
than Cape Town. He moved in 1864 to the present headquarters of the tribe on Molepolole Hill. In 1885 the
Kwena were visited by Sir Charles Warren and were at

last persuaded to accept British protection. Sechele died
in 1892, after a reign of over sixty years.
Sechele's successor, Sebele, had to face a claim to
the chieftainship made on behalf of his brother Kgari.
When Kgari died in 1895, some of his party migrated to
Ramaquabane, and though part returned, there are still
in the Ngwato Reserve a small group of Kgari's former
following. Sebele formed part of the deputation which
approached the Secretary of State in 1895. The Kwena
Reserve was not finally constituted till 1899, and meanwhile the Kwena had to face the result of the trouble
caused by the presence of the Kgatla in what had been
regarded as Kwena territory.
Sebele I died in 1911. His personal conduct had been
such as to lead to an open breach in the tribe which the
Administration had some difficulty in healing; he was no-
toriously intemperate, and his death would have been a
benefit to the Kwena, were it not that his son, Sechele II,
was even more intemperate, and so irregular in his hab-
its that in the end three Councillors were appointed by
the tribe to share his responsibilities. He died in 1917.
His son Sebele II was no better than his father, and in
1926 and again in 1928 the senior members of the tribe
petitioned that he should be removed from the chieftainship. He was deposed by the Administration in 1931,
and succeeded by Khari, his brother by the same mother.
Chief Kgosi Khari Sechele II served with the African
Pioneer Corps in the Middle East during the Second
World War and held the rank of Regimental Sergeant Major. Following his death in 1962, and in the absence of
a male heir, the Protectorate Administration recognized
Neale Sechele as chief. As a result of reports of serious misconduct, a list of charges against Neale was compiled and a large kgotla called on September 21, 1970,
for purposes of impeaching the Chief. At the last minute, Neale was convinced that he should resign rather
than be disgraced in the kgotla. In order to avoid a potentially bitter fight, resignation was made easier by offering Neale a suspension with pay. Chief Bonewemang
was appointed Acting Tribal Authority in October 1970.
The Kwena differ from some other of the tribes
which hold control of Reserves in that they considerably
outnumber all the "allied" tribes, and they can in consequence afford to take a more liberal view of their relations with them. The Kwena are now the third largest
of the Tswana tribes with a population estimated in 1971
as 65,000. The Kweneng District, which essentially

corresponds to tribal boundaries, covers an area of
14,719 square miles.

Kwena Chiefs, with dates of chieftaincy
(early dates not known)

Masilo	Tshosa c. 1803-1807
Malope	Motswasele II c. 1807-1821
Kwena	Morwakgomo c. 1821-1827
Phokotsea	Sechele I c. 1829-1892
Kgabo I	Sebele I 1892-1911
Tebele	Sechele II 1911-1917
Kgabo II	Sebele II 1917-1931
Masilo II	Kgosi Khari Sechele II
Motshodi, died c. 1770	1931-62
Motswasele I c. 1770-	Neale Sechele II 1962-1970
c. 1785	Bonewemang, P. Sechele
Seitlhamo c. 1785-c. 1795	(Acting Tribal Authority)
Legwale c. 1795-c. 1803	1970-
Maleke c. 1803	

KWENENG DISTRICT. The Kweneng District (population
72,000, est. 1971) is responsible for the administration
of the Kwena tribal territory from Molepolole. The
14,719 square mile district extends some 200 miles from
east to west and between 50 and 100 miles north to south.
The population is centered in the eastern third of the district, near the seasonally flowing Metsemotlhaba River
and its tributaries. The western area extends deep into
the Kgalagadi and is characterized by small villages centered around salt pans or government boreholes. The
local economy is based on subsistence agriculture, animal husbandry, and the export of laborers to the mines
of South Africa. The district council has plans to develop the tourist industry within the territory utilizing the
abundant game, as yet unexploited, and a small but
thriving game trophy cottage industry. Ethnically, the
district is dominated by the Kwena, but most of the tribal groups found in Botswana are represented.

-L-

LAND TENURE. Land in Botswana comprises three legal
categories: state land, tribal land and freehold land.
There are 266,000 square kilometers of state land,
274,000 sq. km. of tribal land, and freehold farming
blocks of 20,500 sq. km. Rural land use in Botswana
is mainly divided between crop production, livestock
ranching and hunting/tourism.

In the tribal areas, land is owned by the respective tribes, and is held in trust by the Tribal Land Boards for the tribesmen of the area, and for the economic and social development of all the people of Botswana. Tenure is therefore communal. Land Boards were established by the Tribal Land Act, 1968, but were not activated until 1970. They make land allocations under customary law, as well as under common law. Customary law allocations are made to tribesmen for residential sites, boreholes, and grazing and lands areas, while common law allocations are made for commercial or industrial sites, as well as for public purposes and for non-tribesmen.

State lands are under the direct control of Central Government. Applications for leases of State Land are considered by and, if approved, are granted by the Ministry of Local Government and Lands. Living on State Land are a number of tribes who have hitherto had de facto but not de jure tribal rights over the land. In the case of commercial and industrial ventures on rural State land, the Central Government issues leases on principles similar to those applied to tribal land.

Communal land tenure in the tribal areas presents a number of obstacles to agricultural development. Each household is free to keep as much livestock as it wishes, and no one is responsible for the condition of the range. This factor has contributed to the severe overgrazing in eastern Botswana. Fencing is essential for stock control and modern methods of management, but the fencing of tribal grazing areas is forbidden under customary law. The wealthier livestock owners are able to escape from the overcrowded areas by acquiring rights to boreholes in unused parts of the tribal areas. By this means owners of large herds have effectively obtained exclusive use of large areas without payment of rent. In certain parts of the country, where land is becoming scarce, there is a danger that a large proportion of it will be concentrated in the hands of a few.

LANGUAGE.   The two official languages are Setswana and English.   English is generally spoken only by the educated Africans or those who have worked in South Africa.   Afrikaans is spoken by sections of the white community. Approximately 35 per cent of the population is literate in Setswana and 24 per cent in English.

LEGISLATIVE COUNCIL.   Like the Joint Council which preceded it, the Legislative Council, when established in 1960, consisted of separate representatives of each group;

ten government officials; ten Europeans elected in ten
constituencies; ten Africans chosen by a special electoral
college; one Asian elected by the Asian community; and
four nominated members (two European and two African).
Thus, less than 1 per cent (. 7%) of the population of
European descent had equal representation with the 99
per cent of the population of African origin. The Legislative Council was replaced by the National Assembly
under the 1966 Constitution.

LIMPOPO RIVER. The Limpopo River in southeast Africa
rises as the Crocodile (Krokodil) River in the Witwatersrand, South Africa, and flows on a semicircular course
first northeast and then east for about 1000 miles (1600
km.) to the Indian Ocean. From its source the river
flows northward transversely to the Magaliesburg, cutting
the Hartsbeespoort Gap, site of an irrigation dam. It
then flows across the fertile Bushveld basin to open granite country, where it is joined on the left bank by the
Marico River and is thereafter known as the Limpopo.
(The name may be related to the African uku popozi,
meaning "to rush.") Turning northeastward, the river
forms the border (about 250 miles) between the Transvaal and Botswana, receiving seasonal tributaries. After
swinging eastward between the Transvaal and Rhodesia,
the Limpopo receives the Shashi River and flows about
150 miles to Mozambique, where it reaches the fall line,
dropping 800 feet in 27 miles of rapids. It is unnaviga-
ble until its confluence with the Olifants River 130 miles
from the coast. Partially blocked by a sandbar, the
river can be entered by coastal steamers at high tide.

LINCHWE, CHIEF (1857-1924). Chief of the Kgatla tribe.
He succeeded his father, Kgamanyane in 1875. The earlier part of his rule was taken up with war against his
neighbor Sechele, Chief of the Bakwena. (See also
KGATLA).

LINCHWE II, CHIEF (1936-). Ambassador to the United
States and High Commissioner to Canada, 1969-1972.
Born in Mochudi, completed his primary education at St.
Joseph's College, Botswana; completed Joint Matriculation
Board at Immarentia Secondary School, South Africa, and
proceeded to Essex, England to continue his studies. In
1962 he was recalled to prevent a tribal split and was installed as Paramount Chief, April 6, 1963. He was appointed a member of the Independence Constitutional

Committee and also served on the Economic Advisory
Committee and the Immigrants Selection Board. In 1966
he became chairman of the District Council, Mochudi and
Chairman of the House of Chiefs. After serving as Ambassador to the United States he returned to Mochudi and
reassumed the duties of Paramount Chief, Chairman of
the Land Board, Chairman of the Planning Committee and
President of the Customary Courts in Kgatleng District.

LIVINGSTONE, DAVID (1813-1873). Explorer and missionary.
Born in Blantyre, Scotland. In 1838 he joined the London
Missionary Society and went to South Africa in 1840.
From his headquarters at Kuruman he worked among the
Bechuana and neighboring tribes and in 1849 undertook his
first journey of exploration to Lake Ngami, in company
with Mungo Murray and William Cotton Oswell. Crossing
the Kgalagadi Desert, they reached Lake Ngami on August
1, 1849. While at Kuruman, Livingstone became involved
in a frontier dispute between the Boers and the tribes
under Sechele, and his mission station was destroyed.
Resuming his travels into the interior, he reached the upper Zambezi, where the tsetse fly stopped his scheme of
setting up a mission station. During a two and a half
year trek he reached the Victoria Falls in 1855 and returned to England the next year. In 1857 he published
his Missionary Travels and Researches in South Africa.
His later career was mostly in central Africa, where he
died in 1873.
      Livingstone's Mission Site is easily accessible on the
Kolobeng River. Little remains except the floor of his
dwelling house, two graves and some irrigation ditches.
A few miles to the south, in Manyana Village stands a
large fig tree under which he preached; on the cliffs to
the north of the village are rock paintings.

LOBATSE. South of the capital, Lobatse is the site of the
Botswana Meat Commission (q. v.) one of the largest
meat processing plants in Africa. It also has several
small industries, but a shortage of water has prevented
the town from growing as fast as Gaborone. This water
problem was solved with a pipeline from Gaborone Dam
45 miles to the north and the population is expected to
rise from 12,000 (1971) to 14,000 by 1978. The town has
two hotels and recreational facilities, as well as cinema.
Lobatse is situated amidst a range of low hills. See
also ECONOMY, INTERNAL--(10) Industry.

LOBATSE CONFERENCE   see   CONSTITUTIONAL PROPOS-
ALS

LOBENGULA (1836-1894).   Born in Mosega, Transvaal, now
in the Republic of South Africa.   South African king, the
second and last, of the great Ndebele (or Matabele) nation of Southern Rhodesia. The son of the founder of the
Ndebele Kingdom, Mzilikazi, Lobengula was unable to
preserve the independence of his nation in the face of
growing pressure from British and Boer settlers in southern Africa.

LOCAL GOVERNMENT   see   DISTRICT COUNCILS

LOCH, LORD (HENRY BROUGHAM LOCH) (1827-1900). Governor of Cape Colony and High Commissioner from 1889
to 1895 through the period of increasingly bitter relations
between the British and Transvaal Governments. As
High Commissioner, he supported the Botswana chiefs in
rejecting a transfer of the Protectorate to the Chartered
Company. Loch told the Secretary of State that to hand
over Khama and his people to a commercial company
would be a breach of faith such as no government should
commit.

LONDON CONVENTION OF 1884.   An agreement between the
British and Transvaal governments demarcating the
boundary between the Transvaal and Bechuanaland. With
some modifications it was a repetition of an agreement
in 1881, but excluded from the Transvaal the greater part
of the former republics of Stellaland and Goshen. It con-
ceded some portions of the Tlhaping and Rolong country
to the Transvaal. It also provided that the Imperial government would, if necessary, appoint Commissioners in
Native territories beyond the boundary of the Cape Colony.

LONDON MISSIONARY SOCIETY (LMS).   Founded in 1795, as
a non-denominational missionary society, within a short
time support of the LMS fell mainly upon Congregationalists.   Before the end of the century the Society had established itself in the Cape through Dr. J. T. Vander-
kemp.   The work of the Society gradually expanded
throughout southern Africa.   One of the longest to labor
in the area and one of the most influential missionaries
ever to work in Africa was Robert Moffat (q.v.), who,
with his wife May, established Kuruman in 1820.   This
was the first mission to the Batswana tribes and became

the jumping-off-place for work in the north. After the
transfer of Society headquarters from Kuruman to Tiger
Kloof, an African school was established which attracted
many students from the Protectorate. Until its closing
in 1955 it was the alma mater of most of the Botswana
educated class. At the end of 1955, however, the London Missionary Society gave up its station at Tiger Kloof
largely due to the enforcement of the laws of the Union
Government affecting land occupation (Group Areas Act)
and the prohibition of Bechuanaland Protectorate children
from attending schools in the Union of South Africa, rather than to the effects of the Bantu Education Act. In
1966 the LMS amalgamated with the Commonwealth Missionary Society to become the Congregational Council for
World Missions. (See also MOFFAT; PRICE; WOOKEY;
CAMPBELL; LIVINGSTONE; MACKENZIE; HEPBURN).

LUSAKA MANIFESTO. A common declaration drawn up in
    1969 by the heads of state of East and Central Africa
    meeting in Lusaka concerning the continuation of minority
    white control in Africa. The Manifesto, which consti-
    tutes an important element in Botswana's foreign policy,
    declares: "We would prefer to negotiate rather than de-
    stroy, to talk rather than kill. We do not advocate vio-
    lence; we advocate an end to the violence against human
    dignity, which is now being perpetrated by the oppressors
    of Africa. If peaceful progress to emancipation were
    possible, or if changed circumstances were to make it
    possible in the future, we would urge our brothers in the
    resistance movements to use peaceful methods of struggle
    even at the cost of some compromise on the timing of
    change. "
        However, the Manifesto also commits Botswana as a
    signatory to the implementation of the principles of hu-
    man equality and self-determination throughout Africa.
    It also acknowledges the important fact that the roles in
    the struggle for human equality in Southern Africa will
    be different according to the varied circumstances within
    which each country operates. (See also FOREIGN RELA-
    TIONS).

                            -M-

McCABE, JOSEPH (d. -1865). Early trader and hunter. Lit-
    tle is known of his youth, except that he emigrated from
    the Cape in 1850 and settled in the Transvaal. He was

one of the first white men to cross the Kgalagadi. He
became a trader in Matabeleland, and in 1860 settled in
Botswana at Molepolole, where he died. Apart from his
hunting achievements, he was a pioneer collector of bo-
tanical specimens, many of which he sent to Kew Gar-
dens.

MACKENZIE, JOHN, the Rev. (1835-1899). South African
missionary and diplomat, born in Scotland. In 1854, he
joined the London Missionary Society, which sent him to
South Africa in 1858. At Kuruman he came into conflict
with the policy of the Boers in the neighboring Transvaal
who, through a misunderstanding, destroyed his station.
In 1860 he undertook a trek through present-day Botswana
via Shoshong to the Zambezi, and in 1863 visited Mzilikazi over whom he gained considerable influence. From
1867 onwards he pleaded for the occupation of the interior
by Britain and in 1868 published his book, Ten Years
North of the Orange River. Offered the post of Commissioner for Southern Bechuanaland by Governor Sir Bartle
Frere in 1879, he was barred from accepting by the London Missionary Society. His renewed appeals for British
intervention led to the occupation of Bechuanaland in 1884,
and his appointment as British Commissioner. He persuaded the miniature Boer republic of Stellaland to submit to the British crown, but lost his post through in-
trigue. He retained considerable influence, however,
until his death.

MAFEKING. A town in South Africa originally a kraal (q.v.)
of the Rolong tribe, who gave it the name, meaning
"among the stones." It became a European settlement
after the occupation of the country by the forces of Sir
Charles Warren in 1884. Apart from its importance as
an administrative center for the Bechuanaland Protectorate, Mafeking gained world fame through its successful
defense under General Sir Robert (later Lord) Baden-
Powell in the Boer War. In 1965 the Protectorate administration was removed from Mafeking to the new capital
of Gaborone.

MAFEKING MAIL AND BOTSWANA GUARDIAN. Bilingual
(English and Afrikaans) weekly newspaper with large cir-
culation in Botswana. Commenced publication in 1898 as
Mafeking Mail.

MAHALAPYE. Town in Ngwato District of eastern Botswana

about mid-way on the rail line. Estimated population of
14,000 in 1971.

MAHERERO, Chief Samuel see HERERO

MAKABA II, Chief see NGWAKETSE

MAKGADIKGADI. This enormous salt-pan, approximately
half way between Francistown and Maun, is 73 miles
across at its widest point and some 700 miles in circum-
ference. Once a great lake that dried up little by little
each year, the Makgadikgadi Pan is a satellite of the
Okavango River and the Delta, and its life blood is the
water that floods out of the Delta and is fed into it via
the Boteti River. In bad years, when the Boteti is dry,
it is a gigantic salt-pan, one of the largest in the world.
Otherwise the area is a series of shallow pools. The
white salt sand is flat and featureless and the only breaks
in the white monotone area are islands of grass. A
variety of wild animals thrives near the Makgadikgadi
and great migratory herds of springbok and wildebeest
find their way to it each winter.

MALETE (BAMALETE). One of the eight principal tribes of
Botswana, numbering 14,000 (1971), they are by origin
Transvaal Ndebele (Matabele). While belonging to the
Nguni group the Malete were not subject to Mzilikazi, a
much later arrival. Because they lived for several centuries in the Transvaal surrounded by various Sotho
tribes, they were strongly influenced by Sotho language
and culture. All the early part of Malete history is legendary, but in the middle of the 18th century they apparently settled in the valley of the Taung River near Ramotsa. After various wanderings and conflicts with other
tribes, they settled along the Marico River during the
chieftaincy of Mokgosi I (1820?-86) in what is now the
Kgatleng District. Mokgosi, allied first with the Kwena
and later with the Ngwaketse, acquired a considerable
number of cattle, and under him the tribe gained some
prominence. They came into contact with the Boers about
1850 who demanded their labor. Pressed by the Boers
they accepted in 1852 an invitation from the Kwena Chief
Sechele to settle in Kwena country where they remained
until 1863. Unwilling to pay tribute, however, Mokgosi
took his people in 1875 to Ramotsa, then in Ngwaketse
country. Although the tribe signed a document in 1885
acknowledging their dependence upon the Ngwaketse, the

Malete claimed that it was signed under duress. Later
the same year representatives of the British South Africa
Company extracted from Ikanong, acting for his father,
and Chief Montshiwa of the Rolong, the transfer of their
countries to the Company. Ikaneng was formally granted
power by his elderly father in 1886, an action which
stirred serious controversy. By Proclamation No. 10 of
1895, the British government legalized the transfer to the
Company of the administration of the Malete and the Rolong and Dr. Leander Starr Jameson (q. v.) was designated
as Resident Commissioner of the two territories thus
ceded. In London, meanwhile, Chiefs Khama, Sebele and
Bathoen were seeking to ward off such a fate for their
peoples. But Jameson's embarrassing raid into the
Transvaal in December 1895 brought an end to the Company's plans in the Protectorate.   By Proclamation No. 1
of 1896, the Company's authority over the countries of
chiefs Ikaneng and Montshiwa (see ROLONG) was revoked.
One of the by-products of this entire land transferal epi-
sode was the clear legal recognition of the Malete as an
independent tribe.

Chief Ikaneng died in 1896 and was succeeded by
Mokgosi II who died in 1906 after an uneventful reign.
His brother, Baitlutle, became Regent for the heir, Seboko, who assumed power in 1917. Seboko died in 1937
while the heir, Mokgosi III, was still a minor. Consequently, Seboko's brother, Ketswerebothata, acted as Regent until 1945 when Mokgosi III succeeded to the chieftaincy.

Malete Chiefs, with dates of chieftaincy
(early dates not known)

Badimo	Marumo
Phatle	Poo I
Malete	Mokgojwa c. 1780-c. 1805
Lesokwana	Poo II c. 1805-c. 1820
Mokgware	Mokgosi c. 1820-1886
Digope	Ikaneng 1886-96
Dira	Mokgosi II 1896-1906
Mmusi	Baitlutle 1906-17
Maphalaola	Seboko 1917-37
Mongatane	Ketswerebothata 1937-45
Maio	Mokgosi III 1945-1966
Kgomo	Kelemogile, 1966- (Regent)
Mokgwa	

MALLORY, CHARLES SHANNON see ANGLICAN CHURCH

MARICO RIVER. Main headstream, with the Crocodile River, of the Limpopo River, in west Transvaal. It flows generally north through the Marico Valley and forms a portion of Botswana's eastern boundary.

MASA ("DAWN"). Organ of the BPP which commenced publication in Cairo in January 1964 and continued to be produced there until independence in 1966 when it was moved to a new location.

MASIRE, DR. QUETT K. J. (1925-). Vice-President of Botswana, born at Kanye. He received his education in Kanye and Tiger Kloof, South Africa. He founded Seepapitso Secondary School in 1950. First a reporter and later director of African Echo, in 1958 he became a member of the Ngwaketse Tribal Council. A member both of the Legislative Council and the Executive Council, he was a founding member of the Botswana Democratic Party, its Secretary General and editor of the party newspaper, Therisanyo. In 1965 he was elected a member of the National Assembly but lost his seat in the 1969 elections. As Deputy Prime Minister, 1965-66, he attended the Independence Conference in London in February, 1966. After independence he became Vice-President and Minister of Finance (a title later expanded to Minister of Finance and Development Planning).

MATABELE see MZILIKAZI, LOBENGULA

MATANTE, P. G. Politician, member of Parliament. Although his birthplace is disputed he grew up in Johannesburg, South Africa, where he became a member of the African National Congress (q. v.). At the outbreak of World War II he went to Botswana and was recruited for military service. But he did not leave the country until 1945 when the war was over. In 1946 he was assigned to guard duty with other High Commission Territory troops in the Suez Canal having gained the rank of Regimental Sergeant Major. In 1960 he was one of the founders of the Bechuanaland People's Party (see BOTSWANA PEOPLE'S PARTY). As a result of internal rivalry and his own strong identification with the Pan African Congress, the party was considerably weakened. But in 1965 he was elected a member of the National Assembly and was recognized as Leader of the Opposition. He was reelected to office in 1969.

MATHIBA, Chief   see   TAWANA

MATTHEWS, JOSEPH G. (1929-). Politician, attorney,
  civil servant. A former leader of the African National
  Congress of South Africa. Born at Durban, the son of
  Professor Z. K. Matthews (q. v.), he was educated at St.
  Peter's, the African school in Johannesburg run by the
  Community of the Resurrection until it was closed in protest against the Bantu Education Act. There he came
  under the influence of Oliver Tambo who was the mathe-
  matics master and active in Congress politics. In 1944
  he joined the African National Congress Youth League at
  its formation, and from 1948 to 1950 was active in student politics while studying at Fort Hare University College in the Eastern Cape. In 1948 he presided at the
  first National Conference of the Youth League and became
  the League's National Secretary in 1951. In 1951 he began reading law at the University of the Witwatersrand,
  Johannesburg, but left a year later to organize the De-
  fiance Campaign in the Eastern Cape, which soon became
  one of the centers of resistance to the white minority
  government. In the same year he was banned under the
  Suppression of Communism Act and in 1953 was twice
  convicted under the Act and given suspended sentences.
  He then became articled to a solicitor in Port Elizabeth.
  In December 1956 he was arrested on a charge of high
  treason, though it was withdrawn in 1958. Marked for
  detention by the declaration of the State of Emergency,
  he escaped to Basutoland, where he practised as an attorney in Maseru until leaving for London. In 1973 he
  was requested by President Khama to join his staff.

MATTHEWS, ZACHARIAH K. (1901-1968). Academician,
  lawyer, politician and diplomat. Born at Kimberley into
  a strongly Christian home, of a Bechuana father who had
  been a mine-worker and then became the owner of a
  small cafe, he was educated at the African High School,
  Lovedale, and at Fort Hare University College where, in
  1932, he became the first African graduate of the College,
  as he was later to become the first African graduate in
  law anywhere in South Africa. Having received a bache-
  lor's degree in arts and his education diploma, he was
  appointed in 1925 as Principal of Adam's College, Natal.
  In 1933 he continued his studies at Yale, where he received a master of arts degree, and in 1934, he went to
  the London School of Economics for a further year, doing
  postgraduate studies in anthropology.

Returning to South Africa, he campaigned in 1935 against the removal of African male voters in the Cape from the common electoral roll, rejecting the compensation offered them of four white Native Representatives in the House of Assembly. He was one of the principal organizers of the All African Convention, a conference of all African organizations which gathered at Bloemfontein to protest against the Representation of Natives Act. In 1936 he was appointed professor and head of the Department of African Studies at the University College of Fort Hare. From 1936 to 1939 he did anthropological research into the Rolong of Bechuanaland and he served as a member of the Royal Commission on Higher Education for Africans in British East Africa and the Sudan. In 1941 he was elected to the Native Representative Council, and held his seat until 1950 when he resigned in protest against government policy. In 1942 he joined the African National Congress and was immediately elected to the National Executive. In 1947 he joined the Executive of the South African Institute of Race Relations and was appointed Professor of Native Administration and Law at Fort Hare.

In 1952 New York's Union Theological Seminary appointed Mr. Matthews Professor of World Christianity. He was the first Black to join the seminary's faculty and the first South African Christian scholar ever called to a senior teaching post at an American theological seminary. Between 1932 and 1963 Professor Matthews authored more than twenty books and articles.

The South African Government cancelled Mr. Matthew's passport and he was forced to return there, resuming his teaching duties in African Studies. In 1954 he was refused a passport to attend a world conference on race relations in Honolulu. In December 1956 the South African Government set up what was described as a "far reaching mass treason inquiry" aimed at the opponents of its race segregation policies. Although he was detained, the indictment was quashed in April 1959. After 135 days of detention in 1960 he was admitted as an attorney to practice in Bechuanaland in 1961. Following Botswana's independence he was designated Ambassador to the United States and Permanent Representative to the United Nations, posts which he held from 1966 until his death in 1968.

MAUN. The tribal capital of the Tawana is in the northwest of the country. It is the center of the safari and game

industry for the Okavango Delta and the Moremi Game
Reserve. Maun is 400 miles west of Francistown by
road, but is served throughout the week by Botswana Airways Corporation. Most of the safari companies which
operate into the Moremi and Okavango have offices in
Maun and there are plans to build another hotel to supplement the present accomodations provided by the single
hotel and safari camps and lodges. Population was estimated at 10,000 in 1971. See also TOURISM.

MERRIWEATHER, DR. A. M. (1918-). Physician, missionary, public servant. Born in Bradford, England; educated at George Heriot School, Edinburgh and University
of Edinburgh where he graduated M. B. Ch. B. in 1941.
After serving in the Indian Army Medical Corps (1941-
1944) he arrived in Molepolole in October 1944. Returning to Scotland in 1947 to continue his medical studies,
he received the M. R. C. P. degree at the Royal College
of Physicians and also the D. T. M. O. H. degree at University of Liverpool. Ordained a minister of the United
Free Church of Scotland in 1948, he returned to Molepolole in 1949 to become Medical Superintendent of the
Scottish Livingstone Hospital. In 1956 he received his
M. D. from the University of Edinburgh. Nominated to
the Legislative Council in 1961, he was elected Speaker
of the Legislative Council and Legislative Assembly,
1963-1968.

MILNER, SIR ALFRED (Lord) (1854-1925). Governor of Cape
Colony, and High Commissioner from 1897 to 1901. Following the South African War, he urged an active interest in the lands to the north. To enable him to devote
his attention to this area he successfully urged the separation of the office of the governor of Cape Colony and
the High Commissionership. From 1897 to 1905 he held
the title of High Commissioner alone and endeavored to
further the union of South Africa by inviting representatives of the colonies and protectorates to confer with him.

MINING see ECONOMY, INTERNAL--(4) Mining

MINISTRIES. Botswana's first "shadow" ministries were established in 1965 in preparation for independence. These
included Home Affairs, Agriculture, Finance, Labor and
Social Services, Local Government, Mines, Commerce
and Industry, Works and Communications. Certain adjust-
ments were made after independence and in 1973 the ministries were as follows:

State
Finance and Development
  Planning
Health, Labor and Home
  Affairs
Agriculture
Education

Commerce and Industry
Information and Broadcast-
  ing
Local Government and Lands
Works and Communications
Mineral Resources and
  Water Affairs

MISSIONARIES see LONDON MISSIONARY SOCIETY

MITCHISON, LADY NAOMI (1897-). Wife of Lord Mitchison,
a former Labor member of the British Parliament. A
well-known journalist, author of over 70 books. Having
met the young Chief-designate, Linchwe II in London, she
has spent three months of each year for the past ten
years in Mochudi. Honorary member of the Kgatla.

MOCHUDI. Mochudi was settled by the Kgatla in 1871 when
they occupied a well-watered defensive site which had
earlier been used by the Kwena. The original Kgatla
migrants could only have numbered between three and
four thousand people, but this was increased, after the
hit-and-run wars with the Kwena, by later arrivals. Although it took fifty years to persuade the government that
it should construct a bridge across the Notwane River,
Mochudi did benefit from its proximity to the railway line
and in being one of the first tribal centers to be provided
with telegraph and telephone facilities. The construction
of main roads within Mochudi has ensured easy access to
all parts of the village. By cutting the first road from
Mochudi to Pilane in 1921, the Regent Isang Pilane en-
abled greater use to be made of the railway and brought
Mochudi into closer contact with neighboring communities.
This road was improved by Chief Molefi in 1934.
    Mochudi can boast of a very respectable tally of edu-
cational institutions, for, apart from its five primary
schools, it has two secondary schools, one government
and one private, and the only women's training center in
the country. The origins of this educational achievement
must be traced to the early efforts of the Dutch Reformed
Mission, to the enthusiasm of Chief Linchwe I and to the
extraordinary initiative and drive of Isang Pilane. Mochudi also possesses a hospital, community center, library, prison and other civil facilities, and is relatively
well endowed. Population was estimated in 1971 to be
7000.

MOENG COLLEGE. One of the varied achievements of Tshekedi Khama (q.v.) as an educationist was his founding of
Moeng College, a large, modern secondary school with a
trades department. Established in 1947, the funds were
derived from a cattle levy which realized £100,000 from
the Ngwato Tribe. In 1955, Moeng College was reorganized as a Territorial Institution under the management
of a Governing Council consisting of tribal, mission, and
British Government interests and of the African Teacher's
Association and two persons associated with higher education in Southern Africa.

MOFFAT, JOHN S. (1835-1918). Missionary and British official. Fourth son of Robert and Mary Moffat; after join-
ing the London Missionary Society in 1857 he served in
Matabeleland and Kuruman. In 1877 he was posted to
Molepolole but resigned from the Society in 1879. No
longer a missionary, he entered British government service in the Transvaal and Basutoland. After the establishment of British Bechuanaland as a Crown Colony in 1885,
Moffat was appointed resident magistrate at Taung and
served until 1887.

MOFFAT, ROBERT (1795-1883). South African missionary.
Born in Scotland, he joined the London Missionary Society
in 1816, and was sent by them to Namaqualand. His first
great success was the conversion of the local chief, Af-
rikaner. With his wife Mary, he established Kuruman in
1820. This was the first mission to the Bechuana tribes
and served as the jumping-off-place for work in the north.
David Livingstone married one of the Moffats' daughters
and it was from Kuruman that Livingstone set out to live
among the Bechuana and learn their language in preparation for his first trip north.
    Moffat translated the Bible into Tswana--first the
New Testament, completed in 1830, and later the Old
Testament. On this work he labored forty years, printing it himself on a small press he brought by ox-wagon
from Cape Town. In 1859 Moffat moved to the Ndebele
country, where he set up the first mission station, but
had to give it up in 1870.

MOGAMI, THEBO D. (1942-). Botswana diplomat, educated
at the University of Botswana, Lesotho and Swaziland and
Columbia University. Assistant Secretary, office of the
President, 1968-1971; Under-Secretary for External Af-
fairs, 1971-1972; Permanent Representative to the United
Nations, July 1972- ; delegate to several OAU conferences.

MOGODI, KHUKHU, the Rev. (1829-1925). Born in the
Transvaal he was sent to train as an evangelist at the
Moffat Memorial Institution in Kuruman. After completing his training under the Rev. John Mackenzie, he was
sent to Lake Ngami, where a new mission was to be established. Despite threats by the chief and the leading
men of the tribe who opposed his teachings, he succeeded
in stopping among the Tawana the ill-treatment or the
killing of the Sarwa (Bushmen) without cause. In articles
he contributed between 1882-1888 to Mahoko, a Bechuana
newspaper established by the London Missionary Society,
he reported his adventures and struggles in this work of
evangelism. Through his initiative the congregation became firmly established. As more people were converted
among the Tawana tribe, a day school was put up and
taught by him.

MOGOPA, Chief see KWENA

MOKGOSE I, Chief see MALETE

MOLELHE, TOPO JAMES (1927-). Botswana diplomat born
in Mafeking, South Africa. He received his education at
Fore Hare College. First a teacher in South Africa, he
then took up positions in Botswana from 1957 to 1966,
and was appointed Vice-Principal of the Teacher Training
College in Lobatse in 1966. Appointed Assistant Secretary for the Department of External Affairs in 1966, he
was made Private Secretary to the President in 1967.
He was Premanent Representative to the United Nations
in 1968-1972, and thereafter was associated with the
Ministry of Health, Labor and Home Affairs as Assistant
(Principal) Secretary.

MOLEMA, MODIRI SILAS (1892-1965). Born in Mafeking, the
son of a journalist, he received his education in Heald-
town in the Cape Province. He graduated and then taught
school at the Lyndhurst Road Public School in Kimberley
for several years. About 1913, Molema left South Africa
and went to Glasgow University to study medicine, grad-
uating in 1919. He returned to Bechuanaland but spent
most of the rest of his life in Mafeking. He was a life-
long Methodist, and supported the Botswana Government
until his death. Though he was a member of the Rolong
people, part of the Tswana-language group, Molema published only in English. His works are: The Bantu, Past
and Present (1920); Chief Moroka, His Life and Times,
His Country and His People; Montshiwa, Barolong Chief

and Patriot (1815-1896) and an unpublished biography of Tshekisho Plaatie.

MOLEPOLOLE. Capital of the Kwena tribe, Molepolole has a seasonal population of over 30,000 and a stable population of about 10,000 (1971). Feeder roads lead to Ghanzi, Tshane, Hukuntse and Lehututu.

MOLOPO RIVER. Watercourse which together with the Ramatlabama forms the southern boundary of the Republic of Botswana. It formerly flowed more frequently but when it does flow it ultimately enters the Orange River.

MONTSHIWA, Chief see ROLONG

MOREMI I, Chief see TAWANA

MOREMI II, Chief see TAWANA

MOREMI WILDLIFE RESERVE. The Moremi is on the edge of the Okavango Delta and is soon to be expanded to include a major part of the Delta itself. The Reserve contains an incredible spectrum of wildlife in surroundings as varied as the palm-covered islands in the Delta to the thick Mophane forest. Unlike the majority of parks and reserves, visitors to the Moremi are free to approach the animals on foot accompanied by a game scout. The famous Khwai River Lodge is located in the reserve offering first class facilities for both hunting and photographic safaris.

MORSE ECONOMIC SURVEY MISSION REPORT. A mission headed by the American economist, Professor Chandler Morse, published in 1960 as Report of an Economic Survey Mission, which advanced recommendations for each of the High Commission Territories.

MOTSETE, KGALEMAN T. The first President of the BPP was born at Serowe and educated locally. Proceeding to Tiger Kloof in South Africa, he gained his Junior Teacher's Certificate in 1918, took his matriculation, and then went to London University, where he took degrees in Divinity and Arts. Remaining in London to study music, he obtained his teacher's qualifications in the subject and then returned to Bechuanaland, where he ran for a time the Tati Training Institute and then taught at a number of schools in the Republic of South Africa, Nyasaland, and

Bechuanaland itself. On December 6, 1960, the very day
that the Bechuanaland administration proposed the establishment of a Legislative Council, he formed the Bechuanaland People's Party and became its first President.
He appeared on the Northern Protectorate list of ten nom-
inees, from which five Legislative Members had to be
selected, but he was unsuccessful, and he soon afterwards strongly attacked the new Legislative Council,
which he said might be the "wooden horse" of South African expansionism. (See BOTSWANA PEOPLE'S PARTY).

MOTSWASELE II, Chief   see KWENA

MPHO, MOTSAMAI (1921-). Politician, member of Parlia-
ment. Born of the Bayei tribe in Maun, Ngamiland, ed-
ucated at the Botswana National School and Tiger Kloof,
South Africa. After leaving Tiger Kloof he joined the
African National Congress in South Africa in 1952. He
was arrested in 1956 but acquitted of treason charges.
Detained for four months in 1960, he was deported to
Bechuanaland in August 1960 and became the Secretary
General of the newly formed Bechuanaland People's Party
(BPP) then under the formal leadership of Kgaleman T.
Motsete. When the BPP broke up in 1962 he became the
leader of the Botswana Independence Party. In the 1969
general election he won a seat in Parliament. (See also
BOTSWANA PEOPLE'S PARTY; BOTSWANA INDEPEND-
ENCE PARTY.)

MZILIKAZI (c. 1790-1868). Born in Zululand, the son of
Mashobane, of the Khumalo people, Mzilikazi became one
of Chaka's most trusted lieutenants. When, after a major campaign, he refused to hand over looted cattle, he
was forced in 1823 to leave Zululand with 300 followers.
Over the next 15 years or so he moved westward across
the Transvaal in flight from the Zulu armies, until finally
in 1837, after a triple conflict with the Zulu, with Griqua
raiders from the Orange River, and with the expanding
white farmers or Voortrekkers from the Cape, he led his
following (which had now increased to between 15,000 and
20,000) across the Limpopo River into southwest Rhodesia
and Bechuanaland.
    Across the Limpopo, Mzilikazi found it easy to es-
tablish himself, for the once prosperous Rozwi empire
and the various Shona paramountcies had been weakened
by the earlier Nguni invasions. As in the Transvaal, so
in Rhodesia, Mzilikazi rapidly absorbed large numbers of

the local populace into his age-set regiments; a caste-like society evolved, with the original Nguni nucleus at the top, the Sotho in the middle, and the Shona constituting the lowest rung in society. Beyond their immediate settlement, the Ndebele established a variety of relationships with the surrounding peoples, ranging from regular tributary status to occasional raiding and warfare. Mzilikazi's reign was marred by bloodshed and tyranny, but he was revered by his subjects, and among his closest friends were white pioneer missionaries such as Robert Moffat, scientists, explorers, hunters and traders.

-N-

NATIONAL ASSEMBLY   see   CONSTITUTION

NATIONAL DEVELOPMENT BANK   see   ECONOMY, INTERNAL--(9) Banking

NATIONAL DEVELOPMENT PLAN.   The 1968-73 plan replaced the Transitional Plan for Social and Economic Development published in 1966.   The declared object of the Plan was to create a united nation, to overcome all parochial, tribal and racial rivalries and to safeguard territorial independence.   Special efforts were to be made to strengthen the institutional structure of the country by mobilizing local savings for investment and to establish an industrial sector.   Although prospects for the development of large-scale mining were seen as hopeful, the Plan did not depend upon these projected revenues for success.
     The National Development Plan, 1973-78, is divided in two parts; Part I sets forth policies and objectives, while Part II describes all Central Government development projects in detail.   Although dependence upon foreign grants for the ordinary budget had been obviated in 1972 as the result of an exceptional economic growth rate, it was noted that a high degree of discipline would be required.   The Plan calls for extensive state intervention to promote new activities.   Yet, it assumes that sustained development will be based on a steady increase in the income earning activities of citizens in the private sector.   According to President Khama, not only is a far greater agricultural production necessary but also, "Batswana must increasingly become engaged as businessmen in trade, in manufacturing and in providing an expanding

variety of basic services. " In his view, the nation must look firstly to its own people for initiative and entrepreneurship outside the traditional sector. See also ECONOMY, INTERNAL--(12) Planning.

NATIONAL LIBRARY SERVICE. The Botswana National Library Service is a department of the Ministry of Health, Labor and Home Affairs. Under the Director there is a staff of seven librarians and 13 library assistants. Its headquarters are adjacent to the Gaborone Public Library. The current stock level exceeds 60,000 volumes. A program of construction of rural libraries is currently being undertaken. The project involves the construction of six libraries--at Francistown, Mahalapye, Maun, Molepolole, Lobatse and Serowe.

NATIVE ADMINISTRATION PROCLAMATION see PROCLAMATIONS OF 1934; JUSTICE

NATIVE ADVISORY COUNCIL see AFRICAN ADVISORY COUNCIL

NATIVE TREASURY'S PROCLAMATION see PROCLAMATION OF 1938

NDEBELE see MZILIKAZI, LOBENGULA

NEWSPAPERS see PRESS

NGAMI LAKE. A shallow depression at the southeastern (lowest) corner of the 4000-square-mile inland delta of the Okavango River in Ngamiland in the North West District. It lies 43 miles by road from Maun, and 320 miles from the railway through eastern Botswana. The lake was reached by David Livingstone in 1849. Lying 3000 feet above sea level, it is 40 miles long and 6 to 10 miles wide. Although Ngamiland is part of the great sandy Kgalagadi Desert, around Lake Ngami the country is well timbered with scrub and big thorn trees and supports a large cattle population of approximately 10,000 cattle a day. The lake is often covered with flocks of flamingo numbering more than 20,000 and there is an abundance of pelican and countless waterfowl. The local village is Sehithwa, midway along the northern margin of the lake.

NGAMILAND see NORTH WEST DISTRICT

NGWAKETSE (BANGWAKETSE). The section deriving from
Ngwaketse, after parting from the Kwena (q. v.) of
Kgabo's community, were for some years involved in
conflicts with them and also with other tribes. The tribe
seems to have settled at one time near Lobatse and at
another time at Makolontwane near Moshaneng in the
present Ngwaketse Reserve. It was not until the chieftaincy of Makaba II, about 1795-1825, that they began to
occupy a position of importance among their neighbors.
Makaba II, moreover, appears to have made himself one
of the most formidable chiefs of his time in Bechuanaland.

On the death of Makaba II there was a prolonged period of chaos, owing partly to the raids of the Makololo
under Sebetwane, and partly to the attacks of the Ndebele,
or Matebele, under Mzilikazi, who had made his headquarters in the western Transvaal. Part of the tribe under Sebego, who ruled about 1825-45 and was a younger
son of Makaba II, took refuge near Lehututu in the Kgalagadi Desert, and part, under Gaseitsiwe, the grandson of
Makaba II and direct heir to the chieftainship, moved to
Tswaneng, in the southeast of the present Ngwaketse Reserve. Though the immediate danger from Mzilikazi was
removed when his forces were defeated by the Boers at
the Marico River in 1837, the two sections of the Ngwaketse remained apart till they met together at Kanye in
1853. When, however, they were visited by James Chapman and Samuel Edwards in 1854, the village of Kanye
had been destroyed by the Transvaalers and the Ngwaketse
were in two camps, one headed by Gaseitsiwe and one by
his cousin Senthufi. They did not come under the rule of
a single chief till 1853, when Senthufi agreed to recognize
Gaseitsiwe as Chief of the whole tribe. During the long
reign of Gaseitsiwe, which did not end till 1889, the
Ngwaketse received a considerable accession to their numbers from a variety of different sources.

When Bathoen I died in 1910 he was succeeded by his
son Seepapitso, who carried on his father's program of
"reformed" legislation, and was by general agreement one
of the most advanced chiefs of his time. After a short
reign of six years, however, he was murdered by his
brother, Moyapitso, as the result of a dispute about the
late Chief's, their father's, property, leaving a son (afterwards Bathoen II), who was at the time only eight years
old. There followed a period of stagnation during which
the Ngwaketse had a succession of three Headmen as Acting Chiefs. The situation was only relieved when Ga-

goangwe, the widow of Bathoen I and daughter of the
Kwena Chief Sechele I, a lady of character and public
spirit, took charge of affairs in 1924. On her death,
Ntebogang, the elder sister of Seepapitso, acted as Regent for three years, with the aid of three advisers who
had been selected by Gagoangwe and three others chosen
by herself. She handed over charge to her nephew,
Bathoen II, in 1928 who ruled until 1969, when he abdi-
cated. (See also BATHOEN I and BATHOEN II.)
   In 1971 the population of the Ngwaketse reserve in
the Southern District was estimated at 70,000. The tribal capital and District center is Kanye.

Ngwaketse Chiefs, with dates of chieftaincy
(early dates not known)

Ngwaketse	Bathoen I 1889-1910
Seepapitso	Seepapitso 1910-16
Leema	Kgosimotse 1916-18
Khutwane	Malope 1918-19
Makaba I	Tshosa 1919-23
Mongala	Gagoangwe 1923-24
Moleta c. 1770-c. 1790	Ntebogang 1924-28
Makaba II c. 1790-c. 1824	Bathoen II 1928-69
Sebego 1825-44	Seepapitso IV 1969-1973
Segotshane c. 1846	Mookami Gaseitsve (Acting
Gaseitsiwe c. 1846-1889	Chief) 1973

NGWATO. Son of Malope and grandson of Masilo, legendary
   founder of the Tswana nation. According to most tradition, Kwena, Ngwato, and Ngwaketse, all sons of Malope,
   each became the father of a Tswana tribe.

NGWATO (BAMANGWATO). According to tradition, the followers of Ngwato (see above) separated from the Kwena
   several generations after his lifetime, probably during
   the last half of the 18th century. The early successors
   of Ngwato were Molwa, Tamasiga, Serogola, Madirana,
   Kesitilwe, Makgasana and Moleta. Upon the latter's
   death, Mokgadi was appointed regent for the young heir,
   Mathiba. Mathiba at last assumed the chieftaincy about
   1770 but not before his uncle, the regent, was killed.
      After Mathiba's installation, the Ngwato moved away
   from the Kwena altogether and settled at Shoshong. Soon
   after their arrival there a serious split occurred which
   resulted in the formation of the Tawana (q. v.). Although
   Khama I, who took over around 1795, briefly pursued his
   younger brother, Tawana, he at last acquiesced in his

independence. Khama died of old age about 1817 after
moving his headquarters to a place near Serowe.
Khama was succeeded by his son, Kgari, who moved
the town to Serowe. Suffering some attacks from other
tribes, Kgari led his people northward but was killed in
battle while fighting the Shona about 1826. Kgari was followed by Sedimo as regent amid conflict and further separation. Sedimo passed the chieftaincy to Khama II about
1833 but the new chief, unmarried and without a son,
died in 1835 and was succeeded by his half-brother, Sekgoma I.
    At the time Sekgoma came to the chieftaincy the
Ngwato were scattered and disorganized because of military defeats. Setting out to organize his tribe he soon
felt the opposition of the Ndebele. Marching westwards
towards the Makarikari region Sekgoma stopped at the
Boteti River where Khama III, the first of 16 sons, was
born. Eventually the tribe returned to the Shoshong area
at the invitation of the Kaa and Talaote.
    The appearance in 1857 of Matsheng, a claimant to
the chieftaincy who had lived among the Ndebele, brought
the temporary displacement of Sekgoma. However, Matsheng's harsh rule, which reflected his Ndebele experience, stirred considerable discontent and in 1858 Sekgoma
was again installed. Shortly thereafter, in 1862, Mackenzie and Price of the London Missionary Society arrived to work among the Ngwato. Mackenzie later recorded the 1963 attack of the Ndebele upon the Ngwato
and described in detail the courage and skill of Khama
and his father, Sekgoma.
    The conversion of Khama and his brother, Kgamane,
to Christianity against their father's will stirred considerable conflict in the family. By 1866 the dissension between father and sons flared up into open warfare so that
the latter fled for their lives. Although a truce was ar-
ranged after some weeks and the sons returned to Shoshong, new troubles followed with the reappearance of
Matsheng. Matsheng secured the chieftaincy in 1866 but
brought only five more years of misrule. At last,
Khama III, aided by Chief Sechele of the Kwena, ousted
Matsheng and assumed the chieftaincy.
    Almost immediately Khama met opposition from his
erstwhile ally and brother, Kgamane. Khama therefore
recalled his father, Sekgoma, to take up the power once
more. But further conflict followed until at last, in 1875,
Khama drove out both his father and brother. Khama was
again installed and ruled until 1923. The remarkable

history of Khama III and his heirs thereafter largely over-
shadowed all events in the Protectorate. (See KHAMA
III; SEKGOMA II; KHAMA, TSHEKEDI; KHAMA, SERETSE;
FLOGGING CASE; KGAMANE, RASEBOLAI; MACKENZIE;
PRICE.)

Ngwato Chiefs, with dates of chieftaincy
(early dates not known)

Ngwato	Khama II c.1833-c.1835
Molwa	Sekgoma I c.1835-1857; 1858-
Tamasiga	1866; 1872-75
Serogola	Matsheng 1857-58; 1866-72
Madirana	Khama III 1872, 1875-1923
Kesitilwe	Sekgoma II 1923-25
Makgasana	Tshekedi (Regent 1926-1950)
Moleta	Rasebolai Kgamane-African
Mokgadi c.1770	Authority 1953-64
Mathiba c.1770-c.1795	Leapetswe Tshekedi Khama-
Khama I c.1795-c.1817	African Authority 1964-
Kgari c.1817-1826	Molwa Sekgoma
Sedimo c.1826-1833	

NORTH EAST DISTRICT. The North East District towards
the Rhodesia border is administered from the industrial
center of Francistown. It was formerly contained within
the Tati Concession which was acquired in 1911 by the
Tati Company. The District has an area of 26,000
square miles and a population of only 2062 (1971).

NORTH WEST DISTRICT. The North West District (area
50,212 square miles) covers Ngamiland and the Chobe,
the home of the Tawana tribe, the Bayei, and the Herero
and Bendero from South West Africa. Unlike the rest of
Botswana the area has abundant water mainly consisting
of the Okavango Swamps which drain southward towards
the open plains of the Kgalagadi Desert. The North West
District, from its center at Maun, plays a vital role in
the economy of Botswana, bringing in over R1.5 million
per annum from tourists and hunters. The game in the
area is unrivalled elsewhere in Africa and the District
Council itself administers the Moremi Wildlife Reserve.
The world famous Chobe National Park attracts thousands
of visitors to view the many species of wildlife and game.
The population of the District is 53,000 (1971).

NWAKO, M. P. K. (1922-). Botswana politician, born in
the Ngwato area. He received his education at Tiger
Kloof, South Africa. He was treasurer of the Kwena and

Ngwato Tribal Administrations from 1948-52; Secretary-
Treasurer of Moeng College 1954-64 and served on the
African Council. A member first of the Legislative
Council then the National Assembly, 1965, he has served
as Minister of Agriculture 1965-66; Minister of State for
External Affairs, 1966-69; Minister of Health, Labor and
Home Affairs, 1969- .

-O-

OKAVANGO RIVER AND DELTA. The Okavango Delta, with
its swamps and perennial water, is a major feature of
Ngamiland. Malaria is endemic to Ngamiland, and parts
of the area are infected with sleeping sickness. The
delta supports great herds of buffalo, hippopotamus and
other animals. The Okavango River rises in Angola and
has a catchment area of 205,000 square kilometers. The
delta covers an area of about 16,000 sq. km. (about 3
per cent of the total area of Botswana), of which about
half is permanently flooded. The rest is seasonally
flooded. Because of the high rate of evaporation, however, the average annual outflow from the delta into the
Boteti River and Lake Ngami is little more than 5 per
cent of the total inflow.

ORDER IN COUNCIL of May 9, 1891   see   HIGH COMMIS-
SIONER

ORDER IN COUNCIL of May 16, 1904. By this Order all the
area which was to be placed at the disposal of the Crown
was proclaimed as Crown Land and this applied only to
"the lands abandoned by the Chiefs Khama, Sebele, and
Bathoen." It was subsequently recognized that the Order
was not sufficiently definite, and it was supplemented
therefore by the Order of January 10, 1910, which had
the effect of extending the definition of Crown Lands to
include all lands in the Protectorate, except (a) those defined in the Order of 1904; (b) the lands in the Tati District; (c) any land which might be in future declared a
Reserve; (d) any grant made by or on behalf of the Crown,
or the 41 Barolong Farms.

ORDER IN COUNCIL of December 21, 1960   see   CONSTITU-
TIONAL COMMITTEE

ORGANIZATION OF AFRICA UNITY. Intergovernmental

organization, established in 1963, to which all independent
African states (except South Africa and Rhodesia) belong.
Botswana was admitted to membership immediately upon
attaining independence on September 30, 1966 and has
since played an active role in its operation.

-P-

PAC see PAN AFRICAN CONGRESS

PALAPYE. A traditional village, once a seat of Paramount
Chiefs in the Ngwato Reserve. It was founded by Khama
I but its importance has declined through the rise of
Serowe. It has a seasonal population of 20,000; it is the
rail station for Serowe.

PAN AFRICAN CONGRESS (PAC). In 1958, the more uncom-
promising Africanist grouping within the African National
Congress (ANC) broke off to form the Pan-African Congress. The PAC took strong exception to participation
by the ANC in the Congress Alliance consisting of the
South African Indian Congress, the Colored People's Congress, the Congress of Democrats and the South African
Congress of Trade Unions, each of which had a strong
Communist orientation. When PAC broke away from the
ANC, it claimed that the latter was dominated by the non-
Africans in the other congresses, many of whom were
said to be Communist. For its part, the PAC advocated
a strictly Africanist program so as to maintain control of
the nationalist movement. From 1960 to 1964, over
1400 South African refugees entered the Bechuanaland
Protectorate and, through numerous contacts and discussions, played a decisive role as a catalyst in the development of modern Botswana nationalism. Here, as in the
other High Commission Territories, PAC and ANC refugees assisted the political parties then being organized
under the twin banner of pan-Africanism and militant opposition to the apartheid policies of South Africa. In the
Protectorate the BPP, led by P. G. Matante, was reorganized with strong PAC associations. See also AFRI-
CAN NATIONAL CONGRESS.

PIM REPORT (Cmd 4368). In the early 1930's the whole of
the organization of government in Bechuanaland was re-
viewed by Sir Alan Pim, who had just completed a similar review of Swaziland and Basutoland. Although one of

the main purposes of his inquiry was to study the means
of reestablishing the financial stability of the Protectorate,
his report contained much that directly concerned the organization of the Native Administration. Generally speaking, Pim found that the administration of the Protectorate had been conducted on the principles laid down in
1895 which were designed to maintain the position and
power of the chiefs. At the same time, no attempt had
been made to define their powers or formally to harmo-
nize administrative procedures between appointed civil
servants on the one hand and Native Authorities on the
other. Referring to the administration of justice, Pim
argued that the practice of leaving this responsibility in
the hands of tribal authorities was "almost equivalent to
saying that it remained in the hands of the chiefs, because by existing custom among Bechuana tribes the Chief
is much more independent of the advice and consent of the
tribal council than is usual among Bantu tribes. ... " The
result, said Pim, "was that a practical autocracy (was)
developed by a number of strong chiefs of whom Khama
is best known. "

The Pim Report also referred obliquely to a situation
having serious consequences for political development in
each of the High Commission Territories, namely, the
practice of selecting South Africans for administrative positions. Inasmuch as the Territories had come under the
Commonwealth Relations Office, the services of South
Africans could be enlisted without legal impediment. Little concern was felt about the fact that these administrators might have no inclinations to advance the well-being
of the Territories. Without probing deeply into the implications of this practice, Pim did suggest that linking
up of the service of the three High Commission Territories with that of the colonies might bring great advantages.

While the observations and recommendations of the
Pim Report had some notable effect on the economy of
the Protectorate, the Report's impact on Native Administration was less direct. By the time it was issued in
1935 (See Proclamations of 1934) the discussion of reform
proposals suggested by the Government had already reached
an advanced stage.

PITSO. A system of government found among many tribes of
southern Africa, including the Batswana. The tribal
council or pitso, together with the chief, constituted the
legal authority of the tribe.

POLICE. The police in Botswana perform the normal role
of a civil police force in preserving peace, and prevent-
ing and detecting crime. Its other major responsibility
is to maintain national security, in the absence of a military establishment. It also provides communications and
ambulance and fire-fighting services in the rural areas.
The performance of the force's functions is made difficult
by the sparseness of the population and poor communications. Many border areas, in particular, are inaccessible and therefore vulnerable to violation, and the borders
are extremely long. As a consequence of economic development and the increasing urban population it has been
required, in addition to maintaining and expanding its existing services, to meet the new problems of sophisti-
cated crime, increased road traffic and the protection of
precious stones. The police force grew from 734 to
1,270 men of all ranks between 1966 and 1972.

POLITICAL PARTIES see BECHUANALAND PROTECTO-
RATE FEDERAL PARTY; BOTSWANA DEMOCRATIC
PARTY; BOTSWANA INDEPENDENCE PARTY; BOTS-
WANA NATIONAL FRONT; BOTSWANA PEOPLE'S PARTY

PRESS. No independent newspapers are published in Botswana, but Rhodesian and South African papers, including
the weekly Mafeking Mail and Botswana Guardian (q. v.)
circulate. The Government Information Services publish
and distribute free a cyclostyled version of the broadcast
news bulletins and other information under the title of the
Daily News (q. v.), and a monthly magazine Kutlwano.
Both are published in English and Setswana. Several political monthlies are also circulated--Masa, Puo Phaa
and Therisanyo (all q. v.).

PRETORIA CONVENTION OF 1881. The Pretoria Convention
defined the boundaries of the Transvaal on all sides for
the first time but still did not curb Boer encroachment
upon Bechuanaland. Having set off from the Cape Colony
in 1835, the Great Trek brought the Voortrekkers across
the Vaal River to the frontiers of Bechuanaland. The
Boers, disliking the proximity of the powerful, independent chiefs, thought that the penetration of Bechuanaland
by the missionaries of the London Missionary Society and
by British traders and hunters would curb Boer expansion
northward. They, therefore, claimed a western boundary
that included the "missionary road," the high road from
the Cape to the interior, which ran through Bechuanaland.

They came into sharp conflict with David Livingstone and
Chief Sechele of the Kwena. In 1867 gold was discovered
near the Pati River, in country claimed by both the
Ngwatetse and by the Ndebele. President Pretorius of
the Transvaal in 1868 proclaimed the annexation of a huge
area, including the goldfields, but the British government
refused to recognize this. In the south the arbitration
award of R. W. Keate, Lieutenant Governor of Natal, in
1871, purporting to define a boundary between the colony
and the Transvaal, did nothing to abate Boer encroachment. See also LONDON CONVENTION OF 1884.

PRICE, ROGER, the Rev. (1834-1900). London Missionary
Society (LMS) missionary who with his wife sailed for
South Africa in 1858 accompanied by three other LMS
missionaries--John Mackenzie, William Sykes and Thomas
Morgan Thomas. The party arrived at Kuruman, Robert
Moffat's station and the fountainhead of LMS activity in
Bechuanaland, on the last day of the year. The LMS had
decided to begin two new missions in Central Africa, one
among the Ndebele and the other among the Makololo, of
the Zambezi valley. Sykes and Morgan Thomas were to
go to the Ndebele. They were to be led by Robert Moffat, who was to see the young missionaries settled in the
country. The Makololo mission consisted of Price, Mackenzie and the experienced Halloway Helmore. At the
last moment it was decided that Mackenzie should stay
at Kuruman to look after the station in Robert Moffat's
absence.

The Makololo expedition ended in tragedy. Helmore
and Price, their wives and children and a number of African attendants arrived at their destination, Linyanti, in
February 1860. The party fell ill almost immediately
and died one by one, probably of malaria. Of the Europeans only Price, his wife and two Helmore children
managed to struggle away from Linyanti, and Isabella
Price died on the Mababe plain in July 1860, on the way
back to Ngamiland. Later in the year Mackenzie rescued
Price and the Helmore children in Ngamiland and brought
them back to Kuruman in February 1861.

After a period of recuperation Price was asked to
reinforce the Ndebele mission. In October 1861 he married Elizabeth Lees Moffat. In February 1862 Price set
off with his new wife to his new field of labor. But
Mzilikazi, chief of the Ndebele, refused to receive any
more missionaries, and Price decided to await events at
Shoshong. There he was joined by John Mackenzie,

appointed to open a station there, and John Smith Moffat, who had also arrived at Shoshong from Matebeleland. The three men decided to revive the Makololo project, but the plan was frustrated (1863-64) when the tribes whom the Makololo had subjugated rose and destroyed their masters. Price remained at Shoshong until 1866, and was then transferred to Molepolole to work among the Kwena under Chief Sechele. Early in 1876 the LMS decided to open a mission on Lake Tanganyika. Price was chosen to lead a reconnaissance from the east African coast inland to Mpwapwa. Price returned to Bechuanaland in 1879 and after six years of pastoral work at Molepolole he was moved to Kuruman in 1885 to succeed Mackenzie as the tutor of the Moffat Institution, which closed in 1897.

Toil and anxiety took a heavy toll of Price's constitution and in 1898 he and his wife sailed to England on furlough. Soon after their return to Kuruman in 1899 his health broke down altogether. He lived long enough to witness the outbreak of the Second Anglo-Boer War and the capture of Kuruman by the Boers. Some weeks later he died and was buried in the mission cemetary at Kuruman.

PROCLAMATION[S]: the following entries are in chronological order.

PROCLAMATIONS of June 10 and September 4, 1891 and September 1892. Brought the Tati District (hitherto regarded as part of Matabeleland) within the area of the Bechuanaland Protectorate.

PROCLAMATION 9 of March 29, 1899. Established the Ngwato, Kwena, Ngwaketse, Tawana and Kgatla Reserves as recommended by Boundary Commissioner Captain H. Goold-Adams.

PROCLAMATION 10 of March 1899. Imposed a Hut Tax at the rate of 10 shillings a hut, later revised upward, which provided the Chief, as tax collector, with 10 per cent of the proceeds.

PROCLAMATIONS 4, 12 and 13 of 1905 see TULI BLOCK DISTRICT

PROCLAMATION 28 of 1909. Created Malete Reserve. See also MALETE.

PROCLAMATION 44 of 1933.   Created Tlokwa Reserve.   See
    also TLOKWA

PROCLAMATIONS 74 and 75 of 1934.   Proclamations had
    been drafted both in Basutoland and Bechuanaland with the
    intention of defining the powers of the chiefs so as to
    bring them under control and to prepare for new develop-
    ments of indirect rule.   This new concept of indirect rule
    was cautiously applied to the Protectorate through the Na-
    tive Administration (No. 74) and Native Tribunal Procla-
    mations (No. 75) of 1934.   While providing for the legal
    recognition of chiefly authority, these measures were not
    designed so much for the purpose of using indigenous in-
    stitutions as agencies for local government but rather as
    a means of preventing the misuse of power by the chiefs.
    It was in this spirit that tribal councils were required to
    be formally constituted and judicial tribunals were given
    a fixed composition.   Chiefs were legally obliged to obey
    the instructions of the Resident Commissioner, and be-
    come responsible for promoting the social and economic
    welfare of the people as directed by the Administration.
    In addition, Chiefs were forbidden to demand tribal levies
    without the Resident Commissioner's approval, which
    would only be given if the kgotla approved.   Further, the
    kgotla as a judicial body was replaced by a tribunal of
    limited membership and well-defined jurisdiction.   These
    developments did not fail to capture the attention of the
    Union Government which was distressed by the accompany-
    ing authoritative statement on the importance of African
    interests, a statement not in accord with the trend of
    legislation in South Africa.
        Neither did the new policy commend itself to various
    chiefs who were accustomed to look to the Protectorate
    administration to uphold, rather than control, their own
    privileges.   To the embittered chiefs, the Proclamations
    of 1934 appeared as an abrupt departure from tradition.
    The people also saw them as a menace to the system of
    trial to which they were deeply attached and a relegation
    of the kgotla to a subordinate position.   In an attempt to
    remove their apprehensions about the purpose of this
    legislation, the proclamations were accompanied by a
    memorandum in which the High Commissioner insisted
    that it was not the intention of His Majesty's Government
    to interfere unnecessarily with the chiefs.   Because the
    government had given no sign during the previous forty
    years of its intentions to make any substantial change in
    the procedure initiated by the Proclamation of 1891, some

provisions of the Proclamation of 1934 seemed so wide a
departure from custom that they were difficult if not impossible to operate in practice.

Although some of the chiefs accepted the innovation
contained in the Proclamations of 1934 and attempted to
put them into operation, Tshekedi, together with Chief
Bathoen II of the Ngwaketse and Chief Latlamoreng of the
Rolong, opposed them. Their decision to sue the High
Commissioner was based on their belief that the Proclamation infringed the internal sovereignty reserved to
them by treaty, and contravened native law and custom.
The validity of the Proclamations of 1934 was tested in
a special court of the Protectorate in 1936. But when
the court applied to the Secretary of State for a decision
as to the nature and extent of British jurisdiction in the
Protectorate in terms of the Foreign Jurisdiction Act, it
was laid down that His Majesty's Government "had unfet-
tered and unlimited power to legislate for the government
and administration of justice among the tribes of the
Bechuanaland Protectorate and that his power was not
limited by Treaty or Agreement. "

PROCLAMATION 35 of 1938. Through the cooperation of the
Resident Commissioner, Arden-Clarke, the finances of
the local tribal treasuries were regularized through the
Native Treasury's Proclamation, No. 35Q of 1938.
Chiefs were given a fixed stipend and 35 per cent of the
tribal collection of native tax was credited to these treasuries, while, after 1940, monies provided under the Colonial Development and Welfare Act also became available
for developmental purposes. The effect of this reform
was to give the chiefs and their newly established finance
committees responsibility in such fields as education and
agriculture. Thereafter increased attention was given to
education, the cattle industry and agriculture.

PROTECTORATE, Establishment of the. In 1885, when
Britain reluctantly established a protectorate, Bechuanaland's only apparent value was as a place to pass through
on the way to trading in the more lucrative African interior. A protectorate was viewed as a necessity in
order to maintain access to the "missionary road" (the
so-called "Suez Canal of Southern Africa"), a potentially
vital link in Rhodes' scheme of a Cape to Cairo railway.
Direct encroachment by Boer settlers and freebooters
from the mini-republics of Goshen and Stellaland, as well
as the possibility of eventual domination either by the

Transvaal or by Germany (South West Africa), had to be
resisted. A combination of missionary propaganda and
wise diplomacy on the part of three great chiefs, Sebele,
Bathoen and Khama, created British public sympathies
favorable to protection.

PUO PHAA ("STRAIGHT TALK"). Official organ of the Botswana National Front. Published irregularly in Mahalapye
beginning in 1966.

-R-

RADIO BOTSWANA. Radio Botswana achieved 119 broadcasting hours a week in 1973, in English and Setswana.
From 1936 to 1964 Radio ZNB at Mafeking provided a
regular program for Bechuanaland with the assistance of
the South African Broadcasting Corporation and the technical services of Bechuanaland Government enthusiasts.
It was replaced in 1965 by a 2-kilowatt transmitter situated at Gaborone (Radio ZND) operated under the direction of the Information Service. A new 50-kilowatt transmitter has been installed at Sebele, north of Gaborone,
and has improved reception considerably. Three smaller
transmitters (two of 10 kw and one of 1 kw) are still in
use. Radio Botswana is participating in a project to purchase radio sets in bulk and sell them at cost to the
public. The radio license fee has been abolished as an
incentive to wider radio ownership, particularly among
the lower income groups. There were an estimated 8500
radio sets in the country in 1972 but no television.

RADITLADI, LEETILE DISANG (1910-1971). The founder and
president of the Federal Party, he was born at Serowe
in 1910 and, after attending tribal school, took his Junior
Certificate at Tiger Kloof High School in South Africa.
Ratidladi then matriculated at Lovedale College in Natal,
and went on to Fort Hare University College.
He belonged to the dissident house of the Bamangwato
royal family which opposed the Khamas, and in 1937,
after a much discussed fight with Tshekedi, he and his
father were banished from the Bamangwato Reserve. Having settled in Francistown, where he worked as a clerk
in the Administration, he later became tribal secretary to
the Queen of Ngamiland, and, after he was allowed to return to the Ngwato people, became secretary of their
tribal council. He thus had by descent and later by

function, strong links with the chieftainship, as well as
considerable administrative experience. In 1959 he
helped found the Bechuanaland Protectorate Federal Party.
He was elected to the Legislative Council in 1961 and
served for several years.
Raditladi published three plays: Motswasele II, chos-
en as Volume IX in the Bantu Treasury Series and win-
ner of the May Esther Bedford Competition, Dintshontsho
tsa Lorato [Love Stories], and his second historical dra-
ma, Sekgoma. His one volume of verse is Sefalana sa
Menate [A Granary of Joy]. Submitted many years prior
to their publication, both his second play and the verse
volume won first prize in their respective genres in the
Afrikaanse Library Competition of 1954.

RAILWAYS see ECONOMY, INTERNAL--(7) Transportation
and Telecommunications; RHODESIA RAILWAYS

RAMATHLABAMA. Village on frontier of Cape Province and
Botswana, headquarters of Protectorate Regiment at the
outbreak of the South African War and sacked by the
Boers in an unexpected attack. The name is derived
from an incident in which the Chief Montsioa killed a lion
at close quarters, and means "to straddle over." The
railway crosses Botswana-South Africa border here.

RAMOTSWA. Botswana's eighth largest town (population estimated 12,000 in 1973), the administrative center of the
South East District.

REFUGEES. Botswana has a long tradition as a place of political refuge. Just as many Herero fled South West
Africa in 1905-06 and were granted refuge, so in the
early 1960's some 400 persons, mostly from South Africa,
gained asylum. But by the middle of 1968 a new movement was under way as hundreds fled the undeclared war
carried out in Angola between the Portuguese authorities
and the African liberation movement. Originally the
fighting was chiefly in the north and east of the country
but in 1968 the people of the southeast of the country became affected as well. Towards the middle of 1968 many
of these people left their homes and faced a seven-day
walk from their villages across the South African controlled Caprivi Strip to a small Botswana border town
called Shakawe on the Okavango River.
At first the local population in and around Shakawe
was able to absorb this influx of refugees and it was not

until October of 1968 that they began to constitute a major problem in the area. By December that year there
were more than 2850 refugees from Angola in the Shakawe
area, three-fourths of them women and children. They
had no cattle and many arrived with only the clothes on
their backs. In December the feeding program was
started with food from the United Nations Food and Agriculture Organization, World Food Program. It became
obvious that with the increasing numbers of refugees coming across the border to seek asylum in Botswana, the
Shakawe area would soon be unable to support them and
the idea of a settlement scheme was first considered. A
meeting was held between representatives of the Batawana
tribe on whose land the refugees were to be settled and
the Botswana Government departments of District Administration and Agriculture. The scheme was discussed
and the tribe agreed to allocate a site 100 square miles
in area, bordering the western boundary of the Okavango
Swamps, 75 miles south of Shakawe and 23 miles northeast of the nearest Batawana village of Gomare. The
Botswana Government was unable to meet the high costs
of the scheme itself. An approach was made to the
United Nations High Commission for Refugees (UNHCR)
whose Southern African representative is stationed in
Gaborone, and they agreed to meet the main costs of the
scheme. The Botswana Government and the UNHCR
sought a third party to administer the project and at the
end of April, 1969 a tripartite agreement was signed between the Botswana Government, the UNHCR and the
World Council of Churches (WCC). An agreement was
also signed with the UNFAO World Food Program to provide food for the settlement scheme. In May 1969 the
WCC appointed a Settlement Officer and in 'hat month also the big move from Shakawe began. The 100 square
miles of land has been divided up into 13 village areas
each capable of supporting several hundred people.
Homes were built and the main body of the refugees were
transported by the government to their new homes in what
is now known as the "Etsha Settlement Scheme." The
numbers continued to swell in 1969 and by August there
were nearly 3500 refugees in Etsha.

RELIGION. The majority of people are nominal Christians,
although only a minority are active churchgoers; many
nominal Christians still show some attachment to traditional religion. Between 20 and 30 per cent are practicing Christians. The majority of these are Anglicans,

Congregationalists, Methodists, and Presbyterians; these
four groups have united to worship as a single congregation. There are also smaller communities of the Dutch
Reformed Church, African Methodist Episcopal Church,
and Roman Catholic Church. See also ANGLICAN
CHURCH; LONDON MISSIONARY SOCIETY.

RESIDENT COMMISSIONER. Although the Protectorate was
established in 1885 it was only in 1891 that Sir Sidney
Shippard, then acting as Administrator of Bechuanaland,
was appointed Resident Commissioner, subject to the
High Commissioner (q.v.). The complete list of Resident
Commissioners* is as follows:

1885(91)-95	Sidney G. Alexander Shippard
1895-97	Francis James Newton
1897-1901	Hamilton John Goold-Adams
1901-06	Ralph Champneys Williams
1907-16	Francis William Panzera
1916-17	Edward Charles Frederick Garraway
1917-23	James Comyn Macgregor
1923-27	Jules Ellenberger
1928-30	Rowland Mortimer Daniel
1930-37	Charles Fernand Rey
1937-42	Charles Noble Arden-Clarke
1942-46	Aubrey Denzil Forsyth Thompson
1946-50	Anthony Sillery
1950-53	Edward Betham Beetham
1953-55	William Forbes MacKenzie
1955-59	Martin Osterfield Wray
1959-65	Robert Peter Fawcus
1965-66	Hugh Selby Norman-Walker

*Title changed in 1959 to Her Majesty's Commissioner
("Queen's Commissioner").

RHODES, CECIL JOHN (1853-1902). Statesman and empire
builder. Rhodes was born in the English town of Bishop's
Stortford. Educated at the local school, he was sent at
the age of 17 to Natal Province, South Africa, where his
brother had already commenced farming. The venture
was not a success, and the discovery of diamonds,
coupled with the founding of New Rush (Kimberley) caused
Cecil Rhodes in 1871 to move to that center. By the
time he was 20 he was able to study at Oxford. He remained there for a year, until 1873, but in 1876 he was
back at Oxford where he remained until 1878. Returning
to Kimberley, his financial genius made him one of its

wealthiest men, and in 1880 he not only founded the De
Beers Diamond Mining Company, but was elected to the
Cape Parliament. Already noted in that Parliament for
his strong British ideas, Rhodes nonetheless had a high
regard for the Dutch-speaking Afrikaaner, and in 1882
took part in the efforts to control Boer freebooters on the
frontiers of Bechuanaland, Stellaland and Goshen. His
settlement of the Bechuanaland question was also soon
threatened, for the deputy commissioner in the new area,
John Mackenzie, a missionary whom Rhodes contemptuous-
ly labelled a "negrophilist," antagonized the Boers. His
first appointment to the Cape Cabinet came in 1884, when
he was, for a short while, treasurer of the Colony. Already his thoughts were turning towards the expansion of
British authority into the north, beyond the Limpopo River.
He recognized that Kruger was his principal opponent, and
made it his life's work to frustrate Boer attempts to ob-
struct him. One of his first major successes was the
proclamation of British authority over Bechuanaland in
1885.

RHODESIA RAILWAYS. Transportation system operating in
Rhodesia and Botswana. Its origin may be traced to the
Bechuanaland Railway Company Ltd., established in London in 1893 to construct a line northwards from the existing terminal at Vryburg. Construction began in May,
1893, and within 17 months had reached Bulawayo. Meanwhile work had begun on another line from the coast, by
the Beira Railway Co. Ltd., formed in 1892. The
Bechuanaland Railway Company changed its name to Rhodesia Railways Ltd. in 1899, and became the dominating
concern in the territory, with a capital of £2,000,000,
and a large debenture issue. It was responsible for linking up Beira with Salisbury and Bulawayo, and for carrying the main line to the Victoria Falls and ultimately to
the Congo boundary. A special subsidiary was later
formed, called the Rhodesia-Katanga Junction Railway and
Mineral Company Ltd., while another concern, the Blink-
water Railway Company Ltd. was responsible for the
branch from Gwelo to Fort Victoria. Rhodesia Railways
were purchased by Southern Rhodesia in 1947 for
£30,000,000, transfer being carried out two years later.
In 1959 an agreement was reached with the South African
Railways under which Southern Rhodesia took over the
operation of the section of the old Bechuanaland Railway
from Vryburg to Bulawayo, which had hitherto been in the
hands of the South African Railways. Race discrimination

on the railroad in Botswana has been eliminated since
1964. See also ECONOMY, INTERNAL--(7) Transportation and Telecommunications, Railways; Kgatla.

ROADS see ECONOMY, INTERNAL--(7) Transportation and
Telecommunications, Roads

ROBINSON, SIR HERCULES GEORGE R. (1824-1897). Governor of the Cape Colony and High Commissioner, 1881-89;
1895-97. Like Cecil Rhodes, Robinson was a staunch
champion of imperial interference in Bechuanaland. In
1884, without consulting his ministers, he sent an occupation force into the country and appointed Rhodes as
Special Commissioner. The following year Bechuanaland
was formally annexed.

ROCK PAINTINGS. Southern Africa is the home of some of
the world's finest examples of prehistoric art. Loosely
referred to as "rock paintings" and "rock art" this form
of antique expression is of the greatest interest because
of both its inherent excellence and the primitiveness of
the race (the Bushmen, or Sarwa) thought responsible for
it. In Botswana these paintings are widespread, from
Kalakamati, north of Francistown, to Tsodilo, northwest
of Maun, and south to Manyana. Most are in a reasonable state of preservation. The Tsodilo Hills contain
some of the most striking examples of this art yet discovered. Here, in granite, is an art gallery of Bushmen
paintings, some still bright in color and form. It is believed that the Sarwa began this art at roughly the same
time as the ancient Egyptians. In the earliest efforts the
subjects were exclusively animal. Where space was small
forms were compressed and where there was enough room,
whole herds were depicted. Then men began to appear in
the paintings and they became more complex. See also
TSODILO HILLS.

ROLONG (BAROLONG). Among the earliest Tswana immigrants were the Rolong, who settled first along the Marico and Upper Molopo Rivers, after expelling or absorb-
ing their Sarwa and Kgalagadi predecessors. Afterwards
they spread farther to the south and are now to be found
mainly in the Cape Province, in the Orange Free State,
and in the southwestern Transvaal. The Rolong tribe is
represented in Botswana chiefly by the inhabitants of the
Barolong Farms in the Lobatse District and in parts of
the Francistown District. It appears that the main Rolong

tribe split up about 1775, and proceeded to form four
separate sections: the BaRolong-boo Ratlou, the BaRolong-boo Ra Tshidi, the BaRolong-boo Seleka and the Ba-
Rolong-boo Rapulana. The Rolong living in the Barolong
Farms area are a detachment from the largest of these
sections, the BaRolong-boo Ra Tshidi.

The Tshidi Rolong suffered from the onslaughts of
European free-booters and particularly from the Boers of
the Republic of Goshen. They, therefore, eagerly accepted the offer of British protection made to them by
John Mackenzie in 1884. The Warren expedition of 1885
assured the tribe of immunity from further attack and of
security in their lands. In 1895 the Rolong of the Protectorate were placed under the administration of the
British South Africa Company and their country was made
the base of the Jameson Raid. After the Raid, the proclamation which placed them under the Company was repealed and the British Government resumed the administration of the tribal area. But the transfer of British
Bechuanaland to the Cape Colony in 1895 cut the country
of the Rolong into two parts. Chief Montshiwa (1849-96)
retained his headquarters at Mafeking, however, but remained ultimately responsible to the Protectorate government for the administration of those of his people who
lived north of the Ramathlabama spruit.

It was Chief Montshiwa who initiated the unusual system of land tenure which largely remains among the Rolong in Botswana and provides for individually owned
farms in tribal land. The idea had been suggested to
Montshiwa by the example of the Rolong of Thaba Nchu
in the Orange Free State, where Moroka, the Chief of
that part of the Rolong tribe, had been advised that the
best way to preserve his territory from falling into the
hands of Europeans was to mark it out into individual
farms to be held by members of his tribe. Montshiwa
was not allowed to carry out his scheme insofar as it
concerned the tribal lands in British Bechuanaland, but
after a long discussion on legal points, he was permitted
to carry it out on the lands allotted to the Rolong in the
Protectorate. Certain conditions were, however, imposed.
It was stipulated by the Government that the grants made
to individual members of the tribe should not be capable
of alienation except to other Rolong. Land was not to be
held in freehold, but under lease, and the title was to
take the form of a "Certificate of Occupation." In issu-
ing these Certificates in 1895 Montshiwa provided that
they should confer rights only for the lifetime of the

holder, subject to an annual rental of £1 10s. payable to
the Chief. With the consent of the Chief, the holder
might transfer his rights to any other member of the
tribe, but was expressly prohibited from mortgaging his
holdings.

In 1896 the Government decided to recognize the titles
of the holders of the Certificates of Occupation in the
Barolong Farms, and they were registered in the Deeds
Office of the Protectorate. In these documents the
grantee was described as "occupant" not as proprietor,
and his rights were limited to his lifetime. But though
he was restricted in his power to sell, transfer or mort-
gage his holdings, the deeds as finally registered omitted
the prohibition against "hiring or leasing" which had appeared in the drafts first submitted to the Administration.

Montshiwa died in 1896 and was succeeded by a young-
er son, Besele. With the outbreak of the South African
War the Rolong Tshidi were actively on the British side.
Besele died in 1903 and was succeeded by his brother
Badirile, who died in 1911. After the regencies of Leko-
ko and Joshua, Bakolopang succeeded in 1917 but had a
brief reign being constrained by tribal law to give way to
Lotlamoreng in 1919.

In spite of the precautions taken by Montshiwa, a
certain part of the Barolong Farm area came under European occupation, by means of lease, for the Certificates
of Occupation as finally registered did not exclude this
contingency. Leases began to be given about 1903, and
the practice does not appear to have met at the time with
any objection from the Administration, though by Section
43 of the Proclamation of June 10, 1891, the leasing of
native lands to Europeans required the approval of the
High Commissioner. It came under adverse notice, however, in 1914, when the High Commissioner took exception to the fact that in some cases the leases had given
the lessees the right to treat as "squatters" any Natives
found to be living on the land and to remove them.

When the five major Native Reserves were constituted
in 1899, the Barolong Farms were not gazetted as a Reserve, since the High Commissioner considered that their
area was too small for the purpose. In 1934 the tribe
claimed that the Native Administration Proclamation (No.
74 of 1934) did not apply to the Farms, as they were not
a Tribal Area as originally defined in it, but the position
was adjusted next year by the issue of an amending Proclamation (No. 77 of 1935) which added the Farms to the
list of Tribal Areas in Section I (I) of the law. Though,

however, the Farms were brought within the scope of the Native Administration and Native Courts Proclamations, they actually differed in a number of respects from the normal Tribal Reserves. The Chief, the grandson of Chief Montshiwa, although gazetted as Native Authority, did not live in the Farm area but in Mafeking, South Africa, in order to maintain his connection with that part of the tribe resident in Cape Province. He had, however, a paid representative in the Lobatse District. With independence, the Rolong chief in Mafeking could not exercise authority over citizens of Botswana and he designated his younger brother as chief over the Farms, independent of his jurisdiction.

Rolong Chiefs (Tshidi Section),
with dates of chieftaincy (many dates not known)

Morolong	Tau
Noto	Tshidi
Morara	Tlhutlwa d. c. 1805
Mabe	Leshomo c. 1805-?
Mabua	Tawana / -1849
Monoto	Montshiwa 1849-96
Mabeo	Besele 1896-1903
Modibowa	Badirile 1903-11
Tshesebe	Lekoko 1911-15
Monnyane	Joshua 1915-17
Setlhare	Bakolopang 1917-19
Masepha	Lotlamoreng 1919-
Mokgopha	Kebalepile Montshiwa
Thibela	Besele Lotlamoreng

RURAL DEVELOPMENT COUNCIL see ECONOMY, INTERNAL--(13) Community Development

-S-

SARWA (BUSHMEN). Name applied by their Hottentot neighbors to an indigenous Khoisan-speaking people of southern Africa. Formerly hunters and gatherers, they have generally become wage laborers on ranches or clients of cattle raising tribes. An estimated 10,000 (1971) are found in Botswana. Regarded as the aboriginal inhabitants of most of Southern Africa, they are of very small stature, rarely over 4 feet tall. They possess a number of physical characteristics peculiar to themselves, notably their wrinkled appearance, extraordinarily keen eyesight, skill as trackers, sense of music and art. They show

considerable links with the pygmies of Central Africa and
are believed to have emigrated from those parts. Their
language abounds in clicks, and has been studied only
with the greatest difficulty. See also ROCK PAINTINGS.

SCHULENBOURG, H. C., the Rev. Hermansburg Lutheran
Missionary. First minister of religion to live in Shoshong where he arrived in 1858. Invited by Chief Sekgoma, who gave him facilities, Schulenbourg baptised two
of the chief's sons, Khama and Kgamane, in 1862. The
London Missionary Society later occupied the Shoshong
mission.

SEBEGO, Chief see NGWAKETSE

SEBELE, CHIEF I. (d. 1911). After the death of the great
Kwena Chief Sechele I in 1863, his firstborn son, Sebele
I, succeeded to the chieftaincy. Sebele's half brother
Khari disputed the succession, basing his assertion on
the grounds that no cattle had been paid for Sebele's
mother and therefore according to Kwena law, he, not
Sebele, was Sechele's rightful heir. Khari and his supporters, probably almost half the tribe, wanted to secede
from the rule of Sebele and settle in the northern section
of the Kwena territory near Lephephe. As a result of
the dispute, the administration ordered Khari's faction to
move to Kolobeng and reasserted its support for Sebele,
and upheld his authority over all the people resident in
the Kwena Reserve. In 1895 Chief Sebele visited England
with Chief Khama and Chief Bathoen to protest the proposed takeover of the Protectorate by the Chartered Company. See also KWENA.

SEBELE, CHIEF II (c. 1931). Chief Sebele II came to power
in 1917 after the death of Sechele II. His general inabil-
ity to serve as Chief was recognized at an early stage in
his career. In 1923, he was accused of embezzling £200
in hit tax money. In 1925 the Kwena tribe petitioned the
government to remove the Chief from office. Before a
kgotla in Molepolole, attended by a magistrate, it was
charged that the Chief assaulted and insulted the people,
took their land and wells, and failed to consult his councillors. In 1928, the Chief's "uncles" (senior advisers)
signed a petition to remove the Chief. In 1929, Sebele
was accused of stealing the hut tax of a miner and the
cattle of a tribesman. The operation of the kgotla was
said to have been subverted through bribery and

favoritism. Furthermore, Sebele forceably reinstituted
traditional circumcision and initiation rights (these had
been abolished earlier) and claimed the "droit du seig-
neur" (first rights of sexual access to a son's bride).
Both practices generated considerable enmity on the part
of the Christian missionaries.

In spite of these numerous infractions and disturbances, the British administration was extremely slow to
act. They feared a negative reaction by the tribe, the
chieftaincy itself being still highly regarded as opposed
to the individual incumbent, and were uncertain of their
own legal authority to depose a chief. The tacit approval
by Kgosidintsi, a senior headman of the tribe, of the removal of Sebele provided the degree of legitimacy viewed
as necessary by the administration. After drafting several secret plans and making complex arrangements for
transport, Sebele was sent to Ghanzi by train via South
Africa, and the tribal kgotla was informed of his exile.
Khari, his brother, assumed the Kwena chieftaincy in
1931 and ruled until his death in 1962.

SEBONI, MICHAEL ONTEPETSE MARTINUS (1912-). Born
at Molepololi, Seboni studied at Molepololi Primary
School, St. Matthews College Practicing School, and the
South African Native College. Later he went to the Fort
Hare University College (1934-36), receiving a B. A. in
education and the University Educational Diploma. He
won a B. Ed. degree in 1956 with the dissertation "The
South African Native College, Fort Hare (1903-1954)" and
a Ph. D. (1958) from the University of South Africa.

His positions, mostly in education, have been as a
teacher at several schools near his home town. He also
served as principal (1940-51) of the Nigel United Christian School, Transvaal which, with Cedric Phatudi, he
improved into the Charterston Secondary School. He has
also been senior lecturer and department head of Fort
Hare's Bantu Languages Department (1951-53) and named
senior lecturer, Department of Education in 1953. A
Councillor to Paramount Chief Kgare of the Bechuanaland
Protectorate and to Chief Sechele II, presently he is professor of empirical education at the University College,
Fort Hare, and a member of Fort Hare's Advisory Council and Senate.

Beginning to write in his mid-60's his first work was
a children's novel, Rammona wa Kgalagadi [Rammone of
the Khalahari Desert]. His two later novels are Kgosi
Isang Pilane [Chief Isang Pilane], and Koketse-kitso ya

lefatshe. He has published one volume of praise poems,
Maboko Maloba le Maabane [Praise Poems, Old and New],
and a collection of Tswana idioms, riddles, tales, prov-
erbs and idiomatic phrases: Diane le Maele a Setswana
[Tswana Proverbs and Maxims]. His translations of
Shakespeare's Merchant of Venice and King Henry IV into
Setswana have been widely acclaimed.

SECHELE, CHIEF (c. 1829-1892). Chief of the Kwena, occupying a territory now part of Botswana, he successfully
defied Mzilikazi and his Ndebele, allowing the introduction of Christianity under David Livingstone in 1841. See
also KWENA.

SECHELE, Chief Neale see KWENA

SECHELE II, Chief see KWENA

SEEPAPITSO, Chief see NGWAKETSE

SEGOKGO, M. K. (1928-). Botswana politician, born 1928,
Tlokweng, and educated at Gaborone and Kanye Teacher
Training College. Head teacher, Batlokwa National
School, Assistant Master, St. Joseph's College, elected
to Batlokwa Tribal Council, 1961; member of the Committee to Study Unified Teaching Service, 1962, elected
to National Assembly, 1965- ; Parliamentary Secretary,
1965-66; Assistant Minister of Finance, 1966-69; Minister of Finance, 1969; Minister of Commerce Industry,
and Water Affairs, 1969- .

SEKGOMA I, Chief see KHAMA III

SEKGOMA II, Chief see KHAMA III

SELBORNE, LORD WILLIAM (1859-1942). High Commissioner for South Africa from 1905 to 1910. In that capacity
he successfully advanced the formation of the Union of
South Africa. It had been clear from the first that the
position to be given to the three High Commission Territories was one of the points most likely to affect the reception given by the Imperial Parliament to the draft Act
of Union, and the Bechuanaland Chiefs took the opportunity of voicing their own objections to any scheme which
would bring the Protectorate under the rule of the proposed Union of South Africa. It was in this connection
that Lord Selborne, when addressing the Chiefs at Mafeking

in March 1910, informed them that the transfer to the
Union Government would not take place in the immediate
future.   It was, he added, impossible to say how long it
might be before the country was handed over, "but in the
natural course of things it would take place some day. "
He returned to England shortly before the South Africa
Act, establishing the union, became effective (May 31,
1910).

SELEBI-PIKWE.   A town in eastern Botswana (Central District) where workable deposits of copper, and nickel ore
were discovered in the early 70's.   Rapid growth followed and an estimated 27,000 were in the area in 1972.

SEROWE.   The chief town of the Ngwato tribe, Serowe is
also the headquarters of the tribal administration.   It has
several government offices, a hospital and an airfield.
The white population consists largely of traders.   Serowe
was first occupied by the Ngwato in 1902 after they had
abandoned their earlier home in Palapye.   The statue of
a duiker (small antelope) stands in memory of Chief
Khama III, tribal leader until 1923.   Like other Botswana
villages, the homes are constructed around the home of
the chief and the kgotla, the tribal meeting place.   Serowe seasonally has a population ranging up to 40,000,
perhaps the largest tribal village in Africa.

SETIDISHO, Dr. N. O. H.   Professor of education at the
Botswana campus of the University of Botswana, Lesotho
and Swaziland, Dr. Setidisho was appointed Pro-Vice
Chancellor of the Gaborone Campus.   He succeeded Mr.
Vernon Jackson who left Botswana in 1973.   After some
years of secondary teaching, Professor Setidisho was for
four years a lecturer in education at the University of
Ibadan, Nigeria.   He then joined the Ministry of Education in Zambia as an inspector of schools.   He later established and became first principal of the Kabwe Secondary Teacher's College, an affiliated institution of the University of Zambia.   Dr. Setidisho was senior education
officer (secondary) for three years in the Botswana Ministry of Education.

SETSWANA see LANGUAGE

SHASHI COMPLEX.   The Shashi Complex is a major development scheme capable of making a dramatic impact on the
economy.   The development of copper mining at Matsitama,

copper/nickel mining at Selebi-Pikwe and diamonds at
Letlhakane, accompanied by industrial development at
Francistown and Shashi Siding, when ample water and
power supplies are made available, and the possibility of
the production of salt and soda ash at Sua, will trans-
form the entire eastern region of the country. A great
deal of infrastructural development is orientated towards
mining development in the Shashe Complex Project. Thus
the copper/nickel prospect has necessitated the creation
of a new township and the related infrastructure including
roads, rail spur, water, power and telecommunications,
and these are being financed by Government through loans
from the World Bank, USAID and CIDA.

SHASHI RIVER. Rising near Kalakamate, the Shashi River,
flowing seasonally in a southeasterly direction, provides
the boundary between the North East and Central Districts
and an international boundary with Rhodesia.

SHIPPARD, SIR SIDNEY GODOLPHIN ALEXANDER (1838-
1902). South African diplomat and lawyer. Born in England and educated at Kings College School and Oxford, he
emigrated to the Cape in 1870 where he settled in Kimberley. From 1873 to 1877 he was Attorney-General for
the High Court of Griqualand. From 1880 to 1885 he was
a judge of the Supreme Court of the Cape Colony and also
served as British Commissioner in the joint Anglo-German Commission to investigate the claims of the two
countries to the coast of South West Africa. Upon the
establishment of the first courts in Bechuanaland, he was
appointed Chief Magistrate and President of the Land
Commission. He was Deputy Commissioner for the
Bechuanaland Protectorate and the Kalahari Desert from
1885 to 1895. He convened the Kopong conference in
1890 in an unseccessful attempt to convince the Bechuana
chiefs that they should submit to a more orderly administration.

SILLERY, ANTHONY (1903-). Professor, Oxford University,
Resident Commissioner of Bechuanaland from 1946 to
1950. Among his many works on Bechuanaland are,
Bechuanaland Protectorate (1952), Sechele; The Story of
an African Chief (1954), Founding a Protectorate (1965)
and John MacKenzie of Bechuanaland: A Study in Human-
itarian Imperialism (1970).

SMUTS, JAN CHRISTIAN (1870-1950). General, Cabinet

Minister, Member of Parliament and Prime Minister of
the Union of South Africa. He fought the British in the
Boer War (1899-1902), but thereafter worked for the formation of the Union of South Africa as a self-governing
part of the British Empire. An architect of the Act of
Union, Smuts argued for the incorporation of the Bechuanaland Protectorate, Basutoland and Swaziland in the
Union. In the face of African and some British opposition Smuts sensed that the incorporation of the protectorates could not be achieved simultaneously with union.
He accepted this policy as only a temporary delay. Thus
he set out to achieve the second best arrangement, entail-
ing an understanding with the Imperial government stipu-
lating that the actual transfer need not be specifically
approved by the British Parliament. As leader of the
opposition he strenuously protested in 1948 the proposed
marriage of Seretse Khama to Ruth Williams on the
grounds that an interracial marriage in the Protectorate
would be seized upon by his Nationalist opponents for
anti-British purposes.

SOUTH AFRICA ACT of 1909. The most imminent threat to
the continued existence of Bechuanaland came with the
passage of the South Africa Act in 1909. The so-called
Act of Union, provided for the establishment of the Union
of South Africa, initially to include the Cape, Natal, the
Orange Free State and the Transvaal. Provision was
made for the eventual inclusion of Bechuanaland, Basutoland, Swaziland and the Rhodesias. Clearly delineated in
the Act were several clauses guaranteeing the status of
Africans to be involved in any future transfer. These
provisions, coupled with British public opinion, and the
emergence of Afrikaaner, rather than British liberal
thinking as dominant in South Africa, were to save the
High Commission territories from total incorporation.
Although there were numerous attempts by the Union
government to secure the administrative transfer which
would have rationalized the existing economic situation
(Customs Union of 1903) all such efforts failed. The feel-
ing that the transfer was inevitable served to mollify
South African demands. Only the date for the formal
transfer remained to be set. The vast mineral resources
of the Witwatersrand made the small gold deposits of the
Tati area of northern Bechuanaland seem relatively unat-
tractive. The result was limited European settlement in
the Protectorate. The apparent lack of resources and
the continuing administrative deficits experienced by the

Protectorate administration helped prevent the demand
for transfer from being pressed more vigorously. The
subsequent withdrawal of South Africa from the Commonwealth in 1961 officially rendered the fifty-two year old
South Africa Act null and void. Legal provisions for the
transfer of the territory thereby ceased to exist.

SOUTH AFRICAN COMMON MARKET AND CUSTOMS UNION
    see ECONOMY, EXTERNAL--(3) Customs and Duties

SOUTH EAST DISTRICT. Around Gaborone and to the south
    is the South East District, one of the least economically
    viable regions of the country. With the center at Ra-
    motswa the South East comprises an area of 1091 square
    miles and consists mainly of the Tlokwa and Malete
    tribes. More than half the land in the district is owned
    by private ranchers and farmers. The shortage of trib-
    al land as opposed to state land makes farming on a large
    economical scale impractical for the majority of the peo-
    ple who often leave the area to seek work elsewhere in
    the country, mainly in the nearby "industrialized" towns
    of Gaborone and Lobatse. There is an irrigation scheme
    underway at the village of Mogobane. Total population
    for the district is 20,000 (1971).

SOUTHERN (NGWAKETSE) DISTRICT. The Ngwaketse Dis-
    trict (area 10,053 square miles) which includes part of
    the Kgalagadi is the home of the Ngwaketse tribe with the
    principal village being Kanye. The Council in Kanye also
    administers the Barolong Farms area to the southeast.
    There is small scale mining of manganese, and plans are
    being made to reopen asbestos and talc mining, but the
    majority of the inhabitants are farmers and ranchers. A
    large scale dam building project has been undertaken to
    provide water for domestic and agricultural purposes and
    plans are being made to open up more grassland for graz-
    ing by providing stock dams. There is also good arable
    land in the district. The barren land of the Kgalagadi to
    the west and north changes from sparse grass plains to
    sand desert in the west. The sparse grass is highly nu-
    tritive and ideal for cattle ranching. Once sufficient
    water is found, these vast grazing lands will be opened
    up. The Molopo farms along the South African border of
    the Cape Province have a high potential as rich cattle
    country, depending on the availability of water. Total
    population is 82,000 (1971).

STELLALAND. Established in 1882 by dissident Boers from the Transvaal as a miniature republic formed by Boer adventurers from portions of present-day Botswana. It was absorbed into Bechuanaland in 1884.

SUMMIT MEETING (Gaborone, November 12, 1973). The first summit meeting between the President of Botswana, Sir Seretse Khama, the Prime Minister of Lesotho, Chief Leabua Jonathan, and the Prime Minister of Swaziland, Prince Makhosini Dhlamini, was held in Gaborone on November 12, 1973. According to an official communique, they had agreed in principle to meet from time to time and to establish at an early date a consultative commission of officials, which would meet at regular intervals to discuss subjects of mutual interest.

-T-

TATI CONCESSION. A triangular tract of more than 2062 square miles including Francistown. In the time of the Ndebele chiefs, Mzilikazi and Lobengula, the area was part of Matabeleland (today a province of Rhodesia). The history of the concessions dates back to 1866 when gold was discovered near the Tati River. The district was claimed by both the Ndebele, who stated they had conquered the land, and by the Ngwato, who argued they had grazed their cattle there from time immemorial.

In 1869 Sir John Swinburne and Captain Arthur Lionel Levert (of the London and Limpopo Company) applied for a concession from the Ndebele. While Swinburne was in Britain trying to raise the necessary finances Captain Levert visited Lobengula and was successful in obtaining for his company a grant of mineral rights over the whole of the Tati District. This was the first Tati concession. Not long after, word arrived from Swinburne that he saw no prospect of forming a company to operate the concession because financiers and so-called experts were of the opinion that there was little or no payable gold in southern Africa. The London and Limpopo Company struggled on for a few years until funds were exhausted when they abandoned their right to the area.

A later concession, from which the Tati Company's title to the Tati District originated, was granted by Lobengula in 1880. Several miners, who had left for the Kimberley diamond fields some years before, returned to Tati with adequate machinery and substantial assets.

With the assistance of W. J. Tainton and Samuel Edwards they persuaded Lobengula to renew the abandoned
concession in their favor in return for a rental equivalent
to R60 per annum and certain presents to be given from
time to time. The concessionaries, Messrs. H. Dobbie,
D. Francis, W. Francis, and S. Dodds, styled themselves the Northern Light Company and promptly began
to mine the precious metal. In 1886 Lobengula confirmed the concession and went so far as to give the
Northern Light Company sole mining rights in the region.
Samuel Edwards, who had accompanied Robert Moffat on
the missionary's visit to Mzilikazi in 1854, had by this
time acquired tremendous influence with Lobengula and it
was he who, between 1880 and 1888, obtained from the
Ndebele King the various documents that established the
concession on a secure basis. In 1887 it was recorded
that Lobengula asked Edwards, now a representative of
the Tati Concession Mining and Exploration Company (successor to the Northern Light Company) to govern the
country on his behalf. The following year the King gave
the company the right to exclude squatters from the concession area.
    In 1895 the Tati Concession Mining and Exploration
Company transferred the concession to Tati Concession,
Ltd. The validity of Lobengula's concessions was recognized by the British Government in 1894 and the official
proclamation of the company's ownership of all the land
within the Tati District was made in January 1911. This
company went into voluntary liquidation for the purpose
of reconstruction and in 1914 a new company, the Tati
Company, Ltd., was formed and acquired the concession.
    The Tati District was owned by the Tati Company,
which had full power to sell or lease any portion except
the area leased for Africans, although the government
had the right to acquire sites for public buildings. The
whole of the three blocks and part of the Tati District
were divided into farms and, until independence, were
held under restrictive title which barred owners from
selling to non-whites. On the eve of independence, pre-
ferring to risk the ill-will of the Africans at this crucial
stage of constitutional development, the Tati whites
stepped up their demands for secession. In February
1964, a petition sponsored by 320 whites, more than 90
per cent of the Tati farmers, asked the administration in
vain for independence or self-government, or, alternative-
ly, permission to merge with a friendly neighboring white
state. In 1969 the Tati Company sold 220,000 acres of

rural land and 1600 acres of urban land and also donated
115,000 acres of rural land and 2000 acres of urban land
to the Republic of Botswana. Botswana paid R200,000 for
the land, a sum made available through a British government grant.

TAWANA (BATAWANA). Towards the end of the 18th century
the Ngwato tribe was broken into two separate bodies by
the secession of Twana, the younger son of the then ruling Chief Mathiba. The breakaway appears to have been
due to a quarrel between him and his elder brother
Khama I, the heir to Mathiba's chieftainship. After re-
pulsing an attack by Khama I, Twana migrated northwest
beyond the Botete River and became the founder of the
Tawana tribe, which now hold the Tawana Reserve in
Ngamiland.
    The Tawana appear to have devoted themselves to the
maintenance of their cattle, and extended their cattle-
posts as far as the "pans" in the present Ghanzi District.
Their Chief, Twana, is reputed to have died in 1820,
when he was succeeded by his son Moremi I, who about
1830 was attacked by Sebetwane and the Makalolo and
driven to take refuge in the Chobe riverain. Here the
Tawana came into contact with the Subia and lived with
them for some time, but they were again attacked here
by Sebetwane, and this time they became subject to the
Makalolo. Little is known of the history of the tribe under Moremi's later successor, Letsholathebe (1840?-74),
but it appears that the Tawana had then recovered their
independence, for when Livingstone visited Lake Ngami in
1849 they were living at or near Toten and were no longer subject to the Makalolo. They were, however, raided
by them again in 1860.
    About 1882 the Tawana, who by now had considerable
herds of cattle, were raided from another quarter, being
attacked this time by the Ndebele under Sikhulumi, one of
Lobengula's lieutenants. Led by their Chief, Moremi II
(1876-91) they put up some resistance, and though they
lost a number of cattle, they retained their independence.
The headquarters seem to have been then at Matshiaren.
They were even more successful in resisting another raid
conducted by a group of Ndebele under the leadership of
Lotshe in 1884, but this was the last of the Ndebele raids.
When Moremi II died in 1891, his son Mathiba was a
child, and the chieftaincy was held for some years by his
uncle, Sekgoma Letsholathebe, though a dispute subsequently arose whether his rightful position was that of

Chief or of Regent appointed to act for the period of
Mathiba's minority. The question involved a complicated
issue in native law and custom, and the dissension within
the tribe was aggravated by the fact that Sekgoma had had
a private quarrel with the Ngwato Chief Khama III, who
as a consequence lent strong support to Mathiba. Sekgoma had moreover become personally unpopular, owing,
it is said, to his efforts to make the tribal organization
efficient.

The matter was eventually settled in Mathiba's favor
by a decision of the Resident Commissioner in 1906.
Sekgoma was removed from the Reserve, taking with him
a number of influential headmen and leaving the tribe divided and weakened. He was detained for a time at Gaborone, but was afterwards allowed to live on the Chobe
Crown lands, where he died in 1913. Mathiba died in
1933, and after a difficult period of inefficiency and misrule, during which several persons were tried out as
Acting Chiefs or Regents, Gaetsalwe, a brother of the
late chief, was dragged from obscurity by the tribe which
insisted that he should become Acting Chief. He carried
on with success for a year, and in 1937 handed over
charge to his nephew, Moremi III. Moremi, who did little to improve the poor reputation of some of the Tawana
Chiefs, was killed in an automobile accident in 1946, and
the widow of the late Chief was instituted as Regent of
the tribe during the minority of the new Chief, Letsholathebe.

In 1971 the Tawana population was set at 42,000.

Tawana Chiefs, with dates of chieftaincy

Twana c. 1795-c. 1820	Sekgoma 1891-1906
Moremi I c. 1820-1828	Mathiba 1906-33
Sedumedi c. 1828-1830	Dibolayang 1934-36
Mogalakwe c. 1830-c. 1840	Gaetsalwe 1936-37
Letsholathebe c. 1840-1874	Moremi III 1937-46
Meno 1875-76	Pulane Moremi (Regent) 1946-
Moremi II 1876-91	Letsholathebe Moremi (1946-)

TAXES see ECONOMY, INTERNAL--(11) Taxes

THEMA, B. C., M. B. E. (1912-). Born near Kanye in the
Ngwaketse area, he received his education in Tiger Kloof
and Heraldtown, South Africa. He studied privately from
1937-48, receiving the B. A., B. Ed. and M. Ed. degrees
from the University of South Africa, while teaching during
most of the period at Tiger Kloof. He founded Tshidi
Barolong Secondary School in Mafeking in 1946 and was

headmaster there from 1946-55. He was the third headmaster of Moeng College, 1955-64; a former general
secretary of Cape African Teacher's Union from 1953-55
and member of Federal Council of African Teacher's Association, 1952-55. He was elected a Member of the
National Assembly in 1965- and has successively been
Minister of Labor and Social Services, 1965; Minister of
Finance, 1965-66; Minister of Health, Education and Labor, 1966-69; and Minister of Education, 1969- .

THERISANYO ("CONSULTATION"). Official paper of the Botswana Democratic Party published in English and Setswana.

TIGER KLOOF see LONDON MISSIONARY SOCIETY

TLOKWA. The Tlokwa are numerically a relatively unimpor-
tant element in Botswana though they have played a part
of some importance in the history of Lesotho. They are
part of a tribe of Sotho origin which is widely distributed
over southern Africa. The section now in the Gaborone
area apparently derives its descent from one Tshwane,
who early in the 18th century was at Tlokwe (Potchef-
stroom) in the Transvaal, whence his section is said to
take its name. It was under a descendant of Tshwane,
that the Tlokwa, then allied with the Ngwaketse Chief
Makaba, came into conflict with the Kwena about the year
1820.
    Soon after this the group was split up between vari-
ous claimants to the chieftainship, and one part went
north to the Zambezi, with Sebetwane and the Kalolo.
Another part, which had stayed in the western Transvaal,
became involved in conflict with the Boers, and in 1864
took refuge with the Kwena Chief Sechele, accompanying
him when he moved to the present tribal headquarters at
Molepolole. These Tlokwa afterwards moved back near
Zeerust in the western Transvaal, and were there in
1875, but they split up into four sections, one of which
joined the Kgatla, two stayed in the Transvaal, and one,
under the Chief Gaborone, moved to the Kwena country in
1887 and settled at Mosaweng, later called Gaberone's or
Gaberones after him. At the time this part of the land
was in Kwena country but a suitable gift from Gaborone
was rewarded by Chief Sechele not only with the land but
by money and cattle.
    In 1895, as the result of discussions in London with
the Secretary of State for Colonies, Sebele, like Khama
and Bathoen, surrendered a strip of land on the east of

his country for the construction of a railway. This strip
included the country of the Tlokwa who continued to live
there as occupants. This tract of land was transferred
to the British South Africa Company by Proclamation No.
12 of 1905 and arrangements were made for Gaborone to
be received in the Kwena reserve. But the old chief was
so loved that his people preferred to pay rent to the Company rather than see him lose his independence. This
arrangement was continued until 1932 when Gaborone died
at the estimated age of 106. He was succeeded by his
grandson, Matala. As a result of negotiations between
the Government and the Company it was agreed that after
payment of rent in full the land occupied by the tribe
should thereafter be transferred to the High Commissioner and proclaimed the Batlokwa Native Reserve. This
was done by Proclamation No. 44 of 1933.

The Tlokwa, the smallest independent tribal unit in
Botswana, continue to live under congested circumstances
and have little land for farming and cattle. The population was set in 1971 at 4000. See also KGOSI GABOR-
ONE, Chief.

Tlokwa Chiefs, with dates of chieftaincy
(early dates not known)

Tshwaane	Kgosi c. 1815-c. 1820
Marakadu	Lesage c. 1820-c. 1825
Mosima Tsele	Basha c. 1825-c. 1835
Monageng	Matlapeng c. 1835-1880
Motlhabane	Gaborone 1880-1932
Mokgwa	Matlala 1932-48
Taukobong	Kgosi Gaborone 1949-
Molefe	Gaborone Gaborone, -1973
Bogatsu c. 1815	Kema Gaborone

TOURISM (see also ECONOMY, EXTERNAL--(5) Tourism).
Botswana has three tourist regions, centered on Gaborone,
Maun and Kasane. Gaborone as the capital and one of the
fastest growing towns in the country, attracts a large
number of visitors and is easily accessible by road, rail
and air. One of its main attractions is the casino on the
outskirts of the town, which was opened in 1972. There
are opportunities for water sports on the nearby Gaborone Dam, and further afield, for the viewing of wildlife
(in season) in the Khutswe Game Reserve.

Maun is a small town 527 kilometers west of Francistown and can be reached by good gravel road. It is also
served by a scheduled air service three times a week and
its airstrip can accommodate both small and medium-

sized planes. Maun provides access, first of all, to the
Okavango Delta, a unique area of lagoons and waterways
covering 16,800 square kilometers. Maun is also linked
to the Moremi Wildlife Reserve and, further north, to
the southern part of the Chobe National Park. Both those
wildlife sanctuaries are noted for their riverine and plains
fauna; access to them is possible only by air or by four-
wheel-drive vehicle. Also within reach of Maun are the
Nxai Pan National Park and the Makgadikgadi Pans Game
Reserve, each providing the tourist with the opportunity
of viewing wildlife in a natural wilderness setting.

The main attractions of the Kasane region are the
Chobe National Park and the Chobe River. The Park, extending for over 11,000 sq. km., contains an abundant
supply of wildlife, with large numbers concentrated on the
frontage of the Chobe River during the dry season. The
river itself, harbours crocodile and hippopotami and offers good opportunities for fishing. The role of Kasane
as a tourist center is enhanced by its proximity (100 km.)
to the important tourist attraction of Victoria Falls and
its consequent capacity to attract tourists who wish both
to enjoy the wildlife of the area and visit the Falls.
Kasane is served by two hotels (one opened in 1973), with
swimming pools, facilities for wildlife viewing, fishing,
water-skiing and other tourist amenities.

Two other areas of interest to visitors to Botswana
are the Kgalagadi Desert and the Northern Tuli Block.
The former contains the two largest wildlife parks in
Botswana, the Central Kgalagadi Game Reserve and the
Gemsbok National Park, as well as the smaller Mabutse-
hube Game Reserve. This whole region, however, is
remote and relatively inaccessible and consequently attracts only the more hardy and adventurous visitor. The
Northern Tuli Block consists of about 1000 sq. kms.
bounded by the Motloutse, Limpopo and Shashe Rivers
and the Tuli Circle. It supports a wide variety of wildlife, which, though largely migratory, provides the basis
of small-scale photographic and hunting safaris, particularly in the winter months.

TRADE UNIONS. The legislative basis for trade unionism in
Botswana is the Trade Union Act, 1969, which required
that all unions should be registered. Unions existed before 1969, but the need to register under the Act provided
a powerful incentive for the labor movement to move from
a system of small and ineffective unions to one of large
national unions based on industries. By 1973, eight

unions were registered. Once a union has been registered and has secured as members 25 per cent of the
workers in that industry, it is considered desirable, that,
for the sake of harmonious relations, both the union and
the management enter into a collective agreement on
wages and conditions of employment.

In many industries, however, either there are no
unions, or those in existence are too small to be afforded negotiating rights. In such situations, the Minister of
Health, Labor and Home Affairs is empowered by the
Regulation of Wages and Conditions of Service Act, 1969,
to establish Wage Councils to make recommendations on
wages and conditions of service.

Trade Unions in Botswana and Membership (Oct. 1972)

National Union of Government Manual Workers	1,647
Commercial and General Workers Union	1,617
Construction Workers Union	1,292
Botswana Mine Workers Union	596
Meat Industry Workers Union	530
Botswana Local Government Workers Union	492
Botswana Railway Workers Union	455
Botswana Bank Employees Union	94

TRIBAL STRUCTURE. Historically the Batswana lacked a
paramount chief who could provide an integrating administrative framework for the whole country. The eight
principal tribes of Botswana are therefore the Kwena,
Ngwato, Ngwaketse and Tawana, who claim a common
legendary ancestor and are generally believed to be descended from a single tribe of which the senior branch
is the Hurutshe; the Kgatla, who are perhaps also of
Hurutshe stock but did not enter the Protectorate until
1871; the Rolong, who claim an ancestry even more remote than the Hurutshe and their offshoots; the Tlokwa,
a very small section of a much larger group of that name
in other parts of southern Africa, traditionally an offshoot
from the Kgatla; and the Lete, who are not really Batswana
at all, but Transvaal Ndebele who have completely as-
similated Sotho culture. Each of these tribes occupies
its own country, and is the cominant tribe in that area.
Associated with each of the dominant tribes are smaller
related or formerly subjected tribes. These subordinate
tribes include the Kuba (Bayei), Mpukusha, Subia, Tswa-
pong, Kalaka, Seleka, Phaleng, Birwa, Pedi, Najwa,
Hurutshe, Talaote, Kaa, Maherero and Rotse. Only the
nomadic Sarwa of the Kgalagadi and the few thousand
Europeans are not included in this traditional system.
See also CHIEFTAINSHIP; LAND TENURE.

TSHIDI ROLONG   see   ROLONG

TSODILO HILLS.   Located in the northwest corner of Ngamiland (North West District) near the Okavango River with
highest altitude of 1375 meters.   Christened by explorer
Laurens van der Post, "The Mountains of the Gods,"
these hills contain some of the most famous Bushmen
rock paintings yet discovered.   The Tsodilo Hills, a
ridge of micaceous quartzite schist, rise 1260 feet above
the surrounding desert 35 miles west of the Okavango
Delta.   There are over 2000 rock paintings of wildlife
covering many styles on their towering honey and rose
colored cliffs.

TSWANA   see   TRIBAL STRUCTURE

TULI BLOCK DISTRICT.   Part of the area ceded to the
British South Africa Company in 1895 for the purpose of
the construction of the railway.   The Company obtained
full title in 1905 by Proclamations 4, 12 and 13 of that
year.   After 1922 the greater part of the land was sold
or leased to European farmers.   The decision to sell the
land to Europeans precipitated the so-called Birwa tragedy, when an Ngwato regiment deputed by Chief Khama
with official approval forcefully removed the Birwa populace.   Molema, the Birwa chief, unsuccessfully appealed
to the British government for redress.   See also TOUR-
ISM.

TWANA, Chief   see   TAWANA

-U-

UBLS [University of ...]   see   EDUCATION

UNITED NATIONS.   Botswana was admitted to membership
in the United Nations in October, 1966.   A permanent
mission to the United Nations is maintained in New York.

UNIVERSITY of Botswana, Lesotho, and Swaziland (UBLS)
see   EDUCATION

-V-

VAN RENSBERT, PATRICK (1931-).   Born in Durban

worked for the South African Ministry of Justice, but
ended his civil service career after nine years by resign-
ing a foreign service post in protest against apartheid.
After a brief period of political opposition to apartheid in
South Africa and abroad, he settled in Botswana where he
founded Swaneng Hill School in Serowe in 1962 and later
Shashe River School near Tonota at the Shashe Dam and
Madiba School at Mahalapye. He contributed a great deal
to the development of the brigade system which was
launched in 1967. The object is to provide young people
with a wide range of skills such as building, tanning,
carpentry, farming, textile work, mechanics and electricity. The cost of their training is covered by the
value of the goods produced. Since their founding it has
always been the fundamental aim of the Serowe brigades
to work closely with the development of the local community. A farm was started by Swaneng Hill School in
1967 and a three-year brigade course for builders, car-
penters, tanners and farmers was begun.

VERWOERD, DR. H. F. (1901-1966). South African professor, editor, and statesman who as Prime Minister (1958-
66) rigorously applied a policy of apartheid (separation of
the races), despite protests at home and abroad. Dr.
Verwoerd led South Africa to republic status on May 31,
1961.
  On September 3, 1963, Dr. Verwoerd offered to
"guide" Bechuanaland and the other High Commission
Territories to independence. Dr. Verwoerd was varying
the half-century old policy aimed at bringing the territories under South African political control. With incorporation now out of the question, the National party government saw new opportunities to achieve the same end.
Border posts, passport control, curtailment of railway
passenger service, air flight restrictions, and repatria-
tion of workers from the protectorates were all simultaneously employed in 1963 to demonstrate South Africa's
ability to affect adversely life in the territories. But al-
ternating with these displays of force, Dr. Verwoerd
showed that he could cooperate with any government in
the territories which sought South African friendship.
Friendly relations, he said, were in accord with the Republic's policy of separate development. In 1964, with
the prospect at hand of the final removal of the Imperial
factor from Southern Africa's politics, the Prime Minister expressed confidence that independent governments

would be better guarantors of their own interests than
the British government.

-W-

WARREN, SIR CHARLES (1840-1927). Administrator and
general. During the Griqualand West Rebellion of 1878
he commanded the Diamond Fields Horse and fought
against the Bechuana tribes of Batthaping and Battharo.
As administrator and commander-in-chief of Griqualand
West he led the Northern Border Expedition in 1879. In
1884, as a major-general, Warren rushed to occupy
Bechuanaland ahead of the South African Republic. With
a force of 4000 men he marched to Vryburg and Mafeking
to assert British authority and put an end to Stellaland
and Goshen, two Boer republics which had been established after 1882. During this bloodless campaign Warren met President Kruger on January 24, 1885, at Fourteen Streams, and an agreement was reached on the
border disputes. He then proclaimed Bechuanaland to the
Molopo a British Crown colony and Bechuanaland further
north a protectorate.

WATER SUPPLY. The main water problems of Botswana
arise not from an overall shortage of water, but from
its uneven distribution, in relation to the centers of population and areas of suitable soils. It is the cost of collecting and distributing the water that is the basic problem. Since the only realistic solution to the improvement of water supplies on a large scale is to move it to
the centers of significant population, the chief feature of
the government's water policy is that it should be treated
as an economic asset.
    Botswana lies entirely in a summer rainfall belt, and
the rains normally begin in late October and end in April.
Average rainfall for the whole country is about 450mm.,
but in the extreme southwest the average is less than
250mm. and in the extreme northeast it is more than
650mm. Annual rainfall is less variable in the north
than in the south, where the coefficient of variation is 80
per cent. The seasonal patterns also vary from north to
south, and rain generally falls as high-intensity, short-
duration showers and storms. Annual evaporation rates
are not highly variable through the country, and figures
of 1.7 to 1.9 meters per annum apply generally to open
water (not pan) evaporation, with daily rates of up to 7mm.

The water of the Okavango is of enormous potential significance to Botswana. About 11.800 x 10^6 cubic meters of water, excluding direct rainfall, flows into the area of the delta annually. Because of the very high rate of evaporation, however, average annual outflow from the delta to the Boteti River and Lake Ngami is a little more than 5 per cent of the total inflow.

The most northerly border of Botswana is formed by the Chobe (or Linyati) River, which rises in Angola, crosses the Caprivi Strip, and then forms the border between Botswana and the Caprivi until its confluence with the Zambezi. Few quantitative data are available on the regime of the Chobe, which is complicated by interaction with the Zambezi system, especially when the latter is in flood. The Chobe is badly infested with Kariba weed and measures are being taken to control it.

The rivers in the eastern watershed are all ephemeral and flow only after intensive rain has fallen in the active part of their catchment areas. Flood peaks are sometimes high and cause disruption to communications. The post-flood recession flow may continue for periods varying from a few days to a few months.

Reservoir sites in Botswana are generally expensive to develop in comparison with those in most other countries because there are few dam sites that provide a good depth of water in relation to surface area, and long and expensive embankments are necessary to obtain a satisfactory depth and volume of impounded water.

WOMEN. Although Botswana has a male-dominated society, women have risen to positions of considerable influence in certain areas. Generally speaking women have full civil and political rights throughout the country except that in tribal areas for purposes of legal rights a woman is considered to be a minor and should be supported by her guardians who is her husband if married and otherwise her nearest male relative.

Women are not allowed to prosecute cases in customary courts (diKgotla) unless there are no male relatives to support them in their action or, as is often the case in divorces, they are given a special dispensation by the courts. Normally women have no right to express an opinion, or to sit in the kgotla, whereas this is the prerogative of all adult male members of the tribe; nor is a woman allowed to take an active part in tribal discussions.

Property rights are not usually vested in women, and,

while a woman may both inherit and possess property, it
is not normal for her to have the right to dispose of such
property without the consent of her guardian or the senior
male person of the place at which she lives. "Property"
in this context refers only to stock and grain; a woman
does have the right to sell without permission her own
produce, poultry and crops other than cereal crops.

By custom, labor is divided fairly equally between
the sexes. Most boys between the ages of seven and 12
years are expected to herd the cattle at the cattle-posts.
Consequently many of the boys have little opportunity to
go to school before the age of 11, while the girls, whose
duties are slight, have the opportunity of going from an
early age. There are more girls in school than boys,
although boys usually stay longer in school than girls.
As a result, the percentage of literate women is considerably higher than that of literate men, although the
standard of literacy among men is considerably higher.

WOOKEY, ALFRED JOHN. Born in England he became a
London Missionary Society missionary and in 1870 was
appointed to the Bechuana mission. He was living at
Bothithong (1874-78) when his house was burned down.
He and his family took refuge in Kuruman. Although he
traveled widely outside southern Africa he was stationed
at Kuruman, Molepolele, Lake Ngami and Vryburg for
many years.

Wookey's principal contribution to mission work was
literary, his first work being a speller and reader for
beginners in 1875. For many decades it probably did
more than any other book to bring literacy to the southern
Tswana. Having run to numerous editions, the book was
revised slightly in 1953 and is still in use. No other
book in Tswana, except the Bible and perhaps Pilgrim's
Progress, has had such an influence for so long a time.

In 1884 Wookey produced in Tswana a commentary on
the Gospel of St. Matthew and in 1890 he published a number of New Testament stories with illustrations. His
book of hymns (London, 1894) appeared in 1894. In 1887,
with Roger Price, he was asked to make a thorough revision of the Tswana Bible. In 1907, after 20 years of
minute revision, the revised version was ready for the
printers. In 1907 Wookey began his revision and enlarge-
ment of J. Tom Brown's Tswana dictionary, but, after
spending ten years at it, died before completing his task.
Wookey published an illustrated history of the Tswana in
1913, a work still considered by the Tswana a valuable
contribution to their history.

-X-

XAU LAKE. A seasonal lake formed by the Boteti and Letro-
ham Rivers in the Western Central District, southeast of
the Makgadikgadi Pans.

-Z-

ZAMBEZI RIVER. One of Africa's greatest rivers, it rises
at Kalene Hill, Zambia, and flows generally southeast-
ward to the Indian Ocean after traversing the territories
or frontiers of Angola, Zambia, South West Africa, Botswana, Rhodesia and Mozambique, a distance of 2200
miles. Victoria Falls and Kariba Dam are located on its
course. Botswana's actual border along the Zambezi is
only 457 meters long. This part of the border, which is
not yet established by international treaty, is a source of
controversy among Botswana, Rhodesia and South Africa
(i.e., South West Africa).

CHRONOLOGY

1700's-1800's	Migrations into region of Bechuanaland
1840's	David Livingstone and other missionaries enter Bechuanaland
1884	Khama III appeals for British protection against Boer encroachment
1885	With the concurrence of the Batswana Chiefs the whole of Bechuanaland was proclaimed to be under the protection of the Queen
1891	Order-in-Council authorizing the High Commissioner for South Africa to exercise jurisdiction in Bechuanaland
1894	The British Government appointed a Deputy Commissioner to the Batswana tribes; Rhodes sought control of the territory by the British South Africa Company
1895	Southern part of the territory, including Mafeking, was incorporated in the Cape Colony, now part of the Republic of South Africa. In the same year, three Batswana Chiefs, Khama III of the Ngwato, Bathoen I of the Ngwaketse, and Sebele I of the Kwena, went to England to protest to Queen Victoria against a move to incorporate Botswana into the administration of Rhodes' British South Africa Company
1920-21	Establishment of African and European Advisory Councils
1950	Establishment of the Joint Advisory Council of Africans and Europeans
1961	New Constitution with Executive Council and Legislative Council

151

1963	Constitutional discussions held in territory; unanimous conclusions reached; office of Resident Commissioner changed to Her Majesty's Commissioner
1964	Proposals accepted by Britain as basis for revision of constitution; abolition of the office of High Commissioner
1965	March 1st. General Election inaugurates self-government
1966	February, Independence Constitutional Conference in London
1966	September 30th. Independent Republic of Botswana
1969	Botswana Democratic Party returned to power
1971	Population census
1972	Mineral Rights Tax Bill

HIGH COMMISSIONERS

1881-1889   Sir Hercules G. R. Robinson, High Commissioner and Governor of Cape Colony

1889-1895   Sir Henry Loch, High Commissioner and Governor of Cape Colony

1895-1897   Sir Hercules G. R. Robinson, High Commissioner and Governor of Cape Colony

1897-1901   Sir Alfred Milner, High Commissioner and Governor of Cape Colony

1897-1905   Sir Alfred Milner, High Commissioner (separated from office of Governor)

1905-1910   William Waldegrave Palmer, Earl of Selborne, High Commissioner (separated from office of Governor)

1910-1914   Herbert John Viscount Gladstone, High Commissioner and Governor General of the Union of South Africa

1914-1920   Sydney Charles Buxton, Earl Buston, High Commissioner, and Governor General of the Union of South Africa

1920-1923   Arthur Frederick Patrick Albert, Prince of Connaught, High Commissioner and Governor General of the Union of South Africa

1924-1930   Alexander Augustus Cambridge, Earl Athlone, High Commissioner and Governor General of the Union of South Africa

1931-1935   Herbert James Stanley, High Commissioner

1935-1940   William Henry Clark, High Commissioner

1940-1941   Walter Clarence Huggard (1), High Commissioner

153

1941-1944   William George Arthur Ormsby-Gore, Baron Harlech, High Commissioner

1944   Walter Clarence Huggard (2), High Commissioner

1944-1951   Sir Evelyn Baring, High Commissioner

1951-1955   John Helier le Rougetel, High Commissioner

1955-1958   Percivale Liesching, High Commissioner

1959-1963   Sir John Primatt Ratcliffe Maud, High Commissioner and (1960) Ambassador to the Republic of South Africa

1963-1964   Sir Hugh Southern Stephenson, High Commissioner and Ambassador to the Republic of South Africa

BIBLIOGRAPHY

Introductory Essay

General background on Botswana up to the 1950's is best provided by Anthony Sillery's Bechuanaland Protectorate (1952) and Lord Hailey's two works, Native Administration (1953) and An African Survey (1957). In the first volume heavy reliance was placed upon the anthropological research of W. F. Ellenberger, G. E. Nettelton and Isaac Schapera. As an outstanding scholar of Oxford University, Dr. Sillery brought to Bechuanaland, where he served as Resident Commissioner from 1946 to 1950, a great respect for Batswana culture and national aspirations. His works therefore reflect an intimate knowledge of traditional and contemporary aspects of Botswana. Two general works on Botswana written in the 1960's in turn relied heavily upon the work of Sillery and Lord Hailey for their understanding of historical and sociological factors. Jack Halpern's South Africa's Hostages (1965) and Richard P. Stevens' Lesotho, Botswana and Swaziland deal with political and constitutional events leading up to independence and underscore the challenge presented to Botswana by South Africa. In the latter work, Dr. H. George Henry, former lecturer in economics at Pius XII University College, outlines the economic situation of each of the former High Commission Territories.

CULTURAL

Very little work has thus far been done in the area of archeology, music and the arts. But thanks to the existence of the journal, Botswana Notes and Records, which began publication in 1968, encouragement has been given to such investigations. Sources on Sarwa rock painting are more abundant and only a few of the more representative works have been cited below.

Linguistics and literature have fared much better than many other disciplines. As a result of the extensive efforts made primarily by the London Missionary Society throughout the 19th and early 20th centuries in providing Setswana

grammars and dictionaries, the foundations were laid for a
respectable vernacular literature. D. D. T. Jabavu's Bantu
Literature, Classification and Reviews (1923) exemplified the
early interest of Africans in this area, an interest still borne
out by the recent writings of Kgasa, Seboni, Tlou and Raditladi. Dr. Isaac Schapera's monumental efforts in Setswana
linguistics and oral tradition have informed the work of all
other investigators. The historical works of Dr. Silas Molema, all of which were written in English, as well as those
of Z. K. Matthews, written before he settled in Botswana,
have also had a significant impact on the country's literary
development.

ECONOMIC

        Reflecting the general lack of interest on the part of
the Protectorate government in the economic development of
the Territory, it was not until the desperate circumstances
of the early 1930's forced the hand of the British government
that an investigating commission was sent to the High Commission Territories. Under the direction of Sir Alan Pim,
the commission noted the contradictions of British rule in
Bechuanaland and the basis was laid for economic and political reform. The commission's conclusions were set forth in
Financial and Economic Position of the Bechuanaland Protectorate (1933). However, another two decades would pass before the British government made any serious efforts to develop any alternatives to stagnation and near total dependence
on South Africa. But studies in 1951, 1952, 1954 and 1960
reflected the quickening pace of British activity. The American economist, Darrell Randall, also produced during this
period a far-ranging analysis in Factors of Economic Development and the Okavango Delta (1957), which merits closer
study for future development. Patrick Van Rensburg's various articles in Botswana Notes and Records touch upon some
of the major human factors inhibiting economic growth. The
U. S. Department of Labor's Labor Law and Practice: Botswana provides a useful reference. The basic character of
Botswana's economy as determined by the flow of migratory
labor to South Africa is clearly set forth by Prof. Schapera.
Articles in the International Labour Review (1933, 1942), although dated, are not without relevance to the present situation.

HISTORICAL

Missionary and explorers' reports on Bechuanaland are among the most comprehensive primary sources for the reconstruction of 19th-century African history. Notwithstanding their religious and racial bias there emerges a fairly clear understanding of the issues affecting tribal life during this period of upheaval caused by Boer encroachment, the introduction of Christian mores and the shifting tides of tribal migrations and warfare. Thus, the accounts of R. Barrow (1806), H. Lichtenstein (1806), W. Burchell (1822), R. Moffat (1842), D. Livingstone (1857), J. Chapman (1868), J. Mackenzie (1877, 1883, 1886, 1887), J. S. Moffat (1885) and J. Hepburn (1895) provide valuable primary source material. More recent historical works of considerable importance for their evaluation and interpretation of these sources as well as original scholarship based on oral tradition are represented by Dr. S. M. Molema's Chief Moroka (1951) and Montshiwa (1966). Again the historical research of Dr. Schapera has contributed to Dr. Sillery's excellent biography, Sechele: the Story of an African Chief (1954). Other worthwhile biographical works are those of J. C. Harris, Khama, the Great African Chief (1923) and Julian Mockford. Mockford's two biographies on Khama (1931) and Seretse Khama (1950) have been widely recognized for their objectivity. The periodical literature on Tshekedi Khama and Seretse Khama, involving in the first instance the celebrated flogging case of 1933, opposition to certain administrative-economic proposals and his nephew's marriage is quite extensive; only some of the more significant articles and reports are mentioned below. Mary Benson's sympathetic account of Tshekedi Khama (1960) justly deserves its good reputation. Such historical studies as those by V. F. Ellenberger, Adam Kuper and Anthony Sillery are basic references.

An extensive literature exists on the proposed incorporation of Bechuanaland and the other High Commission Territories into South Africa. As basic references the Union government's Memorandum on Negotiations (1952-53) provides a comprehensive summary from the South African point of view. M. Perham and Lionel Curtis, in their work, The Protectorates of Africa: The Question of their Transfer to the Union (1935) provide excellent insight into the thinking of many British "liberals," who after urging the transfer of power to the Union government in 1910 at African expense, proceeded to urge the transfer of the Territories as a gesture of confidence in white rule--a move, it was argued, which would enhance the white liberals in South Africa. The official British Memorandum of 1934 and Cmd. 8707 (1952) balance the official South African views. Countering all pro-South African positions were the incisive views set forth by Tshekedi Khama in his Statement to the British Parliament and People (1935) and Bechuanaland and South Africa (1955). As one of the few Batswana with education and international stature capable of commanding world opinion Khama's writings have a special place in the country's history. Dr. H. Verwoerd's Crisis in World Conscience (1964) comes as a final attempt to deal with the question of incorporation by proposing immediate "independence" under South African tutelage. Important general discussions of the issue are provided by G. V. Doxey (1963), Lord Hailey (1963) and R. P. Stevens (1972).

POLITICAL

The literature on Botswana's political, constitutional and international evolution has rapidly expanded. Official constitutional reports and proposals of 1960, 1963, 1964 and 1966 are, of course, basic references. Articles written by R. P. Stevens (1964, 1966), R. H. Edwards (1967), J. H. Proctor (1968), W. A. J. Mccartney (1969) and J. E. Griffiths provide interpretations by outsiders who had acquired considerable knowledge of events in the 1960's. Preliminary to these works are the important articles written by Tshekedi Khama throughout the early 1950's wherein he exposed the contradictions of British political and economic policies.

The existence of several party newspapers, Masa, Therisanyo and Puo Phaa, has greatly facilitated the study of Botswana politics. Useful source material is also provided in the Mafeking Mail and Botswana Guardian, Kutlwano, and the Daily News. P. L. Breutz's article (1971) essentially provides justification for South Africa in dealing with the Bantustans. A very substantial and significant work is Adam Kuper's Kalahari Village Politics (1970).

Rounding out the political side is an extensive literature focusing on Botswana and South Africa, Botswana in the southern African sub-system, and Botswana in African and world politics. Official statements of the President, Sir Seretse Khama (1969, 1970), are straightforward and unequivocal. Some of the more significant writers who have endeavored over recent years to underscore South Africa's threat to Botswana are the South African exiles, Neville Rubin

(1970) and Ronald Segal (1964). Richard Dale has made an important contribution to the systematic study of Botswana's foreign policy both in his articles and in his impressive editing of Southern Africa in Perspective: Essays in Regional Politics (1962).

SCIENTIFIC

Without background or experience it is pointless to single out any of the various scientific works as more important than another. However, the various articles by A. G. G. Best and F. C. Dawson involving geopolitical considerations in the establishment of the country's capital, Gaborone, are interesting and worthwhile. A. C. Campbell, former Chief Game Warden, is a recognized naturalist and presently is Curator of the National Museum and Art Gallery.

SOCIAL

In anthropology, ethnology and sociology Dr. Isaac Schapera has set the highest standards for research. His prolific writing based on intimate personal knowledge of the people and their language put his work in a unique category. However, the works of Lady Naomi Mitchison, an honorary member of the Kgatla, offer tremendous insight into the tribe and chieftaincy which complements a scientific, somewhat patronizing approach on the part of many anthropologists. An abundance of specialized periodical literature covers most of the tribes. R. Mookodi's article, "Women's Life in Botswana" (1972) is a cautious treatment of a much neglected issue. Articles by E. Gluckman (1922), J. Harris (1938), J. W. Joyce (1938), G. G. Silberbauer (1961), although dated, touch upon one of the country's most glossed-over issues-- the existence of subordinate groups which, at least until the recent past, have been virtually serfs if not slaves. The Botswana government is engaged in an extensive effort to uproot these traditions of inequality.

The impact of Christianity in Botswana has been profound--a cause of human development and division. Given the overwhelming importance of the London Missionary Society (LMS), A. J. Hailes' A Brief Historical Survey of the London Missionary Society in Southern Africa (1911) and R. Lovett's History of the London Missionary Society, 1795-1895 are most useful. In addition, all of the various accounts of missionaries

referred to under "history" must be taken into account for a
proper assessment of their presence. In a more critical
vein, Anthony Dachs has set forth very concisely the accusa-
tion of "Missionary Imperialism" (1972) while Sandy Grant offers a sober appraisal of "Church and Chief in the Colonial
Era" (1971). As basic studies in traditional Tswana religious
beliefs and practices the work of Dr. Schapera remains un-
rivaled.

Important assessments of Botswana's education system,
its deficiencies and prospects, have been given by the Rev.
G. A. Auger (1962), former head of the education department
of Pius XII University College (now UBLS), Richard Vengroff
(1972), and E. Watters (1970). Various articles by Patrick
Van Rensburg, although falling here under other headings,
have attracted considerable comment by those who favor or
oppose his insistence upon relevant education in an agricultural context.

The Bibliography

GENERAL

Baring, Evelyn. "Problems of the High Commission Terri-
    tories," International Affairs, Vol. 28 (April 1952), pp.
    184-9.
Couperthwaite, Bruce. "The Bechuanaland Protectorate,"
    Race Relations Journal, Johannesburg, Vol. 18 No. 1
    (1951), pp. 28-71.
Dundas, Charles C. and Ashton, Hugh. Problem Territories
    of Southern Africa: Basutoland, Bechuanaland and Swazi-
    land. Johannesburg: Institute of International Affairs,
    1952.
Edwards, Isobel E. Protectorates or Native Reserves?
    London: Africa Bureau, 1956.
Fabian Society. The Unprotected Protectorates, Basutoland,
    Bechuanaland and Swaziland. London, 1965.
Greaves, L. B. The High Commission Territories. London:
    Edinburgh House Press, 1954.
Hailey, Lord. An African Survey. Oxford: Oxford Univer-
    sity Press, 1957.
_____. Native Administration in the British African Ter-
    ritories: Part V. The High Commission Territories:
    Basutoland, The Bechuanaland Protectorate and Swaziland.

London: HMSO, 1953.

Halpern, Jack. South Africa's Hostages: Basutoland, Bechuanaland and Swaziland. Baltimore: Penguin Books,
1965.

"High Commission Territories: A Remnant of British Africa,"
Round Table, No. 213 (December 1963), pp. 26-40.

"High Commission Territories: Potatoes and Administration,"
Round Table, Vol. 42 (March 1952), pp. 141-51.

Hodgson, M. L., and Ballinger, W. G. Bechuanaland Protectorate. Alice, S. A.: Lovedale Press, 1933.

Houlton, Sir John. "The High Commission Territories in
South Africa: Bechuanaland," Geographical Magazine,
Vol. XXVI (August 1953), pp. 175-81.

Khama, Tshekedi. Bechuanaland, a General Survey. Johannesburg: South Africa Institute of Race Relations, 1957.

Maud, Sir John. "The Challenge of the High Commission
Territories," African Affairs, Vol. 43 No. 251 (April
1964).

Orchard, Ronald K. The High Commission Territories of
South Africa. London: World Dominion Press, 1951.

Pim, Sir Alan. "British Protectorates and Territories. An
Address Delivered At a Meeting of the Royal Empire
Society," United Empire, Vol. 25, No. 5 (May 1934),
pp. 266-79.

Sillery, Anthony. The Bechuanaland Protectorate. London:
Oxford University Press, 1952.

Spence, J. E. "British Policy Towards the High Commission
Territories," Journal of Modern African Studies, Vol. 2,
No. 2 (July 1964), pp. 241-46.

Stevens, Richard P. Lesotho, Botswana, and Swaziland: The
Former High Commission Territories in Southern Africa.
London: Pall Mall, 1967.

United Nations. General Assembly. Information from Non-
Self-Governing Territories. Bechuanaland. United Nations (1959, A/4083/Add. 3), March 4, 1959.

_____. _____. Information from Non-Self-Governing
Territories: Summary of Information Transmitted under
Article 73 e of the Charter of the United Nations: Report of the Secretary-General, Africa and Adjacent Territories: Bechuanaland. United Nations (1962, A/
5079/Add. 5), April 4, 1962.

_____. _____. Special Report, Committee on the Sit-
uation with Regard to the Implementation of the Declaration on the Granting of Independence to Colonial Countries and Peoples. Draft Report: Bechuanaland, Basutoland and Swaziland. (A/AC. 109/L. 81) September 3,
1963.

Bibliography

Middleton, Coral. A Bibliography of Bechuanaland. Cape
    Town: University School of Librarianship, 1965.
Mohome, Paulus and Webster, John B. A Bibliography on
    Bechuanaland. Syracuse University, 1966. Supplement,
    1968.

CULTURAL [containing: Archeology, Arts, Rock Paintings,
              Linguistics/Literature, Music, Press...]

Archeology

Lepionka, L. "A Preliminary Account of Archeological In-
    vestigation at Tautswe," Botswana Notes and Records,
    Vol. 3 (1971), pp. 22-6.
Malan, F. "A Wilton Site at Kai Kai, Bechuanaland Pro-
    tectorate," South African Archaeological Bulletin, Vol.
    5 (1950), pp. 140-2.
"Outlines of Prehistory and Stone Age Climatology in the
    Bechuanaland Protectorate," Institut Royal Colonial
    Belge, Section des Sciences naturelles et medicales,
    Mémoire, Vol. 25, No. 4, 1954.
Pahl, R. "Notes on an Iron Age Settlement on Motsenekatse
    Hill," Botswana Notes and Records, Vol. 3 (1971), pp.
    27-31.
Paver, F. R. "The Position of the Kalahari, 'Lost City',"
    South African Archaeological Bulletin, Vol. 14 (1959),
    pp. 38-40.
Rudner, I. "Archaeological Report on the Tsodilo Hills,
    Bechuanaland," South African Archaeological Bulletin,
    Vol. 20, No. 78 (June 1965), pp. 51-70.

Arts

Lambrecht, Dora. "Basketry in N'gamiland, Botswana,"
    African Arts/Arts d'Afrique (Spring 1968), pp. 20-30.
Schapera, Isaac and Wedgewood, Cammila H. "String Fig-
    ures from Bechuanaland," Bantu Studies, Vol. 4 (1930),
    pp. 251-68.

Rock Paintings

Campbell, Alec C. "Notes on Some Rock Paintings at Savuti,"
    Botswana Notes and Records, Vol. 2 (1970), pp. 15-28.

Cooke, C. K. "Rock Paintings--Botswana and Elsewhere, "
Botswana Notes and Records, Vol. 2 (1970), pp. 24-28.
Maufe, H. B. "The Pigments of the Bushman Rock-Paint-
ings, " Proceedings of the Rhodesia Scientific Association, No. 2 (1933).

Linguistics and Literature

Archbell, J. Grammar of the Bechuana Language. Grahamstown: n. p., 1837.
Brown, J. Tom. Bechuana Dictionary. London Missionary
Society, 1876, 2nd. ed. 1895, reprinted 1921, newly
revised, enlarged and rearranged by J. Tom Brown,
n. d. (1922?).
_____. Sechuana Dictionary. Lobatse: District Commit-
tee of the London Missionary Society, (1954?).
_____. Secwana Dictionary. Tiger Kloof: London Mis-
sionary Society, 1931.
Campbell, Alec C. "100 Tswana Proverbs, " Botswana Notes
and Records, Vol. 4 (1972), pp. 121-32.
Cole, Desmond T. An Introduction to Tswana Grammar.
London: Longmans, Green, 1955.
_____. "Notes on the Phonological Relationships of Bechu-
ana Vowels, " African Studies, Vol. 8 (1949), pp. 109-
31.
Doke, C. M. "A Preliminary Investigation of the State of
the Native Languages of South Africa, " Bantu Studies,
Vol. 7 (1933), pp. 1-98. Bibliography of Bechuana lan-
guage and literature, compiled by G. P. Lestrade, pp.
77-85.
Jabavu, D. D. T. Bantu Literature, Classification and Re-
views. Lovedale, 1923.
Jones, Daniel and Plaatje, S. T. A Sechuana Reader. Lon-
don: 1916.
Kgasa, M. L. A. "The Development of seTswana, " Botswana
Notes and Records. Vol. 4 (1972), pp. 107-9.
Kohler, O. "Observations on the Central Khosian Language
Group, " Journal of African Languages, Vol. 2, No. 3
(1963), pp. 227-34.
Peters, Mark A. "Notes on the Place Names of Ngamiland, "
Botswana Notes and Records, Vol. 4 (1972), pp. 219-
33.
Sandilands, A. "The Ancestor of Tswana Grammars, " Bots-
wana Notes and Records. Vol. 4 (1972), pp. 101-6.
Schapera, Isaac. The Bantu-speaking Tribes of South Africa:
An Ethnographical Survey. London: Routledge, 1937.
_____, ed. Ditirafalo tsa merafe ya BaTswana ba lefatshe

la Tshireletso. Alice, S. A.: Lovedale Press, 1954.
———. "Ethnographical Texts in the Boolongwe Dialect of
    Sekgalagadi," Bantu Studies, Vol. 12 (1938), pp. 157-87.
———. "Kxatla Riddles and their Significance," Bantu
    Studies, Vol. 6 (1932), pp. 215-31.
———. Mekgwa le Melao ya BaTswana. Alice, S. A.:
    Lovedale Press, 1938.
———. Notes on the Noun-Classes of Some Bantu Lan-
    guages of Ngamiland. Cape Town, 1942.
———. Praise-poems of Tswana Chiefs. Oxford: Clar-
    endon Press, 1965.
———. "Some Ethnographical Texts in SeKgatla," Bantu
    Studies, Vol. 4 (1930), pp. 73-93.
Seboni, M. Diane le maele a Setswana. Lovedale, S. A.:
    Lovedale Press, 1962.
Tlou, Thomas. "The History of Botswana through Oral Tra-
    ditions--Research among the Peoples of the North-west
    District (Ngamiland)," Botswana Notes and Records,
    Vol. 3 (1971), pp. 79-90.

Music

Kirby, P. R. "The Musical Practices of the Auni and Kho-
    mani Bushmen," Bantu Studies, Vol. 10 (1936), pp. 373-
    431.

Press, Publications, Library

Botswana Notes and Records. Vol. 1, no. 1, 1968- . Arti-
    cles on subjects of permanent interest in fields of na-
    tural and social science, humanities, law and the arts.
    Includes notes on current research on Botswana.
Jones, J. D. "Mahoko a Becwana--The second SeTswana
    Newspaper," Botswana Notes and Records, Vol. 4 (1972),
    pp. 112-20.
Parker, J. S. Botswana National Library Service: The First
    Three Years: A Report on the Establishment and De-
    velopment of the Botswana National Library Service,
    From November 1966 to October 1969. Gaborone, 1969.
Stiles, D. E. Botswana National Library Services: Report
    on the National Library Service for the Period Novem-
    ber 1969-March 1971. Gaborone, 1972.

ECONOMIC [containing: Agriculture, Development, Finance,
     Industry/Commerce, Labor, South African Rela-
     tions]

Agriculture

Child, G. "Ecological Constraints on Rural Development in
     Botswana," Botswana Notes and Records, Vol. 3 (1971),
     pp. 157-64.
Curtis, Donald. "The Social Organization of Ploughing,"
     Botswana Notes and Records, Vol. 4 (1972), pp. 67-80.
Department of Agriculture. The 1968-69 Agricultural Survey.
     Gaborone, 1970.
Landell-Mills, P. M. "Rural Incomes and Urban Wage
     Rates," Botswana Notes and Records, Vol. 2 (1970), pp.
     79-84.
Tsheko, Tsheko. "The Development of Agriculture," New
     Commonwealth, Vol. 49, No. 2 (February 1970), p. 12.
Weare, P. "The Influence of Environmental Factors on Ara-
     ble Agriculture in Botswana," Botswana Notes and Rec-
     ords, Vol. 3 (1971), pp. 165-68.

Development

Botswana. National Development Plan, 1968-73. Gaborone,
     1968.
_____. National Development Plan, 1973-78, Part I and
     Part II. Gaborone, 1972.
_____. Transitional Plan for Social and Economic Develop-
     ment. Gaborone, 1966.
Brown, J. "New Hope for Africa's Thirstland," Fortnightly,
     Vol. 179, No. 173 (June 1953), pp. 394-8.
"Cooperation Comes to Bechuanaland," Review of International
     Cooperation, Vol. 58 (May 1965), pp. 119-25.
"Development is Slow in Bechuanaland," Commonwealth De-
     velopment, Vol. 8 (Jan. -Feb. 1961), pp. 28-30.
Fosbrooke, H. A. "An Assessment of the Importance of In-
     stitutions and Institutional Framework in Development,"
     Botswana Notes and Records, Vol. 5 (1973), pp. 26-36.
_____. "The Role of Tradition in Rural Development,"
     Botswana Notes and Records, Vol. 3 (1971), pp. 188-
     191.
Galbraith, John S. "Economic Development in the High Com-
     mission Territories," New Commonwealth, Vol. 33
     (January 7, 1957).
"The High Commission Territories: Economic and Social De-
     velopment," Commonwealth Survey, Vol. 1, No. 21

(October 1955), pp. 930-36.

Jackson, Dudley. "Income Differentials and Unbalanced Planning: The Case of Botswana," Journal of Modern African Studies (Dec. 1970), pp. 553-62.

Randall, Darrell. Factors of Economic Development and the Okavango Delta. Chicago: University of Chicago Press, 1957.

Report of a Mission to the Bechuanaland Protectorate to Investigate the Possibilities of Economic Development in the Western Kalahari. London: HMSO, 1954.

Ronald, C. "Development in Botswana during the First United Nations Development Decade," Botswana Notes and Records, Vol. 4 (1972), pp. 1-20.

Van Rensburg, Patrick. "Boiteko," Botswana Notes and Records, Vol. 5 (1973), pp. 12-16.

_____. "A New Approach to Rural Development," Botswana Notes and Records, Vol. 3 (1971), pp. 201-15.

Wass, Peter. "The History of Community Development in Botswana in the 1960's," Botswana Notes and Records, Vol. 4 (1972), pp. 81-93.

Finance

Barclays Bank, D. C. O. Basutoland, Bechuanaland and Swaziland: An Economic Survey. London: Barclays Bank, 1962.

Baring, Evelyn. "Economic Developments under the High Commission in South Africa," African Affairs, Vol. 51, No. 204 (July 1952), pp. 222-30.

_____. "Recent Economic Developments in the High Commission Territories in Southern Africa," United Empire, Vol. 43, No. 3 (May-June 1952), pp. 110-16.

"Botswana: Bond Issue," Standard Bank Review, July 1970.

"Botswana Economic Survey," African Development, (February 1973), pp. B. L. S. 1-12.

"Botswana: Finance," Barclays Overseas Review. London, May 1970.

"Botswana: General," Standard Bank Review. London, April 1970.

Cross, S. J. "Basutoland, Bechuanaland Protectorate, Swaziland; Account of the Territories and of the Economic Developments Taking Place," Board of Trade Journal, Vol. 183 (Sept. 28, 1962).

Erasmus, D. P. "The National Income of Bechuanaland Protectorate: 1955," Finance and Trade Review, Vol. IV (March 1961), pp. 261-75.

"Focus on Botswana," New Commonwealth Trade and Commerce (February 1970).

Great Britain. Colonial Office. An Economic Survey of the
     Colonial Territories, 1951. London: HMSO, 1953.
     4 Vols., Colonial Nos. 281-1, High Commission Terri-
     tories: Northern Rhodesia, Nyasaland, Basutoland,
     Bechuanaland, and Swaziland.
_____. Commission on Financial and Economic Position
     of Bechuanaland Protectorate. Report. London:
     HMSO, 1933, Cmd. 4368. (Generally known as Pim
     Report.)
_____. Commonwealth Relations Office. Report of a Mis-
     sion to the Bechuanaland Protectorate to Investigate the
     Possibilities of Economic Development in the Western
     Kalahari, 1952. London: HMSO, 1954.
_____. Directorate of Overseas Survey. Basutoland,
     Bechuanaland Protectorate and Swaziland: Report of an
     Economic Survey Mission. London: HMSO, 1960.

Industry and Commerce

Ainsworth, James. "The Copper-nickel Project in Botswana:
     International Capital for Mining Enterprise," Optima
     (June 1972), pp. 60-78.
Best, Alan C. "General Trading in Botswana, 1890-1968,"
     Economic Geography, (October 1970), pp. 598-611.
Butler, K. E. "Environmental Constraints to Livestock Pro-
     duction," Botswana Notes and Records, Vol. 3 (1971),
     pp. 169-71.
Curtis, Donald. "Cash Brewing in a Rural Economy," Bots-
     wana Notes and Records, Vol. 5 (1973), pp. 17-25.
Ettinger, Stephen. "South Africa's Weight Restrictions on
     Cattle Exports from Bechuanaland, 1924-41," Botswana
     Notes and Records, Vol. 4 (1972), pp. 21-29.
Gray, Alan. "Cattle Ranching in Bechuanaland: Far-Reach-
     ing Scheme Which Will Bring New Prosperity to the
     Territory," African World, (December 1951), pp. 11-12.
Griffiths, Ieuan L. "Botswana Discovers Its Own Resources,"
     Geographical Magazine (December 1970), pp. 217-23.
Smit, P. "Mining Developments in Botswana," Bulletin of the
     Africa Institute of South Africa, Vol. XI, No. 3 (1973),
     pp. 99-108.
Von Richter, W. and Butynski, T. "Hunting in Botswana,"
     Botswana Notes and Records, Vol. 5 (1973), pp. 191-
     208.
Werbner, Richard P. "Local Adaptation and the Transforma-
     tion of an Imperial Concession in North-Eastern Bots-
     wana," Africa (January 1971), pp. 32-41.

Labor

"Labour Recruiting in Bechuanaland," International Labour
Review, Vol. 45 (February 1942), p. 199.
Schapera, Isaac. "Labour Migration from a Bechuanaland
Native Reserve," Journal of the African Society, Vol.
32 (1933), pp. 386-97; Vol. 33 (1934), pp. 49-58.
_____. Migrant Labour and Tribal Life, A Study of Con-
ditions in the Bechuanaland Protectorate. London: Ox-
ford University Press, 1947.
"Servile Conditions in Bechuanaland," International Laborers
Review, Vol. 28 (October 1933), pp. 549-53.
United States Department of Labor. Labor Law and Practice:
Botswana. Washington, D. C. : 1968.

South African Economic Relations

"Cash and Customs Dealings with South Africa: Black States
Seek a Bigger Say: New Look at Rand Tie-Up," The
Star, Johannesburg, September 1, 1969.
"Customs Agreement: Union of South Africa--Territories of
Basutoland, Swaziland, and the Bechuanaland Protecto-
rate, 1910," in Bechuanaland Protectorate, Orders in
Council and High Commissioner's Proclamations and No-
tices Issued from the 9th May, 1891, to the 30th June,
1914. Edited by M. Williams (Mafeking: Mafeking
Mail, Printers, 1915).
Robson, Peter. "Economic Integration in Southern Africa,"
The Journal of Modern African Studies, Vol. 5, No. 4
(December 1967), pp. 469-90.

HISTORICAL [containing: Early... 19th Century, Tribal,
British Protectorate, South Africa..., Flogging
Case, Seretse Khama Marriage]

Early Missionary, Traveller and Political Accounts in the
19th Century

Agar-Hamilton, J. A. I. The Road to the North. London:
Longmans, Green, 1937.
Baines, Thomas. The Gold Regions of South Eastern Africa.
London: Stanford, 1877.
Barrow, Sir John. Travels into the Interior of Southern Af-
rica, 2nd ed. London: Cadell & Davies, 1806.
_____. Voyage to Cochinchina and an Account of a Journey

to the Residence of the Chief of the Booshuana Nation.
London, n. p., 1806.
Broadbent, S.   A Narrative of the First Introduction of Chris-
tianity Amongst the Barolong Tribe of Bechuanas, South
Africa.   London: Wesleyan Mission House, 1865.
Brown, J. T.   Among the Bantu Nomads: A Record of Forty
Years Spent Among the Bechuana.   London: Seeley
Service, 1926.
Burchell, W. J.   Travels in the Interior of Southern Africa.
London: Longman, 1822.   Reprinted 1953, London:
Batchworth Press.
Campbell, John.   Journal of Travels in South Africa: Among
the Hottentot and Other Tribes: in 1812, 1813 and 1814.
London: The Religious Tract Society, 1840.
_____. Journey to Lattakoo in South Africa.   London:
n. p., 1835.
_____. Travels in South Africa.   London: Black, Parry,
1813.
_____. Travels in South Africa ... Being a Narrative of
a Second Journey.   London: F. Westley, 1882.
Chamberlin, D. (ed.) Some Letters from Livingstone, 1840-
72.   London: Oxford University Press, 1940.
Chapman, James.   Travels in the Interior of South Africa.
London: Bell & Daldy, 1868.
Hepburn, James Davidson.   Twenty Years in Khama's Country
and Pioneering Among the Batauana of Lake Ngami.
London: Hodder and Stoughtion, 1895.
le Roux, Servaas D.   Pioneers and Sportsmen of South Africa
1760-1890.   Published by the author and printed by the
Art Printing Works, Ltd., Salisbury, 1939.
Lichtenstein, Henry.   Travels in Southern Africa in the Years
1803, 1804, 1805 and 1806.   A reprint of the translation
from the original German by Anne Plumptre: Van Rie-
beeck Society, Cape Town, 1928.
Livingstone, David.   Livingstone's Missionary Correspondence,
1841-1856.   Berkeley: University of California Press,
1961.
_____. Missionary Travels and Researches in South Afri-
ca.   London: Murray, 1857.
_____. Private Journals, 1851-1853.   Berkeley: Univer-
sity of California Press, 1960.
Mackenzie, John.   Austral Africa: Losing it or Ruling it.
London: Sampson Low, Marston, Searle & Rivington,
1887.
_____. "Bechuanaland," Contemporary Review, February
1898, pp. 282-97.
_____. "Bechuanaland and Austral-Africa," Society Arts,

Vol. 34 (1886), pp. 356-76.
_____. "Bechuanaland, With Some Remarks on Mashona-
land and Matabeleland," Scottish Geographical Magazine,
Vol. 3 (1887), pp. 291-315.
_____. Day-Dawn in Dark Places. London: Cassell,
n. p., 1883.
_____. Ten Years North of the Orange River. Edinburgh:
Edmonston & Douglas, 1871.
MacKenzie, W. Douglas. John Mackenzie, South African Mis-
sionary and Statesman. London: Hodder & Stoughton,
1902.
Moffat, J. S. The Lives of Robert and Mary Moffat. Lon-
don: T. Fisher Unwin, 1885.
Moffat, Robert. The Matabele Journals of Robert Moffat
1829-1860. (2 vols.), edited by J. P. R. Wallis. Gov-
ernment Archives of Southern Rhodesia, Oppenheimer
series (Chatto and Windus, London, 1945).
_____. Missionary Labours and Scenes in Southern Africa.
London: John Snow, 1842.
_____ and Moffat, Mary. Apprenticeship at Kuruman:
Being the Journals and Letters of Robert and Mary Mof-
fat, 1820-1828. Edited by I. Schapera, Central African
Archives. Oppenheimer series, No. 5, 1951.
Molema, S. M. Chief Moroka: His Life, His Times, His
Country, and His People. Cape Town: Methodist Pub-
lishing House, 1951.
_____. Montshiwa, Barolong Chief and Patriot, 1815-1896.
Cape Town: Struik, 1966.
Moseley, G. B. History of the Bangwaketse. Mafeking
Registry file 79.
Nettelton, G. E. "History of the Ngamiland Tribes up to
1926," Bantu Studies, Vol. 8 (December 1934), pp. 343-
60.
Northcott, Cecil. Robert Moffat: Pioneer in Africa, 1817-
1870. Lutterworth Press, 1961.
Okihiro, Gary Y. "Resistance and Accomodation: baKwena-
ba Gasechele 1842-52," Botswana Notes and Records,
Vol. 5 (1973), pp. 104-16.
Parsons, Q. N. "The 'Image' of Khama the Great--1868 to
1970," Botswana Notes and Records, Vol. 3 (1971), pp.
41-58.
_____. "Khama's Own Account of Himself," Botswana
Notes and Records, Vol. 4 (1972), pp. 137-46.
_____. "On the Origins of the bama Ngwato," Botswana
Notes and Records, Vol. 5 (1973), pp. 82-103.
Price, Elizabeth Lees. The Journals of Elizabeth Lees
Price Written in Bechuanaland, South Africa, 1854-1883.

London: Edward Arnold, 1956.

Schapera, Isaac. "The Early History of the Khurutshe,"
      Botswana Notes and Records, Vol. 2 (1970), pp. 1-5.
————————. A Short History of the Bakgatla-BagaKgafela of
      Bechuanaland Protectorate. Cape Town, University, 1942.
————————. "A Short History of the BaNgwaketse," African
      Studies, Vol. 1, (1942), pp. 1-26.

Sillery, Anthony. Sechele: The Story of an African Chief.
      Oxford: George Ronald, 1954.

Smiles, Paul. Land of the Black Buffalo. London: Faber
      and Faber, 1961.

Smith, Edwin. Great Lion of Bechuanaland. London: Lon-
      don Missionary Society, 1957.

Tlou, Thomas. "The History of Botswana Through Oral Tra-
      ditions: Research Among the Peoples of the North-
      West District (Ngamiland)," Botswana Notes and Records,
      Vol. 3 (1971), pp. 79-90.
————————. "Khama III--Great Reformer and Innovator,"
      Botswana Notes and Records, Vol. 2 (1970), pp. 98-105.

Williams, R. C. The British Lion in Bechuanaland: Story of
      the Expedition Under the Command of Major-General Sir
      C. Warren. Rivingtons: 1885.

Williams, Watkin W. The Life of General Sir Charles War-
      ren. Oxford: Basil Blackwell, 1941.

Tribal

Bruce, L. K. The Story of an African Chief, Khama. Lon-
      don, 1893.

Chirenje, J. M. "Chief Sekgoma Letsholathebe II," Botswana
      Notes and Records, Vol. 3 (1971), pp. 64-73.

Cloete, Stuart. African Portraits. London: Collins, 1946.

Ellenberger, V. F. "History of the Ba-ga-Malete of Ra-
      moutsa (Bechuanaland Protectorate)," Transactions of
      the Royal Society of South Africa, Vol. XXV, Part I,
      pp. 1-72.
————————. "History of the Batlokwa of Gaberones (Bechuana-
      land Protectorate)," Bantu Studies, September 1939, pp.
      165-98.

Harris, John Charles. Khama, The Great African Chief.
      London: Livingstone Press, 1923.

Hole, M. M. The Passing of the Black Kings. London:
      P. Allan, 1932.

Knobel, Louis. "The History of Sechele," Botswana Notes
      and Records, Vol. 1 (1968), pp. 51-63.

Kuper, Adam. "The Kgalagadi in the Nineteenth Century,"
      Botswana Notes and Records, Vol. 2 (1970), pp. 45-51.

Lloyd, E.   Three Great African Chiefs: Khame, Sebele, and
     Bathoeng. London: T. Fisher Unwin, 1895.
Matthews, Z. K.   "A Short History of the Tshidi Barolong,"
     Fort Hare Papers, Vol. 1, No. 1 (June 1945), pp. 9-28.
Mockford, Julian.   Khama: King of the Bamangwato.   Lon-
     don: Jonathan Cape, 1931.
_____. Seretse Khama and the Bamangwato.   London:
     Staples, 1950.
Molema, S. M.   The Bantu Past and Present: An Ethnologi-
     cal and Historical Study of the Native Races of South
     Africa.   Green and Sons, 1920.

British Protectorate

"After the Great Ngami Trek," The Round Table, No. 74
     (March 1929), pp. 325-41.
Chirgwin, A. M.   "Britain and Bechuanaland," East and West
     Review, Vol. 1, No. 2 (April 1935), pp. 124-29.
Doering, O.   "How the Anglo-German Boundary in South West
     Africa Was Made," Royal Engineers Journal, Vol. 18
     (1913), pp. 313-18.
Ellenberger, J.   "The Bechuanaland Protectorate and the
     Boer War," Rhodesians Publications, No. 11 (December
     1964), pp. 1-21.
Gabatshwane, S. M.   Introduction to the Bechuanaland Pro-
     tectorate History and Administration.   Basutoland:
     Morija Printing Works, 1957.
Gill, D.   Report on the Boundary Survey Between British
     Bechuanaland and German Southwest Africa.   Berlin,
     1906.
Gillett, Simon.   "Notes on the Settlement in the Ghanzi Dis-
     trict," Botswana Notes and Records, Vol. 2 (1970), pp.
     52-55.
"Great Ngami Trek," Round Table, Vol. 17 (December 1926),
     pp. 81-102.
Great Britain.   Colonial Office.   Correspondence Regarding
     the Visit to this Country of the Chiefs Khama, Sebele
     and Bathoen: and the Future of the Bechuanaland Pro-
     tectorate. London: HMSO, 1896.
Harrison, C.   South Africa and the Chartered Company,"
     Contemporary Review, March 1896, pp. 339-46.
Headlam, Cecil.   "The Race for the Interior, 1881-1895," in
     Eric A. Walker (ed.) The Cambridge History of the
     British Empire, Volume VIII, South Africa, Rhodesia
     and the High Commission Territories.   Cambridge:
     Cambridge University Press, 1963.
Hodgson, M. L.   "Britain as Trustee in Southern Africa,"

Political Quarterly, Vol. 3 (July 1932), pp. 398-408.
Land for Settlers in the Tati Territory, Bechuanaland. Lon-
     don: n.p., 1924.
Landell-Mills, Joslin. "An Extract from the Diaries of
     C. F. Rey," Botswana Notes and Records, Vol. 5 (1973),
     pp. 67-81. (C. F. Rey was Resident Commissioner for
     Bechuanaland from 1930 to 1937.)
Millin, Sarah G. Rhodes. London: Chatto & Windus, 1933.
Sillery, Anthony. Founding a Protectorate: History of
     Bechuanaland, 1885-1895. London: Mouton & Co.,
     1965.
Truschel, Louis W. "Nation-building and the Kgatla; the Role
     of the Anglo-Boer War," Botswana Notes and Records,
     Vol. 4 (1972), pp. 185-93.
Veal, D. A. E. "British South Africa Company: The Story
     of its Foundation," Empire Review, Vol. 32 (1918), pp.
     195-98.
Will, Denzil and Dent, Tommy. "The Boer War as Seen
     from Gaborone," Botswana Notes and Records, Vol. 4
     (1972), pp. 195-209.

South Africa and Proposed Incorporation

Barker, W. E. "South Africa's Claim to the Protectorates,"
     Race Relations Journal, Vol. 23, No. 1 (1956), pp. 15-
     30.
Booth, Alan R. "Lord Selborne and the British Protecto-
     rates, 1908-1910," Journal of African History, Vol. 10,
     No. 1 (1969).
"British South African Territories," Part 1, "External Rela-
     tions," by E. A. Walker; Part 2, "The Present Internal
     Position," by W. G. A. Harlech, African Affairs, Vol.
     44, No. 174 (January 1945), pp. 37-42.
Doxey, G. V. The High Commission Territories and the Re-
     public of South Africa. Oxford: Oxford University
     Press, 1963.
Fitzgerald, R. C. "South Africa and the High Commission
     Territories," World Affairs, Vol. 4 (July 1950), pp.
     306-320.
Great Britain. Parliamentary Committee for Studying the
     Position of the South African Protectorates. Memoran-
     dum Prepared by the Parliamentary Committee for
     Studying the Position of the South African Protectorates,
     August, 1934.
     ———. Secretary of State for Commonwealth Relations.
     Basutoland, the Bechuanaland Protectorate and Swaziland:
     History of Discussions with the Union of South Africa,

1909-39. Cmd. 8707. London: HMSO, 1952.

Hailey, Lord William Malcolm. The Republic of South Africa and the High Commission Territories. London: Oxford University Press, 1963.

"High Commission Territories and the Union of South Africa," World Today, Vol. 6 (February 1950), pp. 83-94.

Jowitt, H. "The Case Against Incorporation (High Commission Territories)," Race Relations Journal, Vol. 23, No. 1 (1956), pp. 31-43.

Khama, Tshekedi. Bechuanaland and South Africa. London: Africa Bureau, 1955.

_____. A Statement to the British Parliament and People. London: Headley Bros., 1935.

Perham, Margery and Curtis, Lionel. The Protectorates of Africa: The Question of their Transfer to the Union. Oxford: Oxford University Press, 1935.

Pim, A. "Question of the South African Protectorates," International Affairs, Vol. 13 (September 1936), pp. 668-688.

Royal Institute of International Affairs. The High Commission Territories and the Union of South Africa. London: H. I. I. A., 1956. Addenda, 1957.

Stevens, Richard P. "The History of the Anglo-South African Conflict Over the Proposed Incorporation of the High Commission Territories," Southern Africa in Perspective: Essays in Regional Politics, (ed.) Christian P. Potholm and Richard Dale, New York: Free Press, 1972. pp. 97-109.

Union of South Africa. Negotiations Regarding the Transfer to the Union of South Africa of the Government of Basutoland, Bechuanaland Protectorate and Swaziland, 1910-1939. Pretoria: Government Printer, 1952-53.

Verwoerd, Dr. H. F. I. Crisis in World Conscience. II. The Road to Freedom for Basutoland, Bechuanaland, Swaziland. Fact Paper no. 107. Pretoria: Department of Information, 1964.

"Verwoerd at Nat. Congress: Pleads for Protectorates, But Keeps Off Republican Election," The Star, November 13, 1958.

The Flogging Case, 1933: Tshekedi Khama

Barnes, Leonard. "The Crisis in Bechuanaland," Journal of the African Society, Vol. 32, No. 129 (October 1933), pp. 342-49.

_____. "Tshekedi and After," Nineteenth Century, Vol. 114, November 1933, pp. 573-82.

Benson, Mary. Tshekedi Khama. London: Faber, 1960.
"Black and White in South Africa: the Bechuanaland Flog-
gging," Review of Reviews, Vol. 84 (October 1933), pp.
13-16.
Day, J. W. "Tshekedi: The Price of Shame: The Treach-
ery of the Premier and Mr. J. H. Thomas," Saturday
Review, Vol. 156 (October 7, 1933), p. 362.
"Events in Bechuanaland," African Labour Monthly, Vol. IV
(December 1933), pp. 753-60.
Gabatshwane, S. M. Tshekedi Khama of Bechuanaland. Ox-
ford: Oxford University Press, 1961.
Macmillan, W. M. "Real Moral of the Tshekedi Case,"
New Statesman and Nation, Vol. VI (September 23, 1933),
pp. 345-6.
Steer, A. L. "Tshekedi and Mackintosh," Spectator, Vol.
151, September 29, 1933, pp. 364, 404-05.
"Tshekedi Affair," Round Table, Vol. XXIV (March 1934), pp.
438-42.

Seretse Khama Marriage Dispute

"Born to Be Chief," Listener, Vol. 70, August 8, 1963, pp.
201-18.
Creech-Jones, Arthur. "Bechuanaland: Constitution and
Government; Tshekedi: A Dilemma of the Protectorates," Listener, July 26, 1951, pp. 123-4.
Great Britain. Commonwealth Relations Office. Bechuana-
land Protectorate: Succession to the Chieftainship of
the Bamangwato Tribe. Cmd. 7913. London: HMSO,
1950.
Hinden, Rita. "White Queen for Bechuanaland," New Statesman and Nation, Vol. 38 (August 13, 1949), pp. 164-5.
Jeffreys, M. D. W. "Seretse's Exile and Return: The Legal Issues," The Forum, (Johannesburg), Vol. 5, No.
8 (November 1956), pp. 42-3.
Redfern, John. Ruth and Seretse: 'A Very Disreputable
Transaction.' London: Gollancz, 1955.
Wade, W. W. "Khama Case Becomes Focus for African
Tensions," Foreign Policy Bulletin, Vol. XXIX (April
7, 1950), pp. 3-4.

POLITICAL [containing: Constitution..., Government, Law/
Legislation, Political Parties, Foreign Affairs]

Constitutional Development

Bechuanaland Independence Conference, 1966: Report. Colonial Office, London, February 21, 1966 (mimeographed).
Bechuanaland Protectorate (Constitution) Orders 1960 and 1963.
Edwards, Robert H. "Political and Constitutional Changes in
the Bechuanaland Protectorate," Boston University Pa-
pers on Africa: Transition in African Politics (ed. by
J. Butler and A. A. Castagno). New York, 1967, pp.
135-165.
Great Britain. Bechuanaland, Constitutional Proposals, Cmd.
2378, London: HMSO, 1964.
_____. Constitutional Proposals: Bechuanaland Protecto-
rate, Cmd. 1159, London: HMSO, 1960.
Proctor, J. H. "The House of Chiefs and the Political Development of Botswana," Journal of Modern African
Studies, Vol. 6, No. 1 (May 1968), pp. 59-79.
Stevens, Richard P. "The New Republic of Botswana," Afri-
ca Report, Vol. 11 (October 1966), pp. 15-19.
Winstanley, George. "A Note on the Practical Use of the
French Voting System in the First Bechuanaland Elections," Journal of Administration Overseas, Vol. 5, No.
2 (April 1966), pp. 112-14.

Government and Administration

African Advisory Council, Minutes, Mafeking. Annual 1945-
1960.
Bechuanaland Protectorate. Annual Reports. London:
HMSO.
Griffiths, J. E. S. "A Note on Local Government in Bots-
wana," Botswana Notes and Records, Vol. 2 (1970), pp.
64-70.
_____. "A Note on the History and Functions of Local
Government in Botswana," Journal of Administration
Overseas, April 1971, pp. 127-33.
Jeppe, W. J. O. "Comparative Development of the Public
Services in Botswana and the Western (Bantu) Areas,"
South African Journal of African Affairs, Vol. 1 (1971),
pp. 112-38.
Joint Advisory Council, Minutes. Mafeking.
Joint Advisory Council, Report on the Establishment of a
Legislative Council and Executive Council for the Bechu-
analand Protectorate. Mafeking, 1952.

Khama, Sir Seretse. "Outlook for Botswana," Journal of
    Modern African Studies, Vol. 8, No. 1 (April 1970),
    pp. 123-8.
Khama, Tshekedi. "Chieftainship under Indirect Rule,"
    Journal of the Royal African Society, Vol. 25, pp. 251-
    61.
_____. "Developing Representative Government in a Chang-
    ing Africa: Problems of Political Advancement in Back-
    ward Territories," African World, September 1956, pp.
    12-14.
_____. Political Change in African Society. London:
    Africa Bureau, 1956.
_____. "The Principles of African Tribal Administration,"
    International Affairs, October 1951, pp. 251-56.
Mccartney, W. A. J. "Botswana Goes to the Polls: Khama
    Government Retains Power in the Face of Lively Oppo-
    sition and Paves Road to Economic Take-Off," Africa
    Report, December 1969, pp. 28-30.
"Political Developments in the Bechuanaland Protectorate,"
    International Bulletin, Africa Institute, Pretoria, Vol.
    II (February 1964), pp. 42-53.
Stevens, Richard P. "The Reconciliation of Traditional and
    Modern Forces," Africa Report, April 1964, pp. 9-10.

Law and Legislation

Aguda, Justice Akinola. "Legal Development in Botswana
    from 1885 to 1966," Botswana Notes and Records, Vol.
    5 (1973), pp. 52-63.
Bechuanaland Protectorate. African Immigration Proclama-
    tion. Mafeking, 1962.
_____. Government Secretary. Bechuanaland Laws and
    Statutes: Proclamations and Subsidary Legislation.
    Mafeking, 1957.
_____. Legislative Council. Report of the Select Com-
    mittee on Racial Discrimination. Mafeking, 1963.
"Government Will Act Against Racialism--Misisi," Mafeking
    Mail, March 26, 1970.
"Move to Condemn D. R. C. Rejected by Assembly," Mafeking
    Mail, April 3, 1970.
"Private Sector Attacked in Assembly," Mafeking Mail, April
    10, 1970.
Williams, Myles (ed.). Orders in Council and High Commis-
    sioner's Proclamations and Notices Issued During the
    Period from May 9, 1891 to the 30th June, 1914. Mafe-
    king: n. p., 1915.

Political Parties

Botswana Democratic Party, Therisanyo/Consultation.
Botswana National Front, Puo Phaa, VoL i, No. 1, 1966- .
Botswana Peoples Party, Masa, Vol. 1, No. 1, January
    1964- .
Breutz, P. L. "Botswana: Party Power and Tribalism, "
    Bulletin of the Africa Institute of South Africa, March
    1971, pp. 65-79.
Kuper, Adam. Kalahari Village Politics: An African Diplo-
    macy. New York: Cambridge University Press, 1970.

Foreign Affairs

Austin, Dennis. Britain and South Africa. Oxford: Oxford
    University Press, 1966, pp. 70-76.
"Botswana to Make Refugees Citizens, " The Star, September
    27, 1967.
"Botswana-Zambia Border Claim, " Bulletin of the Africa In-
    stitute of South Africa, Vol. 8, No. 5 (June 1970), pp.
    196-7.
Dale, Richard. "Botswana, " in Southern Africa in Perspec-
    tive: Essays in Regional Politics, edited by Christian
    P. Potholm and Richard Dale. New York: Free Press,
    1972, pp. 110-124.
_____. "Botswana and Its Southern Neighbor: The Pat-
    terns of Linkage and the Options in Statecraft, " Papers
    in International Studies. Africa series no. 6 (Athens,
    Ohio: Ohio University Center for International Studies,
    Africa Program, 1970), pp. 6-21.
_____. "The Implications of Botswana-South African Re-
    lations for American Foreign Policy, " Africa Today,
    February-March, 1969, pp. 8-12.
_____. The Racial Component of Botswana's Foreign Poli-
    cy. Studies in Race and Nations, Center on Internation-
    al Race Relations, Graduate School of International
    Studies, University of Denver, VoL 2, No. 4 (1970-71).
"Four Nations Line Up to Do Battle Over the Pinpoint Fron-
    tier, " The Star, June 18, 1970.
"Freedom Ferry: Zambesi Crossing Last Hurdle for Refu-
    gees, " The Star, September 23, 1964.
Khama, Sir Seretse. Botswana's Foreign Policy: Address
    by His Excellency the President to the Botswana Demo-
    cratic Party Conference at Molepolole, on Saturday 28th
    March, 1970. Gaborone: Government Printer, 1970.
_____. President of the Republic of Botswana, Address to
    the General Assembly of the United Nations, September

1969. Gaborone: Government Printer, 1969.
Legassick, Martin. "Bechuanaland: Road to the North, "
     Africa Today, Vol. XI, (April 1964), pp. 7-9.
Munger, E. S. Bechuanaland, Pan-African Outpost or Bantu
     Homeland. London: Oxford University Press, 1965.
"O. A. U. 'Freedom Fighters' Will Avoid Botswana: Sovereign-
     ty to be Respected, " The Star, September 17, 1967.
"Refugees in Botswana: A Policy of Resettlement, " Kutlwano,
     Vol. 9, No. 7 (July 1970), p. 15.
Rubin, Neville. "Botswana's Last Exit to Freedom, " Venture,
     Vol. 22, No. 8 (September 1970), pp. 21-25.
Segal, Ronald (ed.). Sanctions Against South Africa. Balti-
     more: Penguin Books, 1964, pp. 204-33. "Sanctions
     and the High Commission Territories. "
"Seretse Decision: Why S. A. Kept Mum, " The Star, March
     26, 1965.
Smit, P. "Botswana Railway Line, " Bulletin of the Africa
     Institute of South Africa, Vol. 8, No. 7 (August 1970),
     pp. 273-80.
"South Africa-Botswana Exchanges: Proposed Trans-Zambezi
     Highway Creates Disturbing Discord, " Southern Africa,
     Vol. 82 (May 2, 1970), p. 247.
"S. A. Upset by Proposed Zambia Road Link: But Botswana
     Enthusiastic, " Mafeking Mail, April 17, 1970.
"Verwoerd Talks of Khama Visit: Sends His Personal Con-
     gratulations, " The Star, March 4, 1965.
"Verwoerd Statement Causes Astonishment, " The Star, March
     5, 1965.
Villiers, J. "Botswana Balanced on a Tightrope, " African
     Communist, Vol. 45, pp. 51-60.
"Won't Touch Rail Line: A Promise from Sir Seretse, " The
     Star, October 6, 1966.
"Zambesi Row: U. S. Stays Out, " The Star, June 2, 1970.

SCIENTIFIC [containing: Climate, Land/Water, Gaborone
               Location, Vegetation, Wildlife, Medical]

Climate

Andersson, R. J. F. "Climatic Factors in Botswana, " Bots-
     wana Notes and Records, Vol. 2 (1970), pp. 75-78.
Jackson, S. P. "Climates of Southern Africa, " South African
     Geographical Journal, Vol. 33 (September 1951), pp.
     17-32.
Sneesby, G. W. "Some Notes on the Climate of British

Bechuanaland," Scottish Geographical Magazine, Vol. 58, No. 2 (September 1942), pp. 71-74.

Land and Water Resources

Baillieul, Tom. "An Introduction to Gemstones and Orna-
mental Stones of Botswana," Botswana Notes and Rec-
ords, Vol. 5 (1973), pp. 170-8.
Bawden, M. G. and Stobbs, A. R. The Land Resources of
Eastern Bechuanaland. London: Department of Techni-
cal Cooperation, Forestry and Land Use Section, Di-
rectorate of Overseas Survey, 1963.
Bechuanaland Protectorate. Geological Survey Department.
The Mambule Coal Area. Mineral Resources Report,
No. 2, Lobatsi: 1961.
Brown, John. "New Hope for Africa's Thirstland," Fort-
nightly, Vol. 179, No. 173 (June 1953), pp. 394-98.
_____. The Thirsty Land. London: Hodder and Stough-
ton, 1954.
Debenham, J. "Journey in Thirstland: In Search of Water
in Bechuanaland," Geographical Review, Vol. 41, No. 3
(July 1951), pp. 464-69.
_____. "The Kalahari Today," Geographical Journal, Vol.
118, Part I, 1952, pp. 12-23.
_____. Report on the Water Resources of the Bechuana-
land Protectorate, Northern Rhodesia. London: HMSO,
1948.
"Down the River of Dreams, Okavango River of South Africa,"
Libertas, Vol. 6, No. 9 (August 1946), pp. 58-60.
"Flood Channel near Ngami Flats Bechuanaland Protectorate,"
Bulletin of the American Museum of Natural History,
Vol. 79, Article 5 (July 7, 1952), p. 39.
Jennings, C. M. H., et al. "Environmental Isotopes as an
Aid to Investigation of Ground Water Problems in Bots-
wana," Botswana Notes and Records, Vol. 5 (1973),
pp. 179-90.
King, Lester C. "Landscape Study in Southern Africa,"
Transactions and Proceedings of the Geological Society
of South Africa, 1947, Vol. 50 (1948), pp. 23-52.
Legendre, Sidney J. Okavango, Desert River. New York:
Messner, 1939.
"Okavango Swamps, Kalahari, South Africa," Geographical
Journal, Vol. 113 (January-June, 1949), p. 64.
Schwarz, E. H. L. "Bottetle River," Geographical Journal,
Vol. 67 (June 1926), pp. 528-35.
_____. The Kalahari or Thirstland Redemption. Cape
Town: Miller, n. d.

Stigand, A. G. "Ngamiland," Geographical Journal, Vol. 62,
    No. 6 (December 1962).
Tlou, Thomas. "The Taming of the Okavango Swamps--the
    Utilization of a Riverine Environment--1750-1800, "
    Botswana Notes and Records, Vol. 4 (1972), pp. 147-
    59.
Van der Merwe, C. R. Soil Classification, Mapping and Soil
    Survey in Southern Africa (African Regional Scientific
    Conference, Johannesburg), 1949, Communication No.
    B (g) 2.
Van Rensburg, H. J. "Range Management in Botswana, "
    Botswana Notes and Records, Vol. 3 (1971), pp. 112-
    30.
Vernay, A. S. "The Great Kalahari Sand Veldt," Natural
    History, Vol. 31 (1931), pp. 169-82, 262-74.
"Water Resources of the Bechuanaland Protectorate, " Bulletin
    of the Imperial Institute, Vol. 46, Nos. 2-4, 1948, pp.
    378-81.
Wayland, E. J. "Drodsky's Cave Bechuanaland, " Geographi-
    cal Journal, Vol. 103 (May 1944), pp. 230-33.
_____. "More about the Kalahari, " Geographical Journal,
    Vol. 119, Part I, (March 1953), pp. 49-56.
Wellington, John H. "The Okavango Delta and its Irrigation
    Possibilities: A Potential Egypt of Southern Africa, "
    African World, (January 1950), pp. 11-13.
_____. "A New Development Scheme for the Okavango
    Delta, Northern Kalhari, " Geographical Journal, Vol.
    113 (January-June 1949), pp. 62-69.
_____. "Niger and Okavango: Physical and Human Fac-
    tors in their Development, " South African Geographical
    Journal, Vol. 34 (1952), pp. 38-47.
White, Roger J. "Planning of Water, Power, Transportation
    and Township Facilities for the Shashe Project, " Bots-
    wana Notes and Records, Vol. 4 (1972), pp. 241-51.
Wilson, Brian H. "Some Natural and Man-Made Changes in
    the Channels of the Okavango Delta, " Botswana Notes
    and Records, Vol. 5 (1973), pp. 132-53.

Gaborone--Location

Best, Alan G. C. "Gaberone: Problems and Prospects of
    a New Capital, " Geographical Review, January 1970,
    pp. 1-14.
Dawson, F. C. "Botswana Builds a Capital, " Geographical
    Magazine, Vol. 39 (December 1966), pp. 669-81.
"Gaberones, " Journal of the Town Planning Institute, Vol. 51
    (July-August 1965), pp. 190-5.

Vegetation

"Mukushi Forests of the Bechuanaland Protectorate," Empire
Forestry Journal, Vol. 18, No. 2 (1959), pp. 193-201.
Russell, G. E. Gibbs and Biegel, H. M. "Report on Botani-
cal Collecting Trips to Maun and the Northern Okavango
Delta," Botswana Notes and Records, Vol. 5 (1973),
pp. 154-69.
Seagrief, S. C. and Drummond, R. B. "Some Investigations
on the Vegetation of the North-Eastern Part of the
Makarikari Salt Pan, Bechuanaland," Rhodesia Scientific
Association, Proceedings and Transactions, Vol. 46
(1958), pp. 103-33.
Story, R. Some Plants Used by the Bushmen in Obtaining
Food and Water. Pretoria, 1958.
"Vegetation, Bechuanaland Protectorate," Bulletin of the
American Museum of Natural History, Vol. 79, Article
5, July 7, 1942, pp. 36-43.
Weare, P. R. and Yalala, A. "Provisional Vegetation Map
of Botswana," Botswana Notes and Records, Vol. 3
(1971), pp. 131-47.

Wildlife

Campbell, Alec and Child, G. "The Impact of Man on the
Environment of Botswana," Botswana Notes and Records,
Vol. 3 (1971), pp. 91-110.
Child, Graham. "Water and Its Role in Nature Conservation
and Wildlife Management in Botswana," Botswana Notes
and Records, Vol. 4 (1972), pp. 253-5.
Pinhey, Elliot. "An Entomologist in Ngamiland," Botswana
Notes and Records, Vol. 1 (1968), pp. 31-40.
Von Richter, Wolfgang. "Wildlife and Rural Economy in
S. W. Botswana," Botswana Notes and Records, Vol. 2
(1970), pp. 85-94.

Medical

Lambrecht, Frank L. "Notes on the History of Sleeping
Sickness," Botswana Notes and Records, Vol. 1 (1968),
pp. 41-49.
Teichler, G. H. I. "Notes on Eye Diseases in Botswana,"
Botswana Notes and Records, Vol. 4 (1972), pp. 237-
40.

SOCIAL [containing: Anthropology..., Demography, Religion,
Education]

Anthropology, Ethnology, Sociology

Almeida, Antonio de. Bushmen and Other Non-Bantu Peoples
of Africa. Johannesburg: Institute for the Study of
Man in Africa, 1964.
Bosazza, V. L. "The Kalahari System in Southern Africa
and Its Importance in Relationship to the Evolution of
Man," Pan-African Congress on Prehistory 3rd, Living-
stone, 1955. Actes London: 1957.
Brentz, P. L. "Tswana Tribal Governments Today," Socio-
logus (1958), pp. 140-54.
Debenham, Frank. Kalahari Sand. London: Bell, 1953.
Dornan, S. S. Pygmies and Bushmen of the Kalahari. Lon-
don: Seeley Service, 1925.
Dreyer, T. F. "The Bushmen-Hottentots-Standlooper Tangle,"
Transactions of the Royal Society of South Africa, Vol.
19 (1931), pp. 79-92.
Gluckmann, E. Tragedy of the Ababirwas and Some Reflec-
tions on Sir Herbert Sloley's Report. Johannesburg:
n. p., 1922.
Grant, Sandy. "Mochudi--The Transition from Village to
Town," Botswana Notes and Records, Vol. 5 (1973), pp.
2-11.
Harris, J. "Slaves Under the British Flag," Spectator, Vol.
161 (July 15, 1938), p. 99.
Hastings, MacDonald. The Search for the Little Yellow Man.
New York: Knopf, 1956.
Joyce, J. W. "Report on the Masarwa in the Bamangwato
Reserve, Bechuanaland Protectorate," League of Nations
Publications, VI. B. Slavery (C. 112 M. 98. 1938. VI),
Annex 6, pp. 57-76.
Larson, Thomas J. The Ecological Adaptation of the Mbuku-
shu, A Bantu Tribe of Ngamiland. (Unpublished M. A.
thesis, American University, Washington, D. C., 1962.)
_____. "The Hambukushu Migrations to Ngamiland," Af-
rican Social Research, June 1971, pp. 27-49.
_____. "The Hambukushu of Ngamiland," Botswana Notes
and Records, Vol. 2 (1970), pp. 29-44.
Lestrade, G. P. "Some Notes on the Bogadi System of the
BaHuruthse," South African Journal of Science, Vol. 23
(1927), pp. 937-42.
London Missionary Society. The Masarwa (Bushmen): Report
of an Inquiry. Tiger Kloof: LMS Book Room, n. d.
MacKenzie, Leonard A. Report on the Kalahari Expedition,

1945. Pretoria: Government Printer, 1946.
Matthews, Z. K. "Marriage Customs Among the Barolong,"
Africa, Vol. 13, No. 1 (January 1940), pp. 1-24.
Mitchison, Naomi. "At Mochudi," New Statesman, Vol. 65,
June 14, 1963, p. 894.
_____. "Fortunate Isle," New Statesman, Vol. 66, No-
vember 22, 1963, p. 739.
_____. "Letter from a Tribe," New Statesman, Vol. 68,
October 16, 1964, pp. 572-74.
_____. Return to the Fairy Hill. London: Heinemann,
1966.
_____. "The Tribe is a Classless Society," New Society,
23 May 1963, pp. 21-2.
Mookodi, R. "Women's Life in Botswana," Canadian Journal
of African Studies, Vol. 6, No. 2 (1972), pp. 357-8.
Oakley, Kenneth Page. Bushmen in the Kalahari Desert,
Bechuanaland Protectorate. London: n. p., 1953.
Perkins, C. M. and Perkins, M. I Saw You From Afar: A
Visit to the Bushmen of the Kalahari Desert. New
York: Atheneum, 1965.
Roberts, Simon. "Kgatla Law and Social Change," Botswana
Notes and Records, Vol. 2 (1970), pp. 56-61.
Schapera, Isaac. "The Aspirations of Native School Children,"
The Critic (Cape Town), Vol. 2 (1934), pp. 152-62.
_____. "The BaKxatla baxaKxafela: Preliminary Report
of Field Investigations," Africa, Vol. 6 (1933), pp. 402-
14.
_____. The Bantu Speaking Tribes of South Africa. Lon-
don: Routledge, 1937.
_____. "The Bechuana Conception of Incest," Social
Structure: Essays Presented to A. R. Radcliffe-Brown.
Oxford: Clarendon Press, 1950.
_____. "The Bushmen of the Kalahari," Natural History
(New York), Vol. 61, No. 10 (December 1952), pp. 456-
64.
_____. "Contract in Tswana Case Law," Journal of Afri-
can Law, Vol. 9, No. 3 (1965), pp. 142-53.
_____. "The Contributions of Western Civilization to
Modern Kxatla Culture," Transactions of the Royal So-
ciety of South Africa, Vol. 24 (1936), pp. 221-52.
_____. The Ethnic Composition of Tswana Tribes. Lon-
don: London School of Economics and Political Science,
Monographs on Social Anthropology, No. 11, 1952.
_____. "Field Methods in the Study of Modern Culture
Contacts," Africa, Vol. 8 (1935), pp. 215-28.
_____. A Handbook of Tswana Law and Custom. London:
International African Institute, 1955.

_____. The Khoisan Peoples of South Africa: Bushmen and Hottentots. London: Routledge, 1930.

_____. "Kinship and Marriage Among the Tswana," African Systems of Kinship and Marriage. London: Oxford University Press, 1950.

_____. "Kinship and Politics in Tswana History," Journal of the Royal Anthropological Institute of Great Britain and Ireland, Vol. 93, No. 2 (July-December 1963), pp. 159-73.

_____. "Marriage of Near Kin Among the Tswana," Africa, Vol. 27, No. 2 (April 1957), pp. 139-59.

_____. Married Life in an African Tribe. New York: Sheridan House, 1941.

_____. "The Native as Letter-Writer," The Critic, (Cape Town), Vol. 2, 1933, pp. 20-28.

_____. "The Native Land Problem in the Tati District," Botswana Notes and Records, Vol. 3 (1971), pp. 219-68.

_____. Native Land Tenure in Bechuanaland Protectorate. Lovedale, S. A. : Lovedale Press, 1943.

_____. "A Native Lion Hunt in the Kalahari Desert," Man, Vol. 6 (1933), pp. 278-82.

_____. Notes on Some Herero Genealogies, Communications from the School of African Studies, University of Cape Town, No. 14, 1945.

_____. "Notes on the History of the Kaa," African Studies, Vol. 4 (1945), pp. 109-21.

_____. Notes on the Tribal Groupings, History and Customs of the Bakgalagadi. Cape Town: 1945.

_____. "Old and New Cultures in Bechuanaland," Times (London), British Colonies Review, Vol. 21, 1956, p. 23.

_____. The Political Annals of a Tswana Tribe. Cape Town: University of Cape Town, School of African Studies: Communications, n. s. No. 18, 1947.

_____. "The Political Organization of the Ngwato of Bechuanaland Protectorate," in African Political Systems, M. Fortes and E. E. Evans-Pritchard, eds., Oxford University Press, 1940, pp. 56-82.

_____. "Premarital Pregnancy and Native Opinion: A Note on Social Change," Africa, Vol. 6 (1934), pp. 59-89.

_____. "Present-day Life in the Native Reserves," Western Civilization and the Natives of South Africa. London: Routledge, 1934.

_____. "The Social Structure of the Bechuana Ward," Bantu Studies, Vol. 9 (1935), pp. 203-24.

_____. "Some Ethnological Notes in Sekgatla," Bantu

Studies, Vol. 4, No. 2 (1930), pp. 73-94.

_____. "Some Features in the Social Organization of the
Tlokwa, Bechuanaland Protectorate," Southwestern Journal of Anthropology, Vol. 2, No. 1 (Spring 1946), pp.
16-47.

_____. "A Survey of the Bushman Question," Race Rela-
tions, Vol. 6 (1930), pp. 68-83.

_____. Tribal Legislation among the Tswana of the Bechu-
analand Protectorate. London: London School of Economics and Political Science. Monographs on Social
Anthropology, No. 9, 1943.

_____. Tribal Legislation among the Tswana-speaking
Tribes of the Bechuanaland Protectorate. London:
Percy Lund, Humphries and Co., 1943.

_____. The Tswana: Ethnographic Survey of Africa:
Southern Africa, Part III. London: International African Institute, 1953.

_____. "The Work of Tribal Courts in the Bechuanaland
Protectorate," African Studies, Vol. 2 (1943), pp. 27-
40.

Shamukuni, D. M. "The beSubiya," Botswana Notes and
Records, Vol. 4 (1972), pp. 161-83.

Silberbauer, George G. "Aspects of the Kinship System of
the B/wi Bushmen of Central Kalahari," South African
Journal of Science, Vol. 57, No. 12 (1961), pp. 353-
59.

_____. "Marriage and the Girls' Puberty Ceremony of
the G/wi Bushmen," Africa, Vol. 33, No. 1 (January
1963), pp. 12-24.

_____. Report to the Government of Bechuanaland on the
Bushman Survey, 1965.

_____, and Kuper, A. J. "Kgalagari Masters and Bush-
men Serfs, Some Observations," African Studies (Johannesburg), Vol. 25, No. 4 (1966), pp. 171-9.

Syson, Lucy. "Social Conditions in the Shoshong Area,"
Botswana Notes and Records, Vol. 4 (1972), pp. 45-65.

_____. "Unmarried Mothers in Botswana," Botswana
Notes and Records, Vol. 5 (1973), pp. 41-51.

Thema, B. C. "The Changing Pattern of Tswana Social and
Family Relations," Botswana Notes and Records, Vol.
4 (1972), pp. 39-43.

Thomas, E. M. "Bushmen of the Kalahari," National Geo-
graphic Magazine, Vol. 123, No. 6 (1963), pp. 866-88.

_____. The Harmless People. New York: Knopf, 1959.

Van der Post, Laurens. The Lost World of the Kalahari.
London: Hogarth, 1961.

Walker, J. M. "Bamalete Contract Law," Botswana Notes

and Records, VoL 1 (1968), pp. 65-76.
Werbner, Richard P. "Land and Chiefship in the Tati Concession," Botswana Notes and Records, VoL 2 (1970),
pp. 6-13.

Demography and Population

Crone, M. D. "Aspects of the 1971 Census of Botswana,"
Botswana Notes and Records, VoL 4 (1972), pp. 31-37.
Fosbrooke, H. A. "Land and Population," Botswana Notes
and Records, VoL 3 (1971), pp. 172-87.
Kuczynski, R. R. A Demographic Survey of the British
Colonial Empire, VoL II: South African High Commis-
sion Territories, East Africa. London: Oxford Uni-
versity Press, 1949.

Religion

Campbell, Alec C. "Some Notes on Ngwaketse Divination,"
Botswana Notes and Records, VoL 1 (1968), pp. 9-13.
Dachs, Anthony. "Missionary Imperialism--The Case of
Bechuanaland," Journal of African History, VoL 13,
No. 4, (1972), pp. 647-58.
Drennan, M. R. "Some Evidence for a Trepanation Cult in
the Bushman Race," South African Medical Journal
(Cape Town), 1937, pp. 183-91.
de Plessis, J. A History of Christian Missions in South Af-
rica. London: Longmans, 1911.
Feddema, J. P. "Tswana Ritual Concerning Rain," African
Studies (Johannesburg), Vol. 25, No. 4, 1966, pp. 181-
195 (bibl.).
Grant, S. "Church and Chief in the Colonial Era," Botswana
Notes and Records, Vol. 3 (1971), pp. 59-63.
Haile, A. J. A Brief Historical Survey of the London Missionary Society in Southern Africa. London: Mission-
ary Society, 1951.
Lovett, R. The History of the London Missionary Society,
1795-1895. London: Frowde, 1899.
Pauw, B. A. Religion in a Tswana Chiefdom. London: Ox-
ford University Press for the International African In-
stitute, 1960.
Schapera, Isaac. "Christianity and the Tswana," Journal of
the Royal Anthropological Institute of Great Britain and
Ireland (London), Vol. 88, No. 1 (January-June 1958),
pp. 1-9.
_____. "Herding Rites of the Bechuanaland Bakxatla,"
American Anthropologist, Vol. 36, No. 4 (October-

December 1934), n. s., pp. 561-584.

_____. "The 'Little Rain' (Pulanyana) Ceremony of the Bechuanaland BaKxatla," Bantu Studies, Vol. 4 (1930), pp. 211-16.

_____. "Oral Sorcery Among the Natives of Bechuanaland," Essays Presented to C. O. Seligman, edited by E. E. Evans-Pritchard and others. London: Routledge, 1934.

_____. "The Significance of Rainmaking for the Mbukushu," African Studies, Vol. 25, No. 1 (1966), pp. 23-36.

_____. "Some Notes on Cattle Magic and Medicines of the Bechuanaland Bakxatla," South African Journal of Science (Johannesburg), Vol. 27 (1930), pp. 557-61.

_____. "Sorcery and Witchcraft in Bechuanaland," African Affairs (London), Vol. 51, No. 202 (January 1952), pp. 41-52.

_____. "Witchcraft Beyond Reasonable Doubt," Man (London), Vol. 55 (1955), p. 72.

Smith, E. W. "The Idea of God among South African Tribes," in African Ideas of God. London: Edinburgh House Press, 1950, pp. 78-134.

Teichler, G. H. "The Historical Background of the Tswana 'centenary' New Testament by A. Sandilands," Botswana Notes and Records, Vol. 3 (1971), pp. 1-5.

Thema, B. C. "The Church and Education in Botswana During the 19th Century," Botswana Notes and Records, Vol. 1 (1968), pp. 1-4.

Waldron, Derek L. C. Bechuanaland: The Church Says Yes. London: Society for the Propagation of the Gospel, 1961.

Willoughby, W. C. Nature-Worship and Taboo. Hartford, Conn.: Hartford Seminary Press, 1932.

_____. The Soul of the Bantu. London: Student Christian Movement, 1928.

"Witchcraft in Bechuanaland," Nature, Vol. 139 (May 1, 1937), p. 749.

Education

American Council on Education. Overseas Liaison Committee. Secondary Level Teachers' Supply and Demand in Botswana by John W. Hanson, Michigan State University, 1968.

Auger, G. A. Education in the High Commission Territories. Reprinted from Science in General Education, Rome, 1962.

Haile, A. J. Tiger Kloof Native Institution, Bechuanaland.

Letchworth: Garden City Press, n. d.
Lewis, R. Haydon. "Educational Co-operation of Government
   and Missions in Bechuanaland," Oversea Education, Vol.
   9, No. 1 (October 1937), pp. 17-22.
Motsete, K. M. "An Educational Experiment in the Bechuana-
   land Protectorate," Oversea Education, Vol. 5, No. 2
   (January 1934), pp. 58-64.
Thema, B. C. "Moeng College--A Product of Self-Help,"
   Botswana Notes and Records, Vol. 2 (1970), pp. 71-74.
Thomas, M. "Secondary Education in Botswana," Botswana
   Notes and Records, Vol. 4 (1972), pp. 95-99.
United Nations. General Assembly. Investment in Education
   in the Non-Self-Governing Territories, Report A/AC.
   35/L. 354. New York: United Nations, 1962.
Vengroff, Richard. "Education and Political Development in
   Botswana: An Exploratory Study," paper presented at
   ASA, Philadelphia, Pa., November 1972. (Unpublished).
Ward, Jennifer. "Education for Rural Development: A Dis-
   cussion of Experiments in Botswana," Journal of Mod-
   ern African Studies, Vol. 10, No. 4 (1972), pp. 611-
   20.
Watters, Edmond. "Significant Developments in Education in
   Botswana (1950-1970)," paper presented at ASA, Phila-
   delphia, Pa., November 1972. (Unpublished).